This thoughtful, scholarly and incisive c____ __ _____ psychology is a must-read for all trainees, trainers and practitioners. This thoroughly readable book is compassionate and ultimately optimistic – his is not a deconstruction that leaves us without thought or hope for a different future. Craig Newnes is one of a very few clinical psychologists who dare to write both critically and self-reflexively about professional practice – its histories, abuses, legacies, values and promises.

Professor Arlene Vetere, Deputy Director PsychD Clinical Psychology, University of Surrey

Craig, as always, writes from the heart, with warmth, compassion and a wry humour. This ensures that the book is not only interesting and informative but good fun to read. In his usual personable style the book combines a highly knowledgeable overview and reflective critique of clinical psychology with glimpses into his own life. His accounts of his own family merge with accounts of his clients, for example, the lady who stuck pins in her arms to get some attention. Craig dares us to move out of our comfortable professional positions to feel for our 'clients' as human beings, as people suffering and hurting like our own family members. This challenging of the cosy professional separation of 'them' and 'us' to instead consider clinical psychology as 'about us' is so refreshing and inspiring.

Rudi Dallos, Professor of Clinical Psychology and Research Director, Plymouth University

This wide-ranging critique of the theory and practice of contemporary clinical psychology will provoke thoughtful reflection about the profession's past and lead to debate about its future.

Dr Dave Harper, Reader in Clin Psych, University of East London

Clinical Psychology
A critical examination

Craig Newnes

PCCS Books
Ross-on-Wye

First published 2014

PCCS BOOKS
2 Cropper Row
Alton Road
Ross-on-Wye
Herefordshire
HR9 5LA
UK
Tel +44 (0)1989 763900
contact@pccs-books.co.uk
www.pccs-books.co.uk

Clinical Psychology: A critical examination

British Library Cataloguing in Publication Data.
A catalogue record for this book is available from the British Library.

ISBN 978 1 906254 59 9

Cover designed in the UK by Old Dog Graphics
Printed in the UK by ImprintDigital, Exeter

CONTENTS

Dedication

For Harriet

SERIES FOREWORD

The value of critique

'Critique' is the crux of good academic work, and functions as the hinge-point between scholarship, professional activity and practice. Each theory is only as strong as its capacity to withstand sustained critical examination of the assumptions it makes about the world, and so each of these books has been constructed in such a way as to anticipate what would be made of their arguments by the most searching reader.

A founding premise of each book is that learning about a field of professional activity must also be to understand how theory and practice are linked together, and so the role of 'critique' in this process of linking ideas is to question what the impact will be of those ideas on the lives of people outside the classroom. To 'critically examine' an argument is a way of constructing a new practice which will help us understand the world and change it.

Ian Parker
Professor of Psychology
Discourse Unit
Manchester Metropolitan University

Acknowledgements

To the team at PCCS, especially Maggie and Pete for keeping faith, Heather for toning me down and Sandy for fantastic sub-editing. To Kevin Sullivan for friendship, Dorothy Rowe and David Smail for so very much and to my family for tolerating hours and days of the author squirrelling himself away in his study and the kitchen in Davejean.

Abbreviations and acronyms used in the text

ACT   Acceptance and Commitment Therapy

ADD   Attention Deficit Disorder

ADHD   Attention Deficit and Hyperactivity Disorder

A&E   Accident and Emergency

APA   American Psychiatric Association

APA   American Psychological Association

BACP   British Association for Counselling and Psychotherapy

BDI   Beck Depression Inventory

BPS   British Psychological Society

CAMHS Child and Adolescent Mental Health Services

CAT   Thematic Apperception Test–Children

CBT   Cognitive Behaviour Therapy

CORE   Clinical Outcomes in Routine Evaluation

CPF   Clinical Psychology Forum

CPN   Community Psychiatric Nurse, now called Community Mental Health Nurse, CMHN

CQC   Care Quality Commission

DLA   Disability Living Allowance

DBT   Dialectical Behaviour Therapy

DCP   Division of Clinical Psychology within the BPS

DSM   *Diagnostic and Statistical Manual of Mental Disorders*

ECT   Electroconvulsive Therapy

FDA   Food and Drug Administration

HCPC   Health and Care Professions Council

IAPT   Improving Access to Psychological Therapies

ICD   *International Classification of Diseases and Related Health Problems*

IQ   Intelligence Quotient

KPI	Key Performance Indicator
MMPI	Minnesota Multiphasic Personality Inventory
NHS	National Health Service (UK)
NICE	National Institute for Health and Care Excellence (UK)
PALS	Patient Advice and Liaison Service
PCA	Person-Centred Approach
PIP	Personal Independence Payment
POPAN	Prevention of Professional Abuse Network
RCT	Randomised Controlled Trial
RPM	Raven's Progressive Matrices
SCL-90	Symptom Check List
SEAN	Scottish ECT Accreditation Network
SOAD	Second Opinion Appointed Doctors
SRV	Social Role Valorisation
VIA	Values in Action
WAIS	Wechsler Adult Intelligence Scale

INTRODUCTION

A kind of biography

I first applied for clinical psychology training in – I think – good faith. Having worked in a rope factory, at Birds Eye Foods and then as a ceiling tiler, I'd gone to university as a way of keeping out of the building trade for a while. Psychology came easily to me – I assiduously observed Siamese fighting fish and rats in mazes, happily suspended belief in lectures from earnest scholars who talked of Stroop tests, rested my head during hours of lectures on statistics and joined a band. Come my final year a clinical psychologist lectured on his profession. What stood out were the pay scales – not exceptional salaries in themselves but pay which increased incrementally year on year and didn't require the wage earners to go on strike for more. Better yet, clinical psychology appeared to be pretty much a desk job; climbing ladders in a dusty building under construction or getting up well before dawn to cycle to a cold factory wasn't on the cards at all.

After a first round of rejections for a training place I worked for a year in a National Health Service unit for troubled and troubling adolescents. It was run on Kleinian analytic principles and, curious though these seemed to me (and wholly useless in preventing the self-harm amongst the teenagers), I stopped questioning and started reading. Intent on gaining credible experience as a precursor to the grail of clinical psychology I practised psychodrama, tried to look as knowing as some of the unit's analysts and set about applying again for training places.

Interviewed by Dorothy Rowe for a probationer clinical psychology position linked to the Masters Degree in Psychopathology at Leicester University, I found myself moving from London to Lincolnshire. Dorothy told me at interview that I was the *only* applicant to have read Freud (*Studies in Hysteria*), the only male interviewee not to wear a tie and the only one to have said when asked, 'What do you do with really troubled kids?' 'Try and teach them a bit of guitar.'

Duly appointed, I was no longer clear about my reasons for becoming a clinical psychologist. Perhaps it wasn't the money and automatic pay rises after all; maybe I wanted to help complete strangers, perhaps it was an unconscious desire to cure my parents, perhaps the intellectual stimulation? …

Clinical psychologists were, broadly, divided between behaviourists and more analytically inclined therapists. Dorothy was moved by personal construct theory; she was a friend of Fay Fransella and Don Bannister. My colleagues and I were happy to try new techniques and technologies whether that meant personal construct grids, Rorschach ink blots or the Minnesota Multiphasic Personality Inventory. Courtesy of various NHS changes in service boundaries we found our employing authorities in a constant state of metamorphosis and, in our final year, our salaries almost doubled.

I joined the Psychology and Psychotherapy Association, a motley crew of socially aware therapists and dissidents escaping the stranglehold of behaviourism and, as the number of therapies increased, so did my own therapeutic trajectory. I had dabbled with neuropsychological test development for Elizabeth Warrington at Queen's Square and been supervised by a rational emotive therapy practitioner and a peer who preferred, with almost religious zeal, transactional analysis. Now it comes as little surprise that, for clinical psychologists, these were viewed as halcyon days. Leaving Lincolnshire took me first to Slough (where analytic ideas where acceptable if not welcome) and then the United States. By then I had trained at the Institute of Group Therapy and supervision had been gratefully received from Freudians, a psychodramatist, a constructivist and an analyst who specialised in saying nothing at all.

The USA, certainly New England, was conservative by comparison. The object relations perspective was a mystery to my new employers and the invasive demands of insurance companies paying for therapy a mystery to me. Two years on and now sated with psychoanalysis by virtue of courses at the Boston Psychoanalytic Society and Institute and a Horneyian supervisor, my return to the UK health system was a mixture of relief and a kind of despair that so little had changed in the world of clinical psychology and its relationship to psychiatry.

So I drifted, now bereft of professional ambition, but keen to live somewhere less isolated than the magnificent but bleak Peak District. The NHS was being reorganised again as I settled in Shropshire, clinical psychology was in the middle of a dramatic rise in funding for training places and I had to negotiate with eleven consultant psychiatrists to determine both funding for a new department of psychology and the direction that department should take.

Having retired, in 2007, as director of that same NHS Department of Psychological Therapies now employing over 80 administrative staff, art therapists, clinical psychologists, cognitive therapists, counsellors, nurse therapists, several service user consultants and a consultant psychiatrist, I felt reasonably sure I'd been a good-enough boss and a passable therapist and researcher. Along the way I'd picked up the editorship of *Clinical Psychology Forum*, the in-house journal of the British Psychological Society (BPS) Division of Clinical Psychology (DCP), and the *Journal of Critical Psychology, Counselling and Psychotherapy (JCPCP)*, been chair of the BPS Psychotherapy Section, published numerous articles critical of psychiatry and psychology and edited a critical book series for PCCS. It didn't seem so bad. I don't think any of my patients had experienced me as abusive (many of them were NHS staff with plenty of opportunity to spread the word if they found me less than considerate) and I had made many allies amongst the service survivor community.

But the good faith had been whittled away. Despite taking on many staff as critical of the health service and wider society as myself, I knew that we were all part of a vast edifice – the NHS – which, by necessity, considered cost as much as health and could only benefit from *appearing*, through the work of the department, to offer real alternatives to organic psychiatric treatments. Most of the folk in the department eschewed diagnosis, most would have claimed to work very hard indeed to help people in distress and those in community mental health teams battled on a daily basis to put that distress rather than diagnostic terminology and psychiatric drugs at the forefront of team business.

But retirement, via a road accident, has freed me to take a more dispassionate view of the psychology service system. It freed me too to enjoy – after about two years of physical struggles – the fruits of not going to work every day to listen to the misery of staff and patients or use up precious energy fighting at management or DCP National Committee meetings. I gave up *Clinical Psychology Forum* and continue with *JCPCP*. Perhaps I should have let go completely but the business of psychology doesn't seem to let go of me. So, what you have in your hands is one of several books in another PCCS series. The series will critique psychology. This volume focuses on what, to my utter amazement as an ex-ceiling tiler, I know best; clinical psychology. It's not meant to change the world but – actually – the world's not such a bad place some of the time.

CHAPTER 1

The nature of clinical psychology

Psychology, as a discipline, has been with us for barely 120 years. People had been called psychologists before the end of the 19th century but there were no official professional organisations. Many who used psychological ideas in asylums for the insane were psychiatrists, known as alienists before the 1880s.

What we now might understand as 'psychology' of course existed – in the novels of Dickens, Austen, Balzac and Zola. But Austen's comedies of manners are better understood as commentaries on prevailing mores, while Dickens, Balzac and Zola explored love, revenge, hypocrisy and a host of other experiences in the context of writings that suggested class, debt and the struggle for economic survival as the prime movers within society. Meanwhile, psychology, as a professional discipline concerned with the study of human conduct for its own sake, or for the supposed benefit of the objects of study, was restricted to the asylum and law courts. Readers of popular literature and psychiatrists had no difficulty in linking misery to the external circumstances of those who suffered or became deranged. The idea that suffering was a 'mental' disorder produced by faulty brain biochemistry or disordered thinking, however, had yet to take root in the professional and public imagination.

Wundt, a philosopher, had inaugurated a psychological laboratory in Leipzig in the late 1870s. Experiments relied heavily on introspection. Students who came from overseas tended to retain more of the laboratory's scientific methods than its introspective orientation; within 30 years the United States became the centre of experimental psychology where debates centred on the merits of introspection versus controlled experiments and the study of consciousness versus conduct. A flexible view of human nature and controlled experimental methods won the day.[1] An exception might be the postgraduate psychologists from the University of Duquesne, Philadelphia who, perhaps acknowledging a debt to Lévi-Strauss, regard themselves as 'philosophical anthropologists'.

In Europe a more philosophical approach prevailed, an approach still predominant in France and the conferences and publications of the History and Philosophy Section of the British Psychological Society.

The first psychological clinic was set up by Witmer in Pennsylvania in 1896 to be followed by one in Iowa, established by Seashore and Sylvester in 1908.[2]

Thanks, in part, to a combination of the First World War, increasingly varied ways to classify insanity, the popularity of psychoanalysis and the development of drugs and physical treatments for those deemed mad, psychiatry in the 1920s rapidly advanced in power and prestige. 'Clinical' psychology was waiting in the wings.

This book examines the rise of clinical psychology as a Psy discipline, a science, a research, therapy and professional enterprise and a prominent player in the human service industry. It does so by looking at clinical psychology's history, some of the key theoreticians and researchers who have shaped its development and the problems in theory and research inherent in trying to explicate human conduct. I shall critically examine the practice of clinical psychology in both assessment and therapy and the ways in which the discipline *qua* discipline may, while claiming to be a helping enterprise, maintain the very factors that lead to human suffering. The reader will find the book unbalanced, though, I think, fair; the whole is an attempt to add *balancing* rather than balanced argument to the literature of psychology. There are already many thousands of volumes available for those who support the Psy endeavour; this volume adds to the literature proposing a more critical view of the discipline. Chapters include suggestions for a gradual change towards a clinical psychology praxis that takes context and complexity into account.

This opening chapter explores some of the history of the changing nature of the discipline and uses Goldie's ideas on the position of professions in relation to the dominant discourse of medicine[3] in attempting to map the practice of clinical psychology.

The nature of clinical psychology

Long before embarking on a clinical psychology training I had, as a child and teenager, listened to my mother talking about the ups and downs (mostly downs) of her marriage, sat with several girlfriends as they talked over unhappy relationships with their fathers, felt helpless as another turned up one day only hours after discovering her father had hanged himself, nursed my grandmother during a bout of shingles and – generally – found myself amidst woe of varying degrees. On entering training my most recent experience of similar misery had been in a clinic for self-harming teenagers where, as the 'designated nurse' for two particularly violent patients, I had dressed wounds and taken my charges to Accident and Emergency (A&E) outpatient services when the cuts were too deep.

None of this had prepared me for the first patient in the opening week of my placement as a probationer clinical psychologist. Before any lectures and with the prospect of supervision from a Freudian analyst and a Personal Construct specialist I trailed off into the wilds of Lincolnshire to meet with a woman living alone on a housing estate. Her previous – highly trained – clinical psychologist had left the country; I was sent in his stead. Loneliness was, from the outside at least, the least of her problems. During her more miserable moments she would slide needles under the skin of her left arm, carefully pull her sleeve down to cover the signs of harm and then wait for the wounds – needles still in place – to become infected. She had been doing the same thing for years.

The outcome was an unusable arm, repeated visits to hospital and infections that left her in agony. I was in my twenties, physically healthy and had no experience of hurting myself in similar ways – or even wanting to. Some might argue that years of swimming training in the freezing cold of open air pools or dragging myself out of bed to play football in the winter wind and rain showed a masochistic bent – but that was different, wasn't it?

So I visited every week, drank coffee while listening to Jeff Wayne's *War of the Worlds* on the stereo system and dutifully accompanied her to A&E on the days I had opened the door to find her frantically pulling a sleeve down to hide the damage. She said she wanted to stop self-harming but neither of us could work out an easier way for her to get people (nurses and medics mostly) to offer her care in her lonely life. Not all of the hospital staff *were* particularly caring; some regarded self-harm as a waste of their time but she regarded others as friends. The medics were, on the whole, tolerant. Two of them were reassured that she now had a reasonably consistent therapist in tow and only one wanted to 'cut her bloody arm off'. A solution proposed by a behaviourally inclined clinical psychology trainee and friend in Manchester was to cut her *right* arm off.

I saw her throughout other placements when my priority was supposedly children or those deemed mentally handicapped and, on qualification, continued to see her until I left Lincolnshire to take up an appointment over a hundred miles away. Even then, if visiting local friends, I would occasionally call round to see how she was doing.

In those early years I had tried systematic desensitisation (for her fear of people), talked with her about assaults she had endured when younger, attempted relaxation techniques, encouraged her to go to the local shops and taken her through various psychometric protocols including an assessment of her core constructs, the Rorschach inkblots (scored via Klopfer's system rather than the yet-to-be in vogue Exner analysis) and the object relations test. When she managed after a couple of years to visit my office based in a 19th century asylum she hated because of previous admissions I used Kleinian and Freudian interpretative therapy in a search for some kind of insight. As I hazarded interpretations of the transference, a supervisor encouraged me to explore the countertransference.

I consistently suggested she should see a woman therapist though none were available within the local NHS and took heart from popular ideas suggesting that the 'relationship' was key – somehow my consistency, patience, even love would free her. Family therapy and systems notions led us to examine her context and the power of homeostasis. Membership of the Psychology and Psychotherapy Association introduced me to the possibility I was simply a witness to her suffering. It's safe to say I learned a lot.

Our contact finally ended, six years after we first met, when I moved to the USA and she found a friend in a neighbour. She was still pushing needles into her arm and surgeons were still threatening to cut it off.

The profession of clinical psychology

One way to examine a profession is to look at those who practise it. The nature of clinical psychology can be partly explored by reference to the people who train as clinical psychologists. It is a profession with an extremely high graduation rate; in effect, once accepted on a UK training course, the person will graduate.

In the UK there is extraordinary competition for places on doctoral-level clinical psychology courses. In 2011 there were almost three and a half thousand applicants for 547 places.[4] This isn't surprising – the profession is one of only two where monies are provided by the government, via the National Health Service, to ensure that trainees receive a good salary while undertaking a state-funded three-year doctoral training. Those attending for interview for training places were, for many years, advised *not* to suggest they wanted to train in order to help people but to say they wanted to apply *scientific* methods to the core work of the profession – therapy and assessment. Until recently the job market was such that a good career (as a lifetime NHS employee) was the guaranteed outcome of receiving the resulting doctoral qualification. The economic downturn has changed this rosy picture though some might argue that the training is, in itself, a privilege not available to the majority, and certainly not available to those with equal talents in the field of helping others.

The overwhelming majority of clinical psychology training places in the UK, due in part to the skewed nature of the selection procedure (one based largely on previous academic achievement), are taken up by white women (83%) in their mid-twenties (84%). Despite claims by the profession that it tries to be representative of the population it is meant to serve, *all* of those in training are highly intelligent as assessed by their achievement of, at least, an upper second-class honours degree. Their experience seems limited to their academic careers and in work (e.g., acting as assistant psychologists or in a related 'caring' profession) supposedly directly related to their future career path. The vast majority (88%) have no children, haven't needed to balance family and work life and, though undeniably hard working, have no experience of the frequently soul-destroying and arduous work (or unemployment with no prospect of employment) more typical of the 21st century so far.

It wasn't always like this. Clinical psychology training in the UK (where the British Psychological Society's Division of Clinical Psychology was not established until 1968) is rooted in the 1948 Health Bill when three distinct enterprises began: the psychometric school personified by Raven at Crichton Royal Hospital in Dumfries, the experimental school at the Maudsley and Institute of Psychiatry, and the psychoanalytic school at the Tavistock Clinic in London. All three centres soon founded courses in clinical psychology and all three emphasised the importance of assessment, though at the Tavistock projective assessment techniques were favoured. For the Maudsley, the promotion of research skills was preferred to training students in therapy. Indeed, Eysenck at the Maudsley said in a 1949 article, '… clinical psychology demands competence in the fields of diagnosis and/or research, but therapy is something essentially alien to clinical psychology ….'[5] Eysenck also suggested that in addition to an in-service initial training, skilled researchers should go on to study for a PhD and work as 'senior psychologists', a suggestion not taken up at the time.

Psychometrics can be seen as an exemplar of what Goldie, when classifying professions' position in relation to the dominant medical discourse, has described as the *compliant* position.[6] In essence professions and individuals acting compliantly do not challenge the dominant discourse. Instead they support the medical hegemony, often, in the case of clinical psychology, by offering supposedly scientific and statistically sound assessments which confirm or otherwise a medical, usually psychiatric, diagnosis. Clinical psychologists have been progenitors of everything from tests for 'schizophrenigenic thought disorder' via the Minnesota Multiphasic Personality Inventory (MMPI)[7] to questionnaire-based assessments of 'attention deficit hyperactivity disorder' today. Raven developed a widely used intelligence test – the 'Raven's Progressive Matrices' (until the late 1970s it was a compulsory part of training to learn how to administer the RPM). The charge which might be levelled at Raven (of neglecting the immediate needs of incarcerated patients – for drug-free and independent lives – in the pursuit of a scientific psychology) is very similar to the position adopted by Jeffrey Masson in relation to Carl Rogers, the doyen of counselling.[8]

For those close to him Raven's essential humanity has been lauded; for Ralph Hetherington the Crichton approach was 'patient-centred, trying to understand such problems as were experienced by individual patients ... and to only use such tests as were necessary to elucidate any remaining problems'.[9] A trainee-centred perspective is provided by Ralph McGuire, a clinical supervisor on the University of Glasgow Diploma in Clinical Psychology course in the early 1960s, who notes that trainees needed a year of supervision at Southern General Hospital and various Child Guidance Centres in preparation for their time at the Crichton working with 'more chronically disturbed patients'.[10]

Eysenck had been appointed as research psychologist at Mill Hill Emergency Hospital during the Second World War. When Mill Hill was redeveloped as the Institute of Psychiatry in Camberwell, clinical services were offered at the Maudsley Hospital where Eysenck became head psychologist and with his colleague Monte Shapiro (the clinical course director) soon established the first UK training in clinical psychology. In the early 1950s the attempt to establish clinical psychology as a science left practitioners trained as *experimentalists* with little to offer the world outside the laboratory: 'Eysenck's nomothetic approach had almost nothing to offer the clinician, while Shapiro's obsessionally detailed single-case approach was too time consuming.'[11] By the late 1950s trainees on the Institute of Psychiatry/Maudsley course were being trained as diagnosticians and science-based 'behavioural therapists', forerunners of today's cognitive-behavioural therapists. 'Behaviour therapy' itself had grown not from the work of Eysenck and Shapiro but from the 'behaviour modification' techniques of Skinner in the USA and Wolpe, a South African psychiatrist. The diagnostic schemata of psychiatry were supported, if refined, and (largely) physical treatments (electroshock, insulin coma and pharmacology) were unchallenged. Instead, behaviour therapy was offered by clinical psychologists as a scientifically validated alternative or, more often, adjunct to psychiatric treatment. This exemplifies Goldie's second position – *eclecticism*[12] a position embraced enthusiastically in the late 1960s and the decades following.

Eysenck was, in part, reacting to what he saw as the wholly unscientific practice of psychoanalysis and psychodynamic therapies. Within the general discipline of psychology, as represented by the BPS, psychoanalytic therapies had a tradition and place going back to 1919 and the formation of the Society's Medical Section. The British Psychoanalytic Society, with some of the same membership, was founded the same year. Although *animal* experimentation and theories of human behaviour based on that experimentation (e.g., Skinner's theory of *operant conditioning*) had an equally long history within the discipline, until the establishment of the postgraduate training course at the Institute of Psychiatry, psychoanalytic theory and methods were the mainstay of practice with patients. The Institute of Human Relations at the Tavistock Clinic (founded in 1920) included analysts from several schools – Freudian, Kleinian and, latterly, the Independent tradition of Balint, Winnicott and others – and it was here that the third stream of clinical psychology training was established. Again 'eclectic', clinical practice at the Tavistock was grounded in untestable notions such as 'the unconscious' and arcane processes like 'interpreting transference'. Such concerns notwithstanding, the Tavistock course flourished.

In the USA, the profession began in 1913. In 1917 The American Association of Clinical Psychology was formed becoming, in 1919, the Clinical Section of the American Psychological Society. Despite these early beginnings, *no* accredited programme in clinical psychology set practice in the discipline as its goal until 1957 when Adelphi University received accreditation. By 1991 over a third of doctoral clinical psychology students were graduating from professional (as opposed to purely academic) programmes.[13]

The aim of these programmes, as first suggested at the Boulder Conference in 1949, was to produce *scientist-practitioners,* i.e., clinicians who were equally adept at research.[14] The project was problematic from the outset; even assuming the possibility that human beings can objectively research other human beings, psychologists largely entered training to become therapists rather than researchers. If one takes publication as one mark of the researcher, numerous studies have shown the modal number of publications by clinical psychologists to be zero.[15,16] Publications by clinical psychologists on whether their own efforts lead to therapeutic success are rare.[17] The Boulder model appeared to produce scientists who were 'unproductive' and practitioner professionals who were 'incompetent'. Indeed, one of the early Doctor of Psychology (PsyD) programmes at the University of Illinois lasted from only 1968 to 1980 as non-clinical academics who scrutinised dissertations found themselves unable to modify the criteria to suit projects undertaken by those on the practitioner programme.[18]

If the 'nature' of a profession is dictated by its adherents it might be seen from the above that clinical psychology, as a profession, began as a mixture of scientific pretension, ambition and a willingness to support the dominant medical discourse for personal gain and professional standing. The profession in the UK is no longer represented by relatively few male academics. For the past two decades new entrants to the profession in the UK have been predominantly white women in their mid-twenties. The numbers of practising clinical psychologists shows a similar trend; most are now women, a significant change from the gender mix of the early training courses. Those entering training must have at least honours degrees in psychology and frequently hold an additional masters level degree. I shall return to these themes in Chapter 7.

The next section briefly introduces the reader to other key features of the profession's nature.

The industry of clinical psychology

Clinical psychology sees its main role as the application of psychological science and methods to the amelioration of human distress. As a profession it is one of many 'children' (including educational, social, occupational, community, etc.) of the parent discipline of psychology. Psychology itself has a long history, best illustrated by the work of philosophers and novelists, though for some of the 50,000 members of the British Psychological Society the need to focus on the demands of entry to clinical psychology training has necessitated a reduction in the influence of philosophy.

Official psychology in the UK began with the formation of the Psychological Society in 1901. Science was in the ascendant, the industrial revolution had given way to what might be called the industrial era and advances were being proclaimed in numerous areas of human endeavour, from vaccination to printing via increasingly efficient transport systems based on steam engines. H.G. Wells had inspired the populace with *The First Men in the Moon,* and powered flight, telecommunication and the motor car were all on the visible horizon. Any group wishing for prestige and public appeal needed to appeal to the popularity of science. Despite its slippery subject matter – people – psychology presented itself as a natural science.

In the first paragraph of their editorial in the very first *British Journal of Psychology* in 1904 Ward and Rivers wrote: 'Psychology … known among us as mental philosophy … has now achieved the position of a positive science ... "Ideas" in the philosophical sense do not fall within its scope; its enquiries are restricted entirely to facts.'[19] The journal was taken over by the BPS in 1914. The Society had a curious beginning. In October 1901 the inaugural meeting at University College London was attended by ten people, four of whom were medical practitioners.[20] Once formed as the Psychological Society, however, the Society discovered another group with the same name and took on the prefix 'British' in 1904. Given the profound influence of philosophy on psychological ideas up to that point (e.g., the Chair in Mind and Logic at University College London only changed its name to 'Psychology' in 1928), it is important to recognise the context in which the BPS saw fit to ally itself and its members to 'facts' about human and animal behaviour. To Beloff, writing in 1973, the ambition was unfulfilled; he categorically states that psychology has yet to establish a *single* fact about human behaviour.[21]

For many years after the Boulder Conference of 1949 clinical psychologists in the UK defined themselves as scientist-practitioners.[22] Clinical psychologists working as psychotherapists had simultaneously designated espousing attempts to help people as an 'art', albeit an art accessible only to the minority. Psychotherapeutically inclined clinical psychologists in the field of mental health now suggested they were reading subliminal signs in their patients and – via a generally agreed set of 'non-specific variables' – effecting cure. The 'non-specifics' included processes like 'sharing', 'support', 'validation' and other terms meaning 'appearing to understand'. Many patients found the concentrated efforts of a concerned other a relief from the physically invasive practices of psychiatrists but *why* being listened to by a stranger once a week might bring lasting improvement to one's lot was never explained. To some critics this looked uncomfortably like magic and for some clinical psychologists (e.g., Smail[23]) was too much. The existence of organisations like POPAN (the Prevention of Professional Abuse Network) made it clear that some of these clinical psychologists offering unconditional love, support and companionship were simultaneously exploiting their patients in sexual or financial ways.

Clinical psychologists working in services for those described as learning disabled continued, with few exceptions, on the path of assessment and, if not therapy, the supervision of less well paid staff in a variety of treatments based on behaviour modification. So-called 'punishment' schedules designed to eradicate self-harming behaviour like constant head-banging included shocking institutionalised learning disabled people with electric cattle prods.

This can be seen as an example of *death-making*, the term Wolfensberger coined to describe behaviour by service providers aimed at killing the body or spirit of service recipients.[24]

The profession moved on to embrace the 'reflective practitioner' position. Paraphrasing Miller Mair, a later Director of Psychology Services at Crichton Royal Hospital, 'To see if a statement makes any sense, try applying its opposite'. Can you imagine a *non-reflective* practitioner? The impossibility of being objectively reflective would appear only to have occurred to a minority in the profession, though it is possible a majority see the problem of identifying through whichever prism the reflective practitioner looks. If he or she claims that reflecting on what has just occurred in a therapy session, for example, is a personal process, then what are the influences on that personal view? It would require some remarkable existential gymnastics to step outside those influences to make a genuinely 'pure' reflection. If the patient has appeared angry or flustered and the clinical psychologist reflects on her reactions in terms of feelings of fear or a need to hurry the session to an end, what might that tell us about the patient? It seems to simply say that the psychologist is easily frightened and acts as most would when afraid. A clinical psychologist might add thoughtful remarks about gender and, if the patient is from a different ethnic background, race. This can only reflect the contemporary *Zeitgeist* in which such concerns are privileged and dictate what the psychologist must record.

Clinical psychology and the status quo

Thomas Szasz claimed that a key role overlooked by mental health professionals (or the Psy complex) when explicating their function is that of distributing important state and insurance-based resources: time and money.[25] Psy professionals act as the point at which resources are allocated, in effect to check whether the poor are deserving or not.[26] Amongst their genuine efforts to help, heal or simply assess their patients it is not a role that many clinical psychologists would necessarily recognise.

Other commentators have pointed to the ways in which the Psy complex maintains the status quo. Ivan Illich, for example, sees any professions allied to medicine, and, indeed, medicine itself, as part of the problem rather than the solution to the ills of individuals.[27] His thesis is reinforced by Magaro[28] who says, in relation to the manifest failure of US psychiatry to alleviate misery, '... because the mental health industry is financially dependent on "mental illness" there is no real reason to treat effectively'.

Beyond the dual roles of resource distributors and preservers of the status quo, the lethal nature of many service interventions might offer some validity to the possibility that clinical psychologists are involved in death-making – the idea that treatment of distressed and 'marked' individuals is *designed* to kill either the body or spirit (or both) under the guise of aid. Wolfensberger saw this as a largely unconscious process; though there are practitioners who set out to harm, one should hope the majority espouse more charitable motivations. Clinical psychology seems to play a part in death-making, a part its practitioners might vehemently deny. From a critical perspective, the profession is often, at best, a bystander in a medically dominated service world where experimentation (via the lack of acknowledgement, for example, that *all* drugs effect people in different ways and thus need to be systematically monitored) is the norm and, at worst, an active accomplice in a death-making enterprise. Wolfensberger suggests that active killing of the spirit is everyday practice for many Psy professionals. His position echoes that of the sociologist, Gruenberg who coined the term 'the social breakdown syndrome' as a way of describing the institutional impact on psychiatric patients.[29]

Imagine you have little spare money, live in a frequently frightening part of town and regret having the three young children that now live alone with you since their father left. You see a clinical psychologist who reassures you that cognitive behaviour therapy (CBT) or a similar one-to-one therapy is the answer. Better still, it won't take long. But, of course, although the psychologist is patient and kind, the office warm and the buses not too inconvenient in terms of dropping the kids off at your mum's, you don't feel a lot different after a dozen visits. After five more you are told that your time is almost up and you seem to be 'resisting'. Your spirit dies a little. This is not the fault of the psychologist, nor a particular limitation of the therapy produced by the material context of the patient's life. Talking treatments are *bound* to kill a little of the spirit *despite* the best intentions of patient and psychologist; talk is neither going to change the context of the patient's life nor – necessarily – lead to the patient gaining the power essential to change, a fairly dispiriting outcome.

Therapy with a congenial psychologist is one of the more benign elements of an analysis of clinical psychology as death-making. I shall return to this theme in Chapter 6.

The practice of clinical psychology

Whether clinical psychology is considered part of the status-quo-enhancing body of professions that change few of society's ills for its own ends or is actively involved in death-making, the day-to-day practice of clinical psychologists is extremely difficult to ascertain. Certainly, there appear to be differences between countries in terms of what is expected and funded but individual difference, partly due to the invisibility of individual practice, is largely unknown.

Within the USA, for example, the use of diagnosis and psychometric testing is ubiquitous *despite* well-attested evidence that the entire psychiatric diagnostic endeavour is flawed[30] and psychometric measures invalid. Stein, for example, claims that 'Validity and reliability of psychological tests are low, almost worthless ...'.[31] Practice in Australia reflects the influence of the USA while in some centres in India clinical psychologists working in psychiatry are expected to wear white coats as if conducting laboratory experiments, a custom even Eysenck may have resisted at the Maudsley in the 1950s. I shall return to this theme in Chapter 3.

In the UK clinical psychologists working with adults in mental health services in the NHS are restricted, to some extent, by their conditions of employment, circumstances that in an organisation so gargantuan – with over a million and a half employees – leaves remarkable room for innovation and independence while simultaneously placing practitioners in a position where they must be seen to follow central government directives. Such directives include priorities for the kind of patients seen, the type of therapeutic and other work carried out and record-keeping protocols dictated by BPS guidelines and statutory law.

Since the *Agenda for Change* transformation in the way NHS work is remunerated (implemented in 2004 in England and Wales though still not fully implemented in Scotland), practising clinical psychologists have been left in an anomalous position. The justification for their salaries in a national pay scale also covering nursing and other healthcare professions is supported by a job evaluation including a supposed core skill of clinical psychologists – research. Yet the median publication rate of clinical psychologists continues to be zero. The national newsletter of the Division of Clinical Psychology (DCP) of the BPS is a monthly publication with over 4,000 subscribers who receive their copies as part of their DCP membership. The majority of articles in the newsletter, *Clinical Psychology Forum,* are pieces by assistant clinical psychologists hoping to gain places on courses. Trainee psychologists are regular contributors. Research by more senior colleagues of the type found in more academic journals like the *British Journal of Clinical Psychology* is rarely reported. Thus, although practitioners are paid more than similar health care professionals on the basis that they are offering research skills, in fact they do no such thing.

This is not a new phenomenon. Practitioner clinical psychologists, as noted above, have always been loath to pursue research activities and commonly cite reading journal articles rather than writing them as the only research they carry out. The lack of time dedicated to research leaves the majority of non-management clinical psychologists plenty of scope for therapeutic work. There is – an admittedly flagging – drive in Britain to promote cognitive behaviour therapy as a panacea. CBT holds that mood and emotions can be directly influenced by thoughts despite the reality that thoughts, feelings and behaviour are entirely different – rather than mutually influencing – modalities. Further, the therapy is based on the assumption of an internal world that can be accurately conveyed to others through speech. Since the Layard Report[32] those claiming state benefits have been offered CBT. This is conducted by newly trained Improving Access to Psychological Therapies (IAPT) workers. Clinical psychologists, though not specifically trained in CBT, stepped forward, strongly supported by their professional body, to supervise IAPT workers. If benefit claimants do not return to work after between 6 and 12 hourly sessions of CBT their benefits are reduced. This inverts the supposed cause and effect of unemployment and distress; instead of being depressed 'because' of being out of work, the person is unemployed 'because' of a diagnosed condition which must be 'treated'.[33] The absence of decent jobs for the majority doesn't enter the equation at this level though doubtless it occurs to patients, IAPT workers and the supervising clinical psychologists.

It might be argued that clinical psychology in the UK rather missed the boat when it came to truly embracing a psycho-therapeutic discourse, although some practitioners practised humanist therapies (e.g., gestalt therapy) and others took up a body-centred praxis (e.g., bioenergetics), public debates within the profession tended in the 1970s to focus on psychodynamic versus behavioural methods, and more recent debates revolve around CBT versus community psychology approaches. Publicly funded clinical psychology in the UK has neglected hundreds of other therapies it might have embraced. The profession is, however, constrained in the UK in a way not familiar to practitioners from countries such as the USA where health care is based on private insurance or direct payment. Public funding and public accountability in the UK limits clinical psychology training courses and their graduates to certain approved therapeutic modalities of which CBT is, presently, the mandatory market leader. Szasz, writing 35 years ago, estimated the number of psychotherapies for an ever-increasing range of diagnosable distress at around a hundred. Today there are over 500.[34,35] Camping therapy, thumb therapy, pet-facilitated psychotherapy, skydiving, soul healing, mental aptitude patterning and boudoir photography are just a few of the therapies that have been reimbursed by insurance companies in the USA; they have yet to be embraced by UK clinical psychologists.

The position of clinical psychologists as NHS employees, though providing relatively secure work, has become, for some, untenable as they seek to work in the relative freedom of private practice where they remain free of central directives such as the National Institute for Health and Care Excellence (NICE) guidelines. I shall return to this theme in Chapter 7.

The language of clinical psychology

This final section continues the theme of practice in relation to the language of clinical psychology, with particular reference to the language of diagnosis, the positioning of psychologists as experts and the consequences for patients.

A major factor in any medical intervention is the diagnosis. You can't, at the expense of the UK National Health Service at least, just have kidney dialysis because you like the idea. As an, essentially, medical endeavour psychiatry and its ally Big Pharma have a vested interested in diagnosing as many people as possible. Often for the best of intentions, clinical psychologists – even counsellors – will use diagnoses. The outcome is that more and more people are diagnosed mad.

Between 1948 and its publication in 1952 the APA Committee on Nomenclature and Statistics had circulated for comment a draft *Diagnostic and Statistical Manual* (*DSM-I*) to numerous organisations and individuals. The social, cultural and medico-technological climate post-Second World War had been transformed from that immediately after the First World War when the first *Statistical Manual for the Use of Institutions for the Insane* had appeared. Mental disorders were now divided into two main categories; disturbance resulting from impairment of brain function (trauma, alcoholism, multiple sclerosis, etc.) and disorders resulting from an inability to adjust. The second group was further divided into psychotic and psychoneurotic disorders.

Post-war, the psychiatric community, influenced by psychodynamic theory, moved towards a position whereby mental health and illness were on a continuum and sought to treat more individuals diagnosed as psychoneurotic.

DSM-II was published in 1968. Its authors turned their sights to the wider community for corroboration and collaboration. Influenced by the eighth edition of the *International Classification of Diseases* (*ICD-8*), *affective reactions* became *major affective disorders,* now including *involutional melancholia* and listing *psychotic depressive reaction* separately. The overall number of disorders rose to 163.

DSM-III, published in 1980, contained 265 disorders. A new feature of *DSM-III* was its multiaxial orientation, Axis I describing symptom-based disorders, Axis II personality disorders. The remaining three axes specified *medical* conditions (an intriguing feature in a nosology supposedly articulating *all* psychiatric disorders as medical phenomena), severity of stressors and the best level of psychological functioning during the preceding year. The all-encompassing nature of the new volume was commented on by Jay Katz, a professor of psychiatry at Yale: 'If you look at *DSM-III* you can classify all of us under one rubric or another of mental disorder.' [36]

Freud, Marie Jahoda and Karl Menninger were amongst many Psy professionals to already be on record as suggesting that we were all mentally ill at one time or another, to a greater or lesser degree. This position puts those frequently critical of the diagnostic endeavour, for example, clinical psychologists, in a paradoxical position from which they can escape via the Judeo-Christian tradition of charitableness. Distress can be normalised or placed on a continuum wherein it is the *suffering* of the individual (or others, e.g., the family) or the temporary apparent inability to function socially (so-called 'problems in living') which dictates the need for professional intervention; suffering is the only justification needed for referral to a mental health professional.

DSM-III-R, DSM-IV and *DSM-IV-TR* were published in 1987, 1994 and 2000 respectively. The 265 diagnoses in *DSM-III* increased to 292 for *DSM-III-R* and 365 for *both* the later editions. *DSM-5,* published in 2013, has a similar total.

As part of their daily practice clinical psychologists working in psychiatric and outpatient settings regularly use diagnostic labels. Although the BPS recently criticised the huge increase in potential diagnoses in *DSM-5* the authors of the statement didn't demand that BPS members stop using diagnosis and the language of psychiatry.[37] A cursory survey of the language used by clinical psychologists in the UK in their publications in various journals and newsletters would have revealed the impossibility of acceding to such a demand.

The growth in diagnoses suggests that any new edition of *DSM* is likely, by 2020, after a brief plateau, to contain 1000 disorders. Whether the *number* of diagnoses rises or not bears little relation to the diagnostic *rate* or the consequences for those diagnosed. Despite no change in the criteria, for example, of ADHD, in the UK the number of children so diagnosed rose from 20,000 to 300,000 in the lifetime of *DSM-III-R.*[38] Some clinical psychologists working in services for children have abjured the use of psychometric tests designed to confirm the diagnosis. Others have embraced diagnostic testing in much the same way they would embrace the prescribing privileges now enjoyed by clinical psychologists in several US states.

The consequences of such diagnoses include families having access to much-needed financial support and – frequently – psychoactive medication for the diagnosed individual. Between 1994 and 2003 UK prescriptions for stimulants (e.g., Ritalin) rose from 6,000 to 345,000, a change not accounted for by the publication of *DSM-IV-TR* in 2000.[39] Between 1996 and 2003 the percentage of boys in American schools diagnosed as ADHD and prescribed stimulants rose from 6 to 17 per cent.[40]

The well-documented adverse and addictive effects of drugs such as Ritalin and Adderall have not led clinical psychologists to embrace the third of Goldie's positions – *fight or flight*, characterised by resisting the medical *Zeitgeist*. Instead, clinical psychologists in child services have trained in family, systems and narrative therapies as part of an *eclectic* position. This enables them to maintain their professional status without disturbing other members of the multidisciplinary teams within which they work.

The ubiquitous nature of psychiatric terminology is not, of course, limited to professionals. Members of the public can now diagnose themselves with the aid of the Internet, a process supported by the equally ubiquitous – now online – psychometry.[41]

I shall return to these points in more detail in later chapters.

Concluding remarks

To summarise, clinical psychology in the USA and UK has a relatively short history. As a profession it is not yet 100 years old and as a profession formally incorporated within the pay and bureaucratic structures of the NHS, little more than 50. In that time it has struggled with roots in the statistical tradition of British empiricism and the often appealing lure of psychoanalytic theorising and therapy, despite their lack of scientific rigour. In the USA, the profession began with greater acceptance of psychotherapeutic ideals and practice and has struggled to establish its scientific credentials through research.

The profession has been inextricably bound up with the practice of psychiatry, both in its aims to add scientific credibility to the assessment of personal differences by conducting psychometric tests on those diagnosed by psychiatrists, and in offering therapies to psychiatric patients. In moving beyond the hospital, clinical psychologists have taken their procedures into the wider community and continue to compete with psychiatrists, counsellors, nurses and others for a share in the distress industry. For a supposedly reflective profession, clinical psychologists have shown little interest in examining their wider role in maintaining the status quo and, until very recently, have failed to adequately criticise the inherent contradictions and lack of validity in psychiatric diagnoses.

Practitioners have, perhaps, been more critical of institutionalised practice in the field of learning disabilities though, even here, since the publication of *DSM-IV*, retardation has been classified as a mental *illness*. Despite the reclassification of retardation to 'intellectual disability' in *DSM-5*, the illness paradigm is maintained.

This opening chapter will appear unbalanced to some readers. The seduction of the media and the public by Psy professionals seems to me to require some attempt to suggest the emperor is naked. It was tempting to offer a subtitle along the lines, 'I come to bury Caesar not to praise him'. The remaining chapters will continue a critical analysis whilst giving examples of clinical psychological practice that challenges the prevailing norms and reclaims socio-philosophical reflection as integral to that practice.

Endnotes

1. Gardner, H. (1976). *The Quest for Mind: Piaget, Lévi-Strauss and the structuralist movement.* London: Quartet Books.

2. Pilgrim, D. & Treacher, A. (1992). *Clinical Psychology Observed.* London: Routledge.

3. Goldie, N. (1977). The division of labour among the mental health professions. In M. Stacey, M. Reid, C. Heath & R. Dingwall (Eds.), *Health and the Division of Labour.* London: Croom Helm, pp. 141–161.

4. Retrieved 5 February 2013 from http://www.leeds.ac.uk/chpccp/BasicEqualopps.html

5. Eysenck, H. J. (1949). Training in clinical psychology: An English point of view. *American Psychologist, 4,* 173–176, p. 173.

6. Goldie, N. (1977). The division of labour among the mental health professions. In M. Stacey, M. Reid, C. Heath & R. Dingwall (Eds.), *Health and the Division of Labour.* London: Croom Helm, pp. 141–161.

7. Graham, J. R. (2012). MMPI-2: Assessing personality and psychopathology (5th ed.). Oxford: Oxford University Press.

8. Masson, J. M. (1988). *Against Therapy: Emotional tyranny and the myth of psychological healing.* London: HarperCollins.

9. Hetherington, R. (2000). Early days in clinical psychology. *Clinical Psychology Forum, 145,* 6–8, p. 6.

10. McGuire, R. (2000). An apprentice clinical psychologist. *Clinical Psychology Forum, 145,* 14–16, p. 16.

11. Pilgrim, D. & Treacher, A. (1992). *Clinical Psychology Observed.* London: Routledge, p. 60.

12. Eclecticism is a strategy whereby psychologists offer therapies as adjuncts to physical treatments without challenging the dominant medical frame.

13. Peterson, D. R. (1992). The doctor of psychology degree. In D. Freedheim (Ed.), *History of Psychotherapy: A century of change.* Washington DC: APA, p. 834.

14. Raimy, V. C. (Ed.). (1950). *Training in Clinical Psychology.* Englewood Cliffs, NJ: Prentice-Hall.

15. See, for example, Levy, L. H. (1962). The skew in clinical psychology. *American Psychologist, 17,* 244–249.

16. 'Eight per cent of psychologists produce half the published research. The modal number of publications remains zero.' Norcross, J. C., Brust, A., & Dryden, W. (1992). British clinical psychologists II, Survey of findings and American comparisons. *Clinical Psychology Forum, 40,* 25–29.

17. Holmes, G. (2003). An audit: Do the people I see get better? *Clinical Psychology, 24,* 47–50.

18. Peterson, D. R. (1992). The doctor of psychology degree. In D. Freedheim (Ed.), *History of Psychotherapy: A century of change.* Washington DC: APA, pp. 829–849, p. 834.

19. Editorial. (1904). *British Journal of Psychology, 1*(1).

20. Hearnshaw, L. S. (1964). Cited in Pilgrim, D. & Treacher, A. (1992). *Clinical Psychology Observed.* London: Routledge.

21. Beloff, J. (1973). *Psychological Sciences.* London: Staples.

22. Raimy, V. C. (Ed.). (1950). *Training in Clinical Psychology.* Englewood Cliffs, NJ: Prentice-Hall.

23. Smail, D. (1996). *How to Survive without Psychotherapy.* London: Constable.

24. Wolfensberger, W. (1987). *The New Genocide of Handicapped and Afflicted People.* New York: University of Syracuse. 'Death-making' refers to human service practices causing spiritual or physical harm (including hastening death) to their recipients.

25. Szasz, T. (1987). *Insanity: The idea and its consequences.* New York: Wiley.

26. The new Poor Law (1834) had its fair share of critics – from Dickens to Beveridge, via Disraeli, Shaw, the Webbs and Churchill. It punished not only the 'undeserving' poor but the 'deserving' (those indigent through no fault of their own).

27. Illich, I. (1977). *Disabling Professions.* London: Marion Boyars.

28. Magaro, P. A. (1978). *The Mental Health Industry: A cultural phenomenon.* New York: Wiley & Sons, p. 104.

29. Gruenberg, E. (1966). *Evaluating the Effectiveness of Community Mental Health Services.* New York: Milbank Publishers.

30. Newnes, C. (2011). Toxic psychology. In M. Rapley, J. Moncrieff & J. Dillon (Eds.), *De-medicalizing Misery: Psychiatry, psychology and the human condition.* Basingstoke: Palgrave Macmillan, pp. 211–225.

31. Stein, D. B. (2012). *The Psychology Industry under a Microscope!* Plymouth, UK: University Press of America Inc., p. 1.

32. Layard, R., Clark, D., Bell, S., Knapp, M., Meacher, B., Priebe, S., Turnberg, L., Thornicroft, G., & Wright, B. (2006). The depression report: A new deal for depression and anxiety disorders. *The Centre for Economic Performance's Mental Health Policy Group.* London: London School of Economics and Political Science.

33. Pickles, C. (2011). Lives without reason? The imperialism of scientific explanation in psychology. *The Journal of Critical Psychology, Counselling and Psychotherapy, 11*(4), 208–216.

34. Szasz, T. (1978). *The Myth of Psychotherapy: Mental healing as religion, rhetoric and repression.* Syracuse, NY: Syracuse University Press.

35. Feltham, C. (2013). *Counselling and Counselling Psychology: A critical examination.* Ross-on-Wye: PCCS Books.

36. Katz, J. (1983). Cited in Szasz, T. (1987). *Insanity: The idea and its consequences.* Chichester: John Wiley & Sons, p. 145.

37. Retrieved 15 April 2013 from http://apps.bps.org.uk/_publicationfiles/consultation-responses/DSM-5%202011%20-%20BPS%20response.pdf

38. Baker, E. & Newnes, C. (2005). The discourse of responsibility. In C. Newnes & N.

Radcliffe (Eds.), *Making and Breaking Children's Lives*. Ross-on-Wye: PCCS Books, pp. 30–40.

39. Timimi, S. & Radcliffe, N. (2005). The rise and rise of ADHD. In C. Newnes & N. Radcliffe (Eds.), *Making and Breaking Children's Lives*. Ross-on-Wye: PCCS Books, pp. 63–70.

40. *Ibid.*

41. See, for example, online tests for Asperger's Syndrome (all retrieved 15 April 2013) (http://iautistic.com/test_AS.php), Autistic Spectrum Disorder; Autism Spectrum Quotient (http://www.wired.com/wired/archive/9.12/aqtest.html); Depression – sponsored by Pfizer and NHS Direct (http://www.nhs.uk/Tools/Pages/depression.aspx); Attention Deficit Hyperactivity Disorder (http://www.dore.co.uk/learning-difficulties/adhd/?gclid=CM-N9N2Xv7ICFUEMfAodiR4Ang)

CHAPTER 2

Problems with theory and research

Everyone tries to be good. It isn't a popular thesis and one that might bring the response, 'But what about criminals, people who beat their children and worse?' But goodness is a societal and contextual notion. If you have grown up in a family that values looks above all else in a culture that dictates what beauty should look like then cosmetic surgery, despite the extraordinary levels of *amour propre* and physical pain – to say nothing of money – will be the obvious next step. If that surgery requires a partner with the resources to pay as you have few independent means then, if you don't have one already, you will find one. And if that partner happens to be a banker in a profit enterprise whose main aim in life is to please you because 'that's what people in love do' then your partner might take gambles risking prosecution for your sake. Even if not involved in criminal activities, your partner may still be hurting others – via high interest rates or inflated charges for services – in order to be good. Everyday criminals are no different; being told as a child that a good hiding is the way parents show love or being sent away on summer camps is for your own sake and involves considerable sacrifice (in the name of discipline) on your parents' behalf might well show itself in your own parenting in a context where discipline is praised. The cultural context ensures no shortage of role models – whether they be petty criminals or hard-working saints – to reinforce whatever your notion of 'being good' happens to be.

This chapter should, I think, be approached in that spirit. I shall offer examples of theoreticians and researchers who – in a contemporary light – might appear misguided. I shall also offer examples of psychologists, focusing on clinical psychologists, who seem to deserve approbation. In 50 years' time their work might be catalogued as harmful, their ideas quaint and their legacy toxic. Or they will reappear as inspirations for a future generation of Psy practitioners who, like us all, are doing their best to be good.

The theory and research claims of clinical psychologists arise in a context in which examining how particular theories or research is privileged goes largely unexamined by the theoreticians and researchers.[1] The following critique examines that context and includes questions about the nature of psychological theory, the assumptions underpinning research methodology and the claims to be found in research publications.

A beginning in the care industry

Working in my mid-teens as a nursing assistant at a psychiatric hospital there was little sign of psychological theory. Patients were mostly older people, frequently diagnosed with senile dementia. Those I walked with in the grounds or bathed in huge – now much sought after – Victorian bathtubs had fascinating histories to tell: the ex-boxer who had been incarcerated in the 1920s because he had bitten off an opponent's ear, the brother of a famous author who sent his faeces to the Department of Health on the grounds that the hospital treated him like shit so the Secretary of State deserved some of his in return and an elderly woman who had not seen her sister for years even though she lived in an adjacent ward (the staff thought it better they shouldn't meet in case they 'cooked up an escape plan'). Apart from chatting to the patients my role was to help them to get up at six o'clock in the morning as the last act of an invariably boring night shift, serve breakfast, hand out medication (my first experience of the foul-smelling Largactil syrup) and then help them dress (in shared, shabby clothing) before the day proper began. This was mostly spent sitting in pee-stained armchairs in so-called day rooms, the infrequent walk outside, a visit to the chiropodist or occupational therapist, an occasional consultant-led ward round and other low-key medically derived routines. It seemed to me that the hospital was a hospital in name only. The staff would joke it was more like a railway siding where battered old trains would slowly disintegrate before going to the scrap heap.

'Psychology' was represented by a clinical psychologist who would arrive, frequently unannounced though never after five o'clock, to administer various tests. These were intriguing: why assess someone's IQ when the need was for friends and a better place to live? Why test memory when it was clear that little in the patients' day-to-day lives was worth remembering? Ask a retired person which day it is and the answer will come after a struggle; without the routine of employment there is little need to know which day of the week it might be. Ask anyone who is on the throne of England and they will only tell you if they are interested. For the clinical psychologist such questions were tests of 'orientation'. For the patients it was more important to know which of the staff were trustworthy and which medications to secrete rather than ingest – questions the psychologist never asked.

Questions concerning context are certainly raised by clinical psychologists in discussing the lives patients lead. Many conversations, though perhaps framed and recorded in diagnostic terms or descriptions of the patient's internal world, are inevitably about what is happening in the external life of the patient. The patient might, for example, give reasons for being particularly distressed in particular circumstances – shopping, sitting at home with a young family or an angry confrontation at work. Depending on the theoretical orientation and general life experience of the clinical psychologist, these reasons may be met with sympathy, a degree of solidarity, interpretation or attempts to link the experiences to similar events. There might be an effort to demonstrate patterns in the patient's reactions, elucidate alternative ways to respond or link the distress to earlier, sometimes childhood, experiences. The range of theories available to therapists ensures that almost any response by the psychologist can be justified.

Theory in clinical psychology

If he did nothing else, the hospital's clinical psychologist led me to quickly understand that his job was easier than that of most other staff members. Not for him the long nights broken only by the occasional need to help a patient onto a commode or bathe an elderly, apparently frail, woman (with extraordinarily strong wrists that would writhe and twist in a nurse's grip) or administer enemas and medication that reduced dignity and resistance. He took no responsibility for patient care at case conferences where decisions revolved around medication and 'management'. Unlike the domestic staff, he wasn't expected to swab the floors (the beds were made and sheets changed by nursing assistants) or sit with patients as they reminisced, though like many ordinary activities such conversations were later to emerge renamed by professionals as 'reminiscence therapy'. Had he wished he might have cited some theories to account for hospital life.

James Thompson regarded the organisation within the institution as one way of reducing anxiety-provoking uncertainty. Hospital staff will become as institutionalised as their patients. One difference between staff and patients is *power*, whether it be the physical power bestowed by relative youth or the simple power of being able to go home after 12 hours on the ward – a power symbolised by key chains or cars in the staff car park (where consultant psychiatrists and the medical superintendent had their own demarcated places).[2] The clinical psychologist might have explored Menzies Lyth's ideas about the way we unconsciously defend against the fear of growing old ourselves by sending elderly people away to places where the staff, sharing similar fears, develop routines around meal times or medication to protect themselves from the obvious misery all around. These routines are justified in terms of 'patient care' or 'safety' but, for bored staff, they also *comprise* the working day; relief from the suffocating presence of people society doesn't want.[3] A more recent analysis might involve Wolfensberger's ideas on *death-making* – perhaps too uncomfortable for many, but ideas which have the merit of making sense of why it is that older people are hidden from view in the name of care.[4] The patients I met in the hospital were generally surrounded by trained nurses. Recent reviews of staff in nursing homes in the UK have shown low rates of training of any type amongst staff, although the investigation into the regime at Mid Staffordshire NHS Foundation Trust revealed both the role of trained nurses in patient assault and the complicity of numerous managers and consultants.[5]

According to Boyle and Moncrieff, psychiatry mimics medicine in order to assert itself as a bona fide branch of the parent discipline.[6,7,8] In addition to using Latin-derived terms for arbitrary clusters of behaviour, psychiatry prefers physical to social interventions and, for the purpose of team discussion, case conferences and ward rounds. Research by Jenkinson has suggested that the main function of the ubiquitous inpatient ward round is to reinforce the hierarchy of those present.[9] Research on the usefulness of staff, as perceived by psychiatric inpatients, makes uncomfortable reading for some clinical psychologists. Of most importance is the consultant psychiatrist; the person with the power to discharge the patient. Rated in second place are the domestic staff – ordinary, non-professional people, with the time to sit and chat.[10] Clinical psychologists might use a social psychology theory to help understand the latter finding; French and Raven, in examining social power, found *referent* power (i.e., the perception that the other person is essentially similar to you in status or culture) as the most influential. Undeniably, *reward* power and the *legitimate* power of authority are vested in the consultant's ability to discharge the patient, but in day-to-day life on the wards *referent power* is key.[11]

Finding a *clinical* psychology theory to help understand ward life is difficult, if not impossible. This is no less true for *theories of therapy* as espoused by clinical psychologists working one to one or in groups with patients.

Clinical psychologists, by necessity, have tended ·to justify their practice by reference to non-clinical psychological theories. Those working within a broadly analytic tradition can select from numerous models, from Freud (originally a neurologist) to Winnicott or Khan (both psychoanalysts) via Jung and Harry Stack Sullivan and John Bowlby (all psychiatrists). Those more inclined to a humanist tradition might favour Berne or Perls (both psychiatrists) or – if working with groups – the psychodrama of Moreno (another psychiatrist) and the group analytic theories of Bion and Foulks (both military psychoanalysts). In addition to theories specific to psychotherapy, Stein estimates there are 2,000 theories of personality.[12] The contextual paradigm – eclecticism – of practice with patients leaves clinical psychologists free to rationalise their approach utilising any theoretical perspective and, after some exposure to the specifics of, say, psychoanalysis and transactional analysis, claim to use both techniques in their work. Such a magpie approach to theory is not necessarily different from the creative endeavours of other professionals. For example, there is nothing to stop an architect combining inspiration from Bauhaus and *fin-de-siècle* ironwork in designing a balcony for a modern skyscraper. Mollon, however, has suggested that this eclectic approach leaves clinical psychology practitioners with a sense of fraudulence; they *know* they haven't studied Freud sufficiently or undergone analysis (compulsory in any true analytic training programme) yet may still claim analysis as their primary means of conducting therapy.[13]

It is some 25 years since Jeff Masson achieved lasting notoriety through the publication of *Against Therapy*.[14] Already despised by the orthodox Freudian community for his previous bestselling exposé *The Assault on Truth*,[15] Masson now set about the founders of other psychotherapeutic schools. Some of his targets, for example John Rosen, a US psychiatrist specialising in assaults masquerading as therapy on people diagnosed as schizophrenic, were not well known, certainly in the UK, though Rosen did publish a critically acclaimed book on his methods.[16] Other targets, for example Jung and Rogers, were renowned leaders in their field with thousands of professional acolytes and millions who knew their names, if not their theories.

Masson tends, in *Against Therapy*, to offer evidence against the major thinkers in psychotherapy which marks them as flawed, sometimes corrupt, individuals. Jung, for example, he reveals as having altered his theories *post hoc* in order to continue living in the Nazi regime. A similar technique has been used against Masson himself; *In the Freud Archives* portrays the ex-director of the archives as narcissistic and overly proud of his numerous sexual encounters. Whilst acknowledging the gritty determinedness and academic integrity of Masson's oeuvre, the reader's doubts are raised by Janet Malcolm's references to Masson's character rather than any flaw in his methods.[17]

In a rare attack on the theory rather the theorist, Masson dismisses Rogerian ideas as a body of knowledge that might be 'picked up in five minutes of careful study'.[18] It is tempting to speculate how he would have deconstructed the world of psychoanalytic theory and its derivatives. Instead, Masson largely limits himself to providing evidence for a lack of integrity or courage on the part of his subjects. This individualistic approach tends, by default, to reinforce the notion that, though their theories were flawed, they were right to focus on individual pathology. Various critics have also remarked that a character flaw in the theorist doesn't necessarily have any implications for the accuracy of the theory.

Freud, for example, is vilified for his abandonment of the seduction theory, for Masson an example of Freud's failure of courage in not exposing himself to censure by his (mostly male) patrons. David Smail is more compassionate about Freud the man, using Freud's correspondence with Fleiss (translated by Masson) to illustrate the *ordinariness* of Freud's concerns. In Smail's exploration of interest as a driver in people's lives it is an understandable need to preserve his income that leads Freud to invert and amend his patients' stories of parental assault.[19]

In summary, clinical psychologists working as therapists frequently utilise theories from other Psy professionals, notably psychiatrists and psychoanalysts. The theories have been subject to considerable criticism. I return to this in Chapter 7. The theorists and *their* critics have been subjected to personal as well as academic attack. As discussed in the opening chapter, clinical psychology practice is for the most part derived from psychological theories. Psychology focuses on the individual as agent or the individual in groups. The discipline thus enjoins the discourse of the self. Before critically examining psychological theories I shall examine this discourse.

The self as construct

From self-actualisation to self-reliance via self-esteem the existence of the self is taken for granted in Western society. In fact, the self has a shorter history than might be imagined. Medieval peasantry, slaves, industrial workers and members of the military were regarded as *interchangeable*. In effect, all were units of labour. However much any given person might regard him- or herself as unique, for those holding power over them, the uniqueness was irrelevant. This perspective marks modern consumer culture wherein, for marketing purposes, our individuality is subsumed within the terminology of the market. We are bracketed as consumers, customers, poor, middle-class, fashion-conscious or whatever descriptor of supposed group membership the seller designates us with. 'Self-respect' enters the vocabulary of sales of cosmetics just as 'self-actualisation' has entered the vocabulary of therapy.

The anthropologist Clifford Geertz challenged the concept of self-identity proselytised in the post-industrial/consumer era: 'The Western conception of the person as a bounded, unique, more or less integrated motivational and cognitive universe … is … a rather peculiar idea within the context of the world's cultures.'[20] McDonald and Wearing conclude that the 'demise' of institutions such as work, family and religion in Western society has resulted in 'the individualized subject influenced and shaped by consumer culture' – we are what we buy. In the field of social psychology self-identity is now theorised and understood as an individualised cognitive approach.[21] Rose has come to similar conclusions.[22] Baudrillard suggests that, in a consumer culture, aspiration becomes a personal driver as we are surrounded by powerful mythologies to engage us and encourage purchasing.[23] 'Selves' are in a sense for sale, either by buying material objects others value, cosmetic surgery or, via 'self-mastery', changing our very essence. It is the third of these illusions that drives patients to clinical psychologists. These clinical psychologists have similar, recently constructed, notions of the self. Using the same conceptual schema of the 'individualised cognitive approach' the clinical psychologist hopes to help the patient change through changes in personal mood, thoughts or behaviour. Smail has compared this approach to a version of 'pulling yourself up by your own boot-straps'.[24]

Psychological theory

The individualism inherent in the approach of Burt, Spearman, Cattell, Terman, Weschler, Skinner, Beck, Eysenck and Wolpe is contextual. All were *men* of their time, committed to a scientistic psychology and intrigued by the possibility of demonstrating individual difference, usually by statistical means.[25] For some, their ideas, wholly in keeping with the intellectual climate of the age, were nested within a racist ideology. Terman, progenitor of the *Stanford-Binet Intelligence Test* and originator of the Intelligence Quotient (IQ) says, 'Dullness seems to be racial – psychologists and their IQ tests are the beacon light of the eugenics movement.'[26] Tasked with assessing the suitability of Black Americans for military service, Brigham remarked, 'Our data indicate clearly the intellectual superiority of the Nordic race group.'[27]

Retrospectively accusing early 20th century intellectuals of racism is a historiographical error. People absorb the *Zeitgeist* and context is everything. For example, admired though they were as social reformers and early leaders of the Labour movement in the UK, the Webbs, George Bernard Shaw and the Woolfs were all avowed eugenicists, though not quite perhaps to the extent of one leader in the field of personality study. R. B. Cattell, inventor of the 'Cattell 16PF Personality Inventory', opined, 'The vast majority of humans are obsolete, the earth will be choked with the more primitive forerunners unless a way is found to eliminate them – genthanasia.'[28] Similarly, a luminary in the world of statistical psychology, Karl Pearson (famous as the inventor of Pearson's *rho*) expressed his admiration for Hitler in an after-dinner speech at University College London in 1934 beginning, 'To *Reichskanzler* Hitler and his proposals to regenerate the German people.'[29]

In brief, a focus on the individual as an object (the 'subject') of study and theory decontextualises that individual allowing the researcher to seek internal factors in, for example, intelligence, personality and pathology. Examining psychological theory in the *theorists'* context raises concerns about racist ideology underpinning theories and hypotheses. Such concerns are ahistoriographical and, in effect, damn the theorists from a modern perspective. Theories in themselves, however, are open to critique.

According to Steven Rose, a neuroscientist, there is a sequence of inappropriate steps in thinking that typical deterministic arguments and theorising go through. Rose was concerned about the fallacies inherent in work on genetics. The same critique is equally applicable to psychological theorising:

1. Reification (a concept is considered an entity). For example, the idea of 'depression' is seen as describing something real. This leads to the circular reasoning wherein someone might suggest that the unconnected so-called symptoms of their distress (waking early, lethargy, feeling sad, etc.) which have led to the diagnosis of depression are 'caused' by what is actually only a collective noun for those symptoms.
2. Arbitrary agglomeration. There is no *ipso facto* reason, for example, in clustering thought disorder, delusions and other experiences in coming to a diagnosis of psychosis,
3. Improper quantification.
4. Belief in statistical 'normality'.
5. Spurious localisation. The idea, for example, that 'love' is to be located in the pineal gland (a suggestion once made to me entirely sincerely by a neuropsychologist).
6. Misplaced causality with dichotomous partitioning between genetic and environmental causes.[30]

Those who then claim that conduct is rooted in a 'mixture' of genetics and environment seem to be covering all bases while neglecting to note that, if their claim is true, then their own behaviour is determined in the same way and deserves neither reward nor punishment as they have removed individual moral choice from the equation. As will be seen in Chapter 8 I sympathise with this conclusion using a different rationale.

Research critical of psychiatric theorising, especially notions of disturbed brain biochemistry and genetics, can be found in the work of the psychiatrists David Healy, Peter Breggin, Joanna Moncrieff, Ronnie Laing and the Critical Psychiatry Network.[31]

Clinical psychology critics of the medicalisation of distress include Jay Joseph, Dave Pilgrim, David Hill, Lucy Johnstone, Mary Boyle, Dave Harper, Richard Bentall, Mark Rapley and Richard Marshall.[32] Other clinical psychologists have taken Psy theories to task for failing to take into account meaning (Rowe), vested interest (Smail), class (Bromley) and the complexity of being a subject (Mair).[33]

Critique within the Psy disciplines is rich and, for some like Professor Mark Rapley, ex-director of the University of East London Clinical Psychology Doctoral Programme, constituted the core of postgraduate training. In the absence of alternative theories, too much criticism can, however, be disabling to practitioners hoping to learn ways of ameliorating distress. Here clinical psychology favours individualistic paradigms. Still vested in the tradition of cognitive individualism, clinical psychologists might suggest refined versions of CBT[34] or practise narrative therapy and other systems-theory derivatives. 'Mindfulness', as applied to different individualistic approaches and 'positive psychology' are currently popular.[35] Such developments are marked by a tendency to be short lived. Attribution therapy, for example, though briefly popular in the late 1980s and based on attribution theory had all but disappeared by the mid-1990s. This does not necessarily reflect anything wrong with either the theory or practice of attribution therapy but may illustrate Marshall's point that within scientific circles, the most recent theories and publications are regarded as the most important.[36] Whatever the benefits of attribution therapy, within 10 years, except for a core group of practitioners, it was seen as out of date. The intrinsic hierarchy of science also places more technical endeavour at the forefront and 'softer' approaches at the rear. Thus, a highly technicalised process like cognitive analytic therapy will be more prestigious than, for example, co-counselling.

The work of Carl Harris in Birmingham and, in a less formalised way, that of Guy Holmes in Shrewsbury, provides instances of clinical psychologists who draw from wider – political and socially informed – traditions to enhance their practice.[37] I shall return to their work in Chapter 6.

Research

The ubiquity of societal context for research is frequently confronted by historians and explicated by Bernal, an eminent chemist: 'Often enough the ideas which statesmen and divines think they have taken from the latest phase of scientific thought are just the ideas of their class and time reflected in the minds of scientists subject to the same social influences.'[38] Gould, in *The Mismeasure of Man* (a history of intelligence testing), applies the same reasoning to psychology as a science. He suggests that, as in all scientific endeavour, psychology is a socially embedded activity which must be understood as a social phenomenon, at times serving as a mirror of social movements.[39]

One possible critical reading of psychology's persistent scientism might position the profession's stance as survivalism. The last century has seen science so elevated in professional and public discourse that credibility depends on claims to be 'scientific' and 'research' or 'evidence based' whether selling shampoo, new housing policies or CBT. Psychology, as an industry, must sell itself in the same way.

Research has a broad definition; from some background reading on a topic to detailed and frequently extraordinarily costly attempts to reveal the way the natural universe is thought to work. Clinical psychology highlights the evidence base of its practice though the proportion of clinical psychologists conducting research remains some distance from the scientist-practitioner ideal.[40] Behaviour therapy is considered grounded in the work of Skinner and others, while psychoanalysis portrayed itself as a science wherein every analyst–patient encounter was a form of pure research. Assessments from intelligence tests to projective techniques were subjected to research of varying degrees before being used with patient populations. For over 20 years qualitative methods have vied with older quantitative praxis in the hands of practising clinical psychologists and those based in universities. At first glance, clinical psychologists are part of a healthy scientist-practitioner profession.

Any research is subject to a broad range of criticism, from the accusation of fraud to critiques of experimental design. As noted above, research driven within particular ideologies will be directed toward verifying foregone conclusions even if the research requires fraudulence. Famously, Sir Cyril Burt, in attempting to show the inheritability of intelligence was ultimately exposed, some 30 years later, as guilty of a major fraud involving not only the invention of research subjects (various sets of identical twins) but also two co-authors and researchers.[41]

Psychology, as an academic discipline, carries with it the persistent charge of scientism: in its insistence on being a natural science, the discipline – in investigating human subjects – can, at best, only mimic the processes of chemistry or astronomy. As Marshall has succinctly summarised however, psychology fails to reflect on the processes that determine *what* is studied and *how*.[42] No science can stand outside the forces that direct experimenters, principally forces of context and interest. Psychology and its sub-discipline clinical psychology would, in an ideal world, address these human concerns as intrinsic to its subject matter. Why, for example, study children who unproductively spend hours counting things, thereby gaining a label of Asperger's syndrome, rather than study the activity of well-paid accountants who do much the same thing?

Might research routinely reported, for example, in newspapers such as the prestigious *Daily Telegraph* lead to better lives for older people? Beneath the headline, 'A stressful job could increase risk of

Alzheimer's disease in later life', the reader is informed, 'A study on mice shows that those with higher levels of stress hormones had diminished memory function'. The study cited is an unpublished thesis submission from Umeå University in Sweden. The study concludes, 'chronic elevation of allopregnanolone (a "stress steroid") accelerated the development of Alzheimer's disease' in the mice. Unexplained is how a mouse can develop a human disorder – too much sitting in day-rooms watching television, perhaps? While advising that, 'It is important to remember this research was not carried out in people,' the head of research at the charity Alzheimer's Research UK adds, 'some research has already highlighted a *possible* link between chronic stress, cognitive decline and the development of Alzheimer's,' and suggests 'further study' and investment in research to make 'a real difference' in people's lives. Self-interest here seems self-evident: though disguised by the speaker's position as head of supposedly disinterested research the call is not for truth, but more research. 'Some' and 'possible' are important qualifiers in the passage; to expose the subtext in such praxis the study of rhetoric rather than science would prove more revealing in innumerable similar examples.[43]

In the case of Psy-as-science, Richard Marshall has delineated the challenge. Within academic psychology there is a hierarchy. Paraphrasing Liam Hudson, Marshall continues, 'The pure look down on applied, and the experimental, usually physiological or biological in background, look down on the social, clinical and educational and, as in all systems of social snobbery, participants are under continual pressure to appear, indeed to become, what they are not.'[44]

Intrinsic to this hierarchy are practices that define where in the social order researchers lie. These practices include particular types of research with particular research subjects, publishing results and the use of a specific technical lexicon. Many clinical psychology researchers, particularly those involved in therapeutic and community praxis, avoid the constraints faced by academic psychologists. In these next sections I shall examine those constraints. Chapter 8 will explore possibilities for research beyond the more limited type to be found in university departments of psychology.

The subjects of research

During my first degree in psychology I participated in several research projects. Frequently these were simply demonstrations of methodology (of the hypothesis-experiment-analysis of data-conclusion type) or observational activities (watching rats in mazes or Siamese fighting fish). At other times I joined fellow students as subjects in psychological experiments investigating perception and memory. These experiments were conducted by lecturers and other researchers in the psychology department who then submitted their work for publication. In the main corridor of the department notice boards were adorned with photocopies of published papers and lecturers' rooms had notices on the doors inviting students to participate as subjects in further experiments. Thirty-five years on, an observer will discover similar photocopies and requests displayed in any academic psychology department anywhere in the world. Hundreds of thousands of willing research subjects are to be found in the undergraduate psychology community.

In order to generate conclusions about the applicability of their research to the general population, psychologists must first assume some essential similarities between that population and their research subjects. Research into, for example, new treatments for cancer is bedevilled by difficulties of analogy; can the researcher reasonably assume that the multiplication of cancer cells in mice will be analogous to cancer growth in humans? This kind of research relies on a small number of physical similarities in order to draw parallels between rodents and people. Research conducted by psychologists on dogs and rats led first to general theories of behavioural reinforcement and then to behavioural therapies for patients. The animal–human analogy seems problematic to me when considering the complex social contexts of people's lives. In modernist terms it would be possible to suggest that consciousness and the ability to reflect (to 'search for meaning' in Frankl's phrase[45]) make people very different from animals. This difference notwithstanding, clinical psychologists working with children or those deemed learning disabled have designed punishment and reward schedules for their patients for almost a century.

It is apparent that we are, generally speaking, not as similar to animals as psychologists working in academia would prefer to believe (there are millions of experiments that require no such similarity – in the field of animal behaviour, psychologists study animals as animals rather than cheaper, more ethically acceptable, substitutes for human subjects). Those experimental psychologists working with human subjects, however, face a different question: how similar to the general population are the human subjects of psychological research?

An example is provided by a study at the University of Northumbria published in the *Journal of Experimental Psychology*. The reader is informed that 'uplifting' music can enhance 'mental alertness and concentration'. 'Scientists' (again quoted in the *Daily Telegraph* of 19th March 2013) measured the electrical activity in the brains of 14 'young volunteers' (read, 'psychology students') as they listened to Vivaldi's *Spring* (uplifting) and *Autumn* (sombre) concertos from *The Four Seasons* while performing a 'challenging mental task' (pressing a keyboard space bar whenever a green square appeared on the computer screen; other shapes and colours were to be ignored). They also performed the task in silence. Response time was fastest for *Spring*. Response times during silence were slower, and slower again (by an average of 19.5 milliseconds) during *Autumn*. A researcher was quoted as saying, 'The Spring movement ... had an exaggerated effect on the area of the brain that's important for emotional processing.'[46]

Critiquing the praxis of psychological experimenters may be something of a sport amongst editors of national daily newspapers such as the *Telegraph*; I suspect research reports of the type described are published for just that purpose. The researchers are being thrown to the lions amongst the readership. To indulge the editor then, one critique might go as follows: the Northumbria University group ignore the fact their subjects consisted of only 14 people (let us assume the subjects were paragons of student life and had not been drinking the night before), give no data on the context (did the subjects gain credits towards a modular degree for participating?), culture (how do we know the subjects agreed with the experimenters' assessment of the music's uplifting or sombre quality?), and made gross assumptions about 'emotional processing' centres in the brain. *At best* the study might have concluded that 14 psychology students pressed a space bar marginally quicker in response to a visual cue while listening to *Spring*, a conclusion which – though accurate – says nothing about anyone else performing the same task, nor anything about how people in, say, a factory or classroom might perform.

It might appear unkind to attempt a deconstruction of experiments of this type. It is, however, notable that this is a *published* study. Similar publications can be found in any psychological journal; studies that ignore the leaps of faith from small student samples to the wider populace or make unwarranted statements about how the brain might link to anything from 'emotional processing', anger, love or any other construct. Finding a psychological study that takes its subject matter (being human) *seriously* is extremely difficult. Though the proper place for such studies may well be psychological journals, the proper place for the study of why psychologists act as they do is to be found in sociological analysis. A motivating factor for academic psychologists is the publication of their findings. This next section will look in more detail at publication as praxis.

Publication

Research output is used as a means to distribute resources, status and power between individuals within schools/departments; between departments/schools; between universities and higher education institutions. These institutions are rated (and funded) via Key Performance Indicator 'points'. KPI points are gained by publishing in the most KPI-prestigious journals which, for psychologists, are American Psychological Association journals. The APA publishes rejection rates from its journals every year in *The American Psychologist*. A rejection rate of 80 per cent is regarded as a sign of a good-quality journal.[47] To publish in APA journals researchers must learn the rules of the game.

Since 1993, UK research councils have made greater links with industry to better meet corporate needs. Corporate funding is now *de rigueur* in universities and the publishing sector. Consequently, 75 per cent of drug trial research published in three main journals – *The Lancet*, the *New England Journal of Medicine* and the *Journal of the American Medical Association* – is industry funded. Drug companies buy copies of journal articles that report favourably on their products and send them out to health care institutions to persuade physicians to prescribe those products, a lucrative enterprise for publishers where reprints have high profit margins.[48]

For clinical psychologists not working in the academy, eight per cent of psychologists produce half the published research and the modal number of publications remains at zero.[49] Higher education institutions 'identify the academic worth of research with economic market value' where 'doing research' has been reconstructed as 'in receipt of income from a research grant'.[50] Although it is possible for researchers to aim for both quantity and quality it is output that produces funding. Providing the 'quality' of the research studies adheres to the necessarily limiting publishing standards of the APA, research will be published.

It can be seen that funding for research activities and publication is largely controlled by business interests. For over 20 years scientific journals have included a 'declaration of interest' notice asking that contributors reveal sources of funding and any attachments beyond their academic institution. Of course, where a study has shown results that are not in the sponsor's interest, it is unlikely that the study will be submitted for publication in the first place. For drug-company-affiliated studies this can have potentially extremely harmful effects. Stein, for example, notes, 'There is strong suspicion that the Food and Drug Administration [the US regulatory body] has in its possession numerous studies indicating that the stimulant drugs used for controlling ADD/ADHD children can cause life-threatening liver problems. However the FDA will not release these studies because of 'proprietary rights'.[51]

Stein's 'suspicion' should not be surprising; a case of 'He who pays the piper ...'. There is also considerable evidence that numerous articles in medical journals are 'ghost written'. In effect, senior academics sell their names to companies to ensure publication of articles actually written by industry employees. Many clinical psychologists are involved in pharmaceutical company research. For the majority, however, publication is wholly limited to psychological journals. Here, it is the language used and the form of experimental reporting that supports the scientistic programme. Research is typically reported in the form of an hourglass. Gross assumptions (for example, concerning concepts such as 'depression') are made with supporting published evidence followed by a narrower hypothesis, description of methodology and subjects, results usually supported by a statistical analysis and finally a discussion section inexorably leading to a suggestion for more research (and funding). At any point in the hourglass bias, mistaken assumptions, distortion of data and weak methodology is possible. The move in British clinical psychology toward more qualitative research, though welcomed by many opposed to the de-individualising nature of the vast majority of studies wherein subjects are described in group terms ('elderly', 'depressed', 'diagnosed with schizophrenia', etc.) has itself been roundly criticised. [52]

For most of my 20 years as co-ordinating editor of *Clinical Psychology Forum* I ensured that the 'notes to contributors' bucked the academic trend. On the inside cover of each (monthly) issue the following appeared:

Contributors are asked to use language which is psychologically descriptive rather than medical and to avoid using devaluing terminology; i.e., avoid using clustering terminology like 'the elderly' or medical jargon like 'person with schizophrenia'. If you find yourself using quotation marks around words of dubious meaning, please use a different word ... we reserve the right to shorten, amend and hold back copy if needed.

This was an entirely conscious attempt to shape the way submissions were written – an attempt to clarify and de-medicalise the language of the profession. The last phrase sub-clause, however, is more accurately interpreted as legitimising censorship. In effect, at the proofreading stage, I simply changed terminology favoured by authors. For example, 'schizophrenic' would become 'person diagnosed with schizophrenia'. The outcome was a journal that rarely reflected the language commonly used by clinical psychologists. My aim (actually made explicit in a 1995 paper[53]) of shaping praxis via language was unfulfilled. Any desire on my part to increase the range of submitted articles to include more personal and less scientistic writing was equally frustrated. Indeed, in a review of over 1500 articles published in the journal between 1990 and 2001, I identified only 25 unsolicited papers that were *not* scientistic.[54]

Structuralists might argue that we *are* language; language determines what can be said and, via power-based rules of syntax, semantics and expression, how it can be said. For some postmodernists language *is* thought and the way we describe behaviour is determined by what we are constrained, via language, to attend to. Thus, for Derrida and others, it is not what is written but what *cannot* be written that reveals the social order. For many clinical psychologists, such theorising will appear abstruse. The latest 'guidelines for contributors' to the journal, although expanded, still include a version of the above paragraph.[55] The guidelines, however, do not appear to cover other areas of clinical psychology praxis. A recent issue, for example, includes a report (DCP Update) on a sub-section of the Division of Clinical Psychology called The Psychosis and Complex Mental Health Faculty. Allowing, possibly, the term 'psychosis' as marginally less stigmatising than 'schizophrenic', it is not clear to me what 'complex mental health' is other than an obscurantist phrase that, by default, makes its user an 'expert'. The same article includes reference to 'Severe Mental Illness', a phrase that does not comply with the journal's de-medicalising brief.[56]

These concerns are not mere pedantry. Language has been integral to power relations from humanity's first communications. The ability to read distinguished masters from slaves in Ancient Rome; the ability to speak Latin and French was key to the establishment of royal governance in England from the 11th to the 14th centuries. It is no accident that Latin terms such as 'schizophrenia' are the province of the Psy complex. For recipients of services the power of technicalised language continues to be challenged by spokespersons who aim to reclaim '... ordinary language that is grounded in people's lived experience ... – just saying it as it is – ... is a liberatory act.'[57] As noted above, however, the discipline inherent in the academic background of clinical psychology is not, for clinical psychologists, liberatory. In fact, the majority of academic psychology publishing *requires* non-liberatory discourse. The use of ordinary language for those claiming expertise is rarely an option. I shall return to this theme in later chapters in attempting to deconstruct what are, at first glance, transparent terms such as 'mental health,' 'intelligence', 'personality', and 'improvement'.

Summary

Clinical psychology draws from numerous theories in order to support and suggest research and therapeutic work with patients. I have suggested that both the theorists and theories must be viewed in their cultural and temporal contexts and, for the most part, do not reflexively examine why particular theories are preferred over others. The theories are individualistic and involve inappropriate steps in thinking, for example, reification and misplaced causality which lead to research on concepts like 'the self' or 'depression' as if these are substantive realities. A belief in statistical 'normality' and the possibility of generalising findings to whole populations positions psychological researchers as experts who publish results partly to enhance this persona and partly as one way of ensuring continued funding. Clinical psychologists and others have critiqued the profession for its scientism and some have drawn from other traditions to support less individualised praxis.

A final reflection

I cannot leave the subject of critiquing theory and research without a recognition that the various concerns outlined above are themselves supported by research. In citing, for example, the survey by Norcross and Dryden I did not confirm the authors' findings by re-examining their data. Nor did I critique their relatively low response rate or explore the possible vested interest Norcross and Dryden had in the outcome. Like other Psy authors I am here trapped in the paradox of critiquing the inherent scientism of clinical psychology *via* scientism. In my defence I can only say that I have tried to address this before. In a (published) paper in a (refereed) journal I examined the need for clinical psychologists to reference even the blandest statements about people. This praxis is integral to the scientistic project. I made the point that it is perfectly legitimate though absurd to leave a message on one's own answerphone and, after listening back, reference oneself with the usual 'personal communication' in order to enlarge the reference section. The paper had no references but did have a note to the effect that a full reference list was available on cassette tape read by Judi Dench.[58] I received no requests.

Endnotes

1. Feminist critics have, in particular, taken psychological theoreticians to task. Over 45 years ago, in a widely circulated paper – 'Psychology Constructs the Female', Naomi Weisstein notes the uncritical acceptance of gendered societal roles by, amongst others, Freud, Erikson and Bettleheim. She continues, 'The first reason for psychology's failure to understand what people are and how they act is that psychology has looked for inner traits when it should have been looking for social context; the second reason for psychology's failure is that the theoreticians of personality have generally been clinicians and psychiatrists, and they have never considered it necessary to have evidence in support of their theories.' Retrieved 25 October 2013 from http://www.uic.edu/orgs/cwluherstory/CWLUArchive/psych. html

2. Thompson, J. D. (2003). *Organizations in Action: Social science bases of administrative theory* (with a new preface by Mayer N. Zald and a new introduction by W. Richard Scott, Ed.). New Brunswick, NJ: Transaction Publishers. (Original work published 1967)

3. Menzies Lyth, I. (1988). *Containing Anxiety in Institutions: Selected essays* (Vol. 1). London: Free Association Books.

4. Wolfensberger, W. (1987). *The New Genocide of Handicapped and Afflicted People.* New York: Syracuse University.

5.   http://www.midstaffsinquiry.com/pressrelease.html

6.   Boyle, M. (2002). *Schizophrenia: A scientific delusion?* (2nd ed.). London: Routledge.

7.   Moncrieff, J. (2007). *The Myth of the Chemical Cure: A critique of psychiatric drug treatment.* Basingstoke: Palgrave MacMillan.

8.   Moncrieff, J. (2011). The myth of the antidepressant: An historical analysis. In M. Rapley, J. Moncrieff & J. Dillon (Eds.), *De-medicalizing Misery: Psychiatry, psychology and the human condition.* Basingstoke: Palgrave Macmillan, pp. 174–188.

9.   Jenkinson, P. (1999). The duty of community care: The Wokingham MIND crisis house. In C. Newnes, G. Holmes & C. Dunn (Eds.), *This is Madness: A critical look at psychiatry and the future of mental health services.* Ross-on-Wye: PCCS Books, pp. 227–239.

10. Goodwin, I., Holmes, G., Newnes, C. & Waltho, D. (1999). A qualitative analysis of the views of inpatient mental health service users. *Journal of Mental Health, 8*(1), 43–54.

11. French, J. R. P. & Raven, B. (1959). The bases of social power. In D. Cartwright & A. Zander (Eds.), *Group Dynamics.* New York: Harper & Row, pp. 150–167.

12. Stein, D. B. (2012). *The Psychology Industry under a Microscope!* Plymouth, UK: The University Press of America Inc.

13. Mollon, P. (1989). Narcissus, Oedipus and the psychologist's fraudulent identity. *Clinical Psychology Forum, 23,* 7–11.

14. Masson, J. (1989). *Against Therapy.* London: Collins.

15. Masson, J. (1985). *The Assault on Truth: Freud's suppression of the seduction theory.* Harmondsworth: Penguin.

16. Rosen, J. (1953). *Direct Analysis: Selected papers.* New York: Grune & Stratton.

17. Malcolm, J. (1984). *In the Freud Archives.* London: Jonathan Cape.

18. Masson, J. (1989). *Against Therapy.* London: Collins.

19. Smail, D. (2005). *Power, Interest and Psychology: Elements of a social materialist understanding of distress.* Ross-on-Wye: PCCS Books.

20. Geertz, C. (1975). *The Interpretation of Cultures.* New York: Basic Books, p. 48.

21. McDonald, M. & Wearing, S. (2013). *Social Psychology and Theories of Consumer Culture: A political economy perspective.* Hove: Routledge.

22. Rose, N. (1999). *Governing the Soul: The shaping of the private self* (2nd ed.). London: Free Association Books.

23. Baudrillard, J. (1998). *The Consumer Society: Myths and structures* (Tr. C. Turner). Thousand Oaks, CA: Sage. (Original work published 1970)

24. Smail, D. (1996). *How to Survive without Psychotherapy.* London: Constable, p. 238.

25. Scientistic dogma insists that inductive methods of the natural sciences are the only source of factual knowledge; in particular, knowledge about human society. Further, only knowledge which is measurable can be 'real' knowledge. For a historical critique of scientism in a wide range of disciplines, see Boyle, D. (2000). *The Tyranny of Numbers: Why counting can't make us happy.* London: HarperCollins.

26. Autobiography of Lewis M. Terman. In C. Murchison (Ed.), *History of Psychology in Autobiography* (1930, Vol. 2). Worcester, MA: Clark University Press, pp. 297–331.

27. Brigham, Carl C. (1923). *A Study of American Intelligence.* Princeton, NJ: Princeton University Press.

28. Cattell, R. B. quoted in Mehler, B. (1997). Beyondism: Raymond B. Cattell and the new eugenics. *Genetica, 99*(2–3), 153–163.

29. Marshall. J. R. (1996). *Clinical Psychology Forum, 96,* 14–17, p. 15.

30. Rose, S., Kamin, L. & Lewontin, R. C. (1984). *Not All in Our Genes.* Harmondsworth: Penguin.

31. See, for example, Healy, D. (1997). *The Antidepressant Era.* Cambridge, MA: Harvard University Press; Breggin, P. (1993). *Toxic Psychiatry.* London: Fontana; Moncrieff, J. (2008). *The Myth of the Chemical Cure: A critique of psychiatric drug treatment.* Basingstoke: Palgrave Macmillan.

32. See, for example, Coles, S., Keenan, S. & Diamond, B. (2013). *Madness Contested: Power and practice.* Ross-on-Wye: PCCS Books.

33. For example, Smail, D. (2005). *Power, Interest and Psychology,* Ross-on-Wye: PCCS Books; Rowe, D. (1982). *Depression: The way out of your prison.* London: Routledge & Kegan Paul; Bromley, E. (1983). Social class issues in psychotherapy. In D. Pilgrim (Ed.), *Psychology and Psychotherapy: Current trends and issues.* London: Routledge & Kegan Paul, pp. 204–207; Mair, M. (1989/2013). *Between Psychology and Psychotherapy: A Poetics of Experience.* London: Routledge.

34. Mansell, W., Carey, T. A. & Tai, S. J. (2012). *A Transdiagnostic Approach to CBT Using Method of Levels Therapy.* London: Routledge.

35. Crane, R. (2012). *Mindfulness-based Cognitive Therapy.* London: Routledge.

36. Marshall, J. R. (1996). Science, 'schizophrenia' and genetics: The creation of myths. *Clinical Psychology Forum, 95,* 5–13.

37. Harris, C. (2005). The family well-being project: Providing psychology services for children and families in a community regeneration context. In C. Newnes & N. Radcliffe (Eds.), *Making and Breaking Children's Lives.* Ross-on-Wye: PCCS Books, pp. 138–150.

38. Bernal, J. (1965). *Science in History* (3rd ed.). London: Watts.

39. Gould, S. J. (1981). *The Mismeasure of Man.* New York: Norton.

40. Norcross, J. C., Brust, A. & Dryden, W. (1992). British clinical psychologists II, Survey of findings and American comparisons. *Clinical Psychology Forum, 40,* 25–29.

41. Hearnshaw, L. S. (1979). *Cyril Burt: Psychologist.* Ithaca, NY: Cornell University Press.

42. Marshall, J. R. (1996). Science, 'schizophrenia' and genetics: The creation of myths. *Clinical Psychology Forum, 95,* 5–13.

43. Adams, S. (2013). Stress link to Alzheimer's. *Daily Telegraph,* March 19, p. 16. Available at http://www.telegraph.co.uk/health/healthnews/9938599/Stress-link-to-Alzheimers.html

44. Marshall, J. R. (1996). Science, 'schizophrenia' and genetics: The creation of myths. *Clinical Psychology Forum, 95,* 5–13, p. 5. See also Hudson, L. (1972). *The Cult of the Fact.* London: Cape.

45. Frankl, V. E. (1959). *Man's Search for Meaning: An introduction to logotherapy.* New York: Simon and Schuster. (Original work published 1946)

46. Hewett, I. (2013). There is no secret formula to music's mystery. *Daily Telegraph,* March 19. Available at http://www.telegraph.co.uk/culture/music/classicalmusic/9940544/There-is-no-secret-formula-to-musics-mystery.html

47. Fryer, D. & Duckett, P (in press). Community psychology. In T. Teo (Ed.), *Encyclopedia of Critical Psychology.* New York: Springer.

48. House of Commons Health Committee Report. (2005). *The Influence of the Pharmaceutical Industry.* London: The Stationery Office.

49. Norcross, J. C., Brust, A. & Dryden, W. (1992). British clinical psychologists II, Survey of findings and American comparisons. *Clinical Psychology Forum 40,* 25–29.

50. Lorenz, C. (2012). If you're so smart, why are you under surveillance? Universities, neoliberalism, and new public management. *Critical Inquiry, 38*(3), 599–629, p. 626.

51. Stein, D. B. (2012). *The Psychology Industry under a Microscope!* Plymouth, UK: The University Press of America Inc, p. 145.

52. Harper, D. (2013). Reflections on qualitative research in clinical psychology training. *Clinical Psychology Forum, 243,* 20–23.

53. Newnes, C. (1995). Histories of *Clinical Psychology Forum. Clinical Psychology Forum, 84,* 39–42.

54. Newnes, C. (2002). The rhetoric of evidence-based practice. *Ethical Human Sciences and Services, 4*(2), 121–130.

55. Retrieved 8 July 2013 from http://dcp.bps.org.uk/dcp/dcp-publications/clinical-psychology-forum/guidelines-for-contributors.cfm

56. Clarke, I. (2013). DCP update: The Psychosis and Complex Mental Health Faculty in a time of turbulence. *Clinical Psychology Forum, 243,* 11–13.

57. Dillon, J. (2013). Just saying it as it is: Names matter; language matters; truth matters. *Clinical Psychology Forum, 243,* 15–19.

58. Newnes, C. (1992). References. *Clinical Psychology Forum, 42,* 27–29.

CHAPTER 3

Problems with assessment: Pathologising difference

This chapter critically examines the practice of clinical psychology. Practice includes assessment and attempts to change individuals, couples, families and wider systems. The latter include communities, government policy and clinical psychology itself, both the profession's image and its place within the overarching discipline of psychology. I shall first lay out the problems inherent in *knowing* what clinical psychologists do before looking at some of the difficulties surrounding assessment. The next three chapters look in more detail at problems in treatment and other interventions.

Individual practice

There is a, perhaps, significant difficulty in examining what individual clinical psychologists do in their daily practice. In work with individuals, the difficulty arises from the nature of face-to-face meetings. These are, except in cases where practice is observed for the purposes of supervision or, in some forms of family therapy and certain settings (e.g., secure and forensic units for dangerous patients) where the clinical psychologist might be regarded as at risk, *private*. Telephone consultations and online communications between clinical psychologists and patients are, except when recorded, invisible and not open to examination at all.

For the assessment of patients, clinical psychologists are instructed to follow certain protocols. When administering the Wechsler Adult Intelligence Scale, for example, there are explicit instructions about where to sit, the necessity to ensure no interruptions, ensuring the person assessed can hear and see, etc.

When undergoing training, clinical psychologists will sit in on assessment or therapy sessions or indirectly observe a senior colleague via a video or two-way mirror. Later, the senior colleague will in turn sit alongside the trainee for a few sessions until the trainee and the supervisor express confidence in the trainee's ability to practise alone. Such an expression of confidence depends on a range of factors frequently *unrelated* to the trainee's ability. These include the trainee's ability to *pass* as confident, the relationship between trainee and supervisor, and guidelines from the training programme. The *type* of intervention to be observed is important. It is unlikely, for example, a supervisor will want to be present during sessions of psychodynamic therapy. Simple factors, such as the supervisor's availability, play a significant role; in a profession with such a high percentage of part-time workers (due, in part, to the high proportion of senior women practitioners with child-care commitments), many practitioners are no doubt grateful for the opportunity to divert work to trainees leaving time for their own patients and administrative demands. Despite regulations from the British Psychological Society, there is, inevitably, wide variation in the number of times trainees are observed.

In the UK, training involves compulsory work experience (placements) in which designated competencies are developed under supervision. Placements reflect NHS organisational structures. Thus, although competencies are theoretically transferable across patient groups, they are developed in the context of particular administrative structures, for example, child and adolescent mental health services or older adult services. On some of these placements, for example, child and adolescent mental health services, the opportunity for the trainees to observe senior colleagues and be observed is more frequent due to the greater use of video, two-way mirrors, tape recording or joint work with colleagues in therapy sessions involving several family members.

Most states in the USA have a licence for 'psychologists'. They don't specify clinical, neuropsychological, counselling, etc. (New Jersey has a separate 'certification' for non-PhD school psychologists; at PhD level, school psychologists may also be licensed.)

State psychological associations, however, ask that a person by supervised for 'several years' before practising in the chosen specialty.

Once qualified, however, in both the UK and USA it is only if the practitioner embarks on further training in, say, systems therapy with families or wishes to use research techniques such as conversational analysis[1] that he or she will be observed practising. If we assume a career spanning 30 years, this could mean that any given clinical psychologist has been observed one-to-one with patients at most 50 to 70 times – and all of those during training. Simply put, the problem with looking at practice is that we don't know what clinical psychologists actually *do* in sessions with patients. We don't know if assessment protocols are followed to the letter and some, for example, the object relations technique, in any case require an approach tailored to each patient.

Amongst Psy professionals the situation is not unique to clinical psychologists; psychoanalysts in training are even more left to their own devices. But in most health care professions, medical doctors, psychiatrists, social workers and psychiatric nurses are observed (and directly assessed) far more frequently.

Of course clinical psychologists can *say* what they do – to managers, supervisors, colleagues and non-psychologist members of multidisciplinary teams. But saying what you have done is a practice mired in the impossibility of accurate self-report and obscured by the use of technical language. A trainee or (in the USA) intern might, for example, choose to focus in a supervision session on one particular aspect of a recent assessment of a patient. In so doing the supervisee (qualified or not) and the supervisor are ignoring other recent patient interactions and even ignoring other aspects of the interaction. Raising the supervisee's reactions to a patient being late, for example, can result in anything from discussions about 'how to handle lateness' in the context of a service inundated with referrals thus making session time precious to rumination on why the supervisee might have unconscious hostility towards anyone who is late.

Further, in the context where the supervisee is being formally assessed by a supervisor, that supervisee may fail to mention aspects of the session interaction with the patient that don't seem to have gone well, for example, the supervisee's *own* lateness. This is unlikely to be mere *amour propre* – the supervisee *needs* to be seen in a good light by the supervisor and scored accordingly.

In group supervision, especially peer supervision amongst qualified practitioners, other factors come into play; existing *non-work setting* relationships, hierarchical differences and the relative lack of time when compared to a one-to-one supervision session of, typically, an hour.

Thus, although supervision is, in theory, one way of finding out what practitioners do with patients, numerous pressures militate against accurate report. By resorting to technical and generalised terms supervisees add further opacity. This reaches its apogee in writing about clinical psychology practice.

Saying what we do

To describe what we do is a process dictated by proximal and distal power.[2] *Proximal* power refers to immediate influences. In the case of a patient such influence might be the presence of a professional deemed an expert with the power to diagnose, prescribe, incarcerate, allow access to financial and other help or *interpret* what the patient says from an authoritative position implying insight.

For the professional, the *proximal* power of the patient can range from describing experiences to which the professional cannot personally relate to more physically present factors like size, gender, race and class or financial difference. Even simple aspects of the patient's appearance (e.g., clothing or hair style) will influence the professional's perception of the patient – a factor noted by psychoanalysts though one ignored by most Psy professionals who can base judgements, entirely consciously, on the patient's choice of anything from footwear to skirt length. This is a process by no means limited to clinical psychologists, many of whom will receive referrals from general practitioners or psychiatrists wherein assumptions, even diagnoses, are made entirely on the patient's appearance.

In the UK, the British Psychological Society's Division of Clinical Psychology offers members (currently numbering about 5,000) advice on what to wear in order to present a professional appearance at work. The advice in *Guidelines to the Professional Practice of Clinical Psychology* is, broadly, similar to that offered to any similar profession – look smart as defined by contemporary mores. The BPS offered male members an official BPS tie some years ago (provoking a backlash from non-tie-wearing female members of the profession voiced in terms of sexism). In a number of clinical psychology clinics in India, practitioners – in keeping with cultural norms around professions related to science and medicine – are expected to wear white coats.

A clinical psychologist confronted by a patient in muddy boots or visiting an 80-year-old patient who wears clothing the professional admires cannot help but make judgements – positive and negative – about the patient. As noted in the opening chapter, some clinical psychologists claim to be (reflective) scientist-practitioners. Compare this claim with the claim of haematologists to be practising science. A haematology clinic receives for analysis thousands of blood samples every day. The haematologist will know little or nothing of the person whose blood is being tested and is extremely unlikely to know what the patient was wearing when the sample was taken. For a clinical psychologist *every* utterance or procedure is proximally influenced by the patient. (*Conversational analysis* is one method for interpreting the nature of this psychologist–patient interaction but it is a method rarely used in anything other than research studies and is more frequently used by clinical psychologists to analyse the interactions of other Psy professionals.[3])

Proximal power is no less influential in the supervision process. A trainee clinical psychologist is dependent on the supervisor for support, clarification of difficulties during patient interactions and, ultimately, *approval*. This approval is translated into successfully completing the placement or internship – one more hurdle cleared on the road to qualification. It seems unlikely that, faced with such power, all trainees will be entirely honest about what occurs with patients but even those that are will describe their conduct in terms dictated by the professionalisation process. They will mimic senior colleagues and supervisors in talking about 'interpreting transference', 'setting homework tasks', and 'trying some guided imagery', depending on the nature of the placement. They may not mention hurrying the patient through an intellectual assessment task or failing to properly (as directed by guidelines for, for example, the Weschler Adult Intelligence Scale – WAIS) arrange the room, table or seating positions.

The vocabulary of clinical psychology is vast. It borrows extensively from psychiatry and it is not difficult to imagine a clinical psychologist both before *and* after qualification using technical terms to describe meetings with patients in order to be accepted as a bona fide professional. Thus 'assessing' is used instead of 'judging' and 'counselling' rather than 'chatting'. Clinical psychologists can claim to be doing 'grief work' or 'systematic desensitisation' with patients, terms that may mean nothing to other members of a multidisciplinary team. If challenged, the clinical psychologist may explain the terms in more detail but, by concentrating on the technicalities of the procedure, somehow loses a sense of the patient as a *person*. Some clinical psychologists abjure the use of the descriptor 'patient' in conversation or written communication, preferring instead 'client'. Published and informal debates about terminology reflect similar concerns in the service user and survivor movement. It seems likely that interactions between professionals and service recipients will be influenced by the preferred nomenclature used to describe participants and professional praxis; it is most frequently the professional who determines that nomenclature. Clinical psychology remains a profession bound by the context of a largely medical discourse. It might be argued that the use of the term 'client' is a way of distancing clinical psychology from the dominant discourse. There seems a certain irony in such usage given the determination with which the profession in the UK pursued, in the 1980s, the goal of establishing a doctoral degree as the minimum qualification for practitioners. Thus, many clinical psychologists now share what to the general public is a *medical* title with medical colleagues. Confusingly, they prefer a title, 'client', for service recipients more usually associated with the recipients of legal services.

In describing the profession as 'insecure' Mary Boyle has used an individualistic term equally easily applied to practitioners involved in the worrying task of appearing to be helpful to strangers.[4] *Hiding* that insecurity behind the language of assessment and 'formulation' is one way of disguising discomfort.

The process of assessment during interactions with patients is not one way. Clinical psychologists are aware that the patient, especially at the first encounter, will have doubts and concerns about the interaction; a certain wariness is to be expected. A typical example might involve a young grandmother who has struggled for years with housing difficulties, a wayward daughter, an unemployed and miserable husband and a soul-destroying job. Diagnosed both anxious and depressed she also lives with various bodily and experiential changes induced by prescribed medication. She is, in no uncertain terms, a survivor. She arrives at the office of a clinical psychologist who, aged 31, has no children, some experience of a succession of intimate relationships, lives in a well-heated house, drives a new car and is designated 'Doctor'. The clinical psychologist has a long waiting list and has been advised to only see patients at weekly intervals for two months at most. What is the referred person likely to think of any advice that is forthcoming? What does the patient *understand* by the term 'assessment?' While the clinical psychologist is introducing herself and warning of the limitations on her time, the grandmother is worrying about babysitting for her daughter, concerned about being late for work and intrigued by the bookshelf to her left. She doesn't, as a rule, much trust young women and finds this one's accent most off-putting. She is, of course, assessing the younger woman. The clinical psychologist is also harbouring a fear – will the patient ask if she, herself, has any children? For childless clinical psychologists, this fear is articulated as a concern about the practitioner's authority.

Describing what we do via publication

The loss in personhood is made complete in the majority of writings by clinical psychologists. The avenues for publication are numerous; informal newsletters, official newsletters such as *Clinical Psychology Forum*, peer-reviewed journals, textbooks, websites and blogs are a few of the options. Peer-reviewed journals are the most prestigious and, for academic clinical psychologists assessed according to their publication output, a vital means of disseminating their work. Clinical psychologists can submit their research to well over a hundred journals devoted to Psy and any number tangentially related. To do so invariably means using the language of Psy and, frequently, an all-too-predictable format displaying the author's familiarity with playing the publication game. As described in the previous chapter, the format can be described as an hourglass, beginning with a justification for the research in terms of contemporary (preferably global) relevance, via a description of what was tried out with whom in a particular locale, to the need for further research to confirm the (preferably global) implications of the findings.

Such research, by necessity, uses anonymised subjects, frequently grouped by diagnostic categorisation ('depressed', 'autistic spectrum', etc.) or vague demographics ('elderly', 'Black', 'adolescent', etc.) and describes technical procedures as if they are carried out without deviation from official manuals of treatment. Indeed, many research protocols use exclusively manualised treatment. Any variation, however gross, within the practitioner is denied by default; a manual was used so, by definition, all participants used it in the same way. Thus journal articles, sometimes with a bewilderingly large number of authors (again, a function of the academic *demand* to publish) will have titles using the format; *Therapy X for condition Y: A comparison with therapy Z.*

The scientistic discourse of clinical psychology ensures that the unique characteristics of patients *and* researchers/practitioners entirely disappear in these, largely quantitative, studies.

In answer to the question, 'What do clinical psychologists do?' it is tempting, in the light of the above, to suggest that what they do extremely well is hide what they do.

There are notable exceptions to the scientistic and conservative writing of clinical psychologists. David Pilgrim, for example, has postgraduate qualifications and a considerable bibliography in the fields of clinical psychology, psychotherapy and sociology; he has been a foremost critic of the professional ambitions of clinical psychology.[5] Lucy Johnstone, ex-director of the Bristol University Clinical Psychology Doctorate Programme was one of the first clinical psychologists in the UK to outline, in book form, the abuse inherent in psychiatric practice.[6] David Harper, Reader at the University of East London Clinical Psychology Doctoral Programme, has repeatedly exposed the solipsistic theorising around the concept of paranoia[7] and Richard Bentall's work includes two renowned volumes psychologising madness.[8] All of these authors are heavily involved in academic work as well as limited clinical practice. David Smail has similarly critiqued much of the practice of clinical psychology since the 1970s.[9] Another author, Guy Holmes, is rare indeed – a non-academy-based practising clinical psychologist writing in accessible ways about a wholly non-technical intervention (walking and talking).[10]

With the exception of Smail and Holmes, however, these authors, though inspirational to many, do not describe their own work in the volumes cited. Certainly, they have given more detailed accounts of their own practice but, in general, they follow a tradition of academic critique, frequently critique of another profession – psychiatry. This is ironic as psychiatry has a far longer tradition than clinical psychology of criticism from within its own ranks.[11]

Assessing

The preceding sections laid out the problem of describing in detail the day-to-day activities of clinical psychologists when seeing individuals or families. By recourse to the very generalisations that clinical psychologists themselves use it *is* possible to explicate professional praxis. Although some clinical psychologists might be surprised at the general terms I have chosen, it seems fair to suggest that the majority of clinical psychologists are in the business of judging and labelling people (usually complete strangers) and then interfering in their lives. Clinical psychologists use, variously, the terms assessment, formulation, diagnosis, and therapy for these activities. Chapter 4 will examine therapeutic practice in more detail.

The consequences of assessment

As remarked in Chapter 1 clinical psychologists use a variety of assessment procedures for a host of assumed ills. The range of different types of assessment is impressive: direct and indirect observation, self-report, reports from family members, hospital, school and care home staff, so-called 'clinical' observation, paper and computerised questionnaires, observation of children's play, semi-structured interview schedules, formalised schedules, projective tests, the analysis of audio and visual recordings – indeed every technique that can be devised for systematically delineating difference. Clinical psychologists have, from the establishment of the profession, been involved in this key aspect of the gaze.[12]

In the United States, where the majority of health care is paid for via private insurance, insurance companies *insist* on psychometric assessment and subsequent psychiatric labelling before agreeing to fund treatment. The point was not lost on Spitzer and his colleagues when revising *DSM-III: TIME* magazine reported from the first of their meetings that the most important thing, '… is that *DSM-III* is of crucial importance to the profession [because] … its diagnoses are generally recognized by the courts, hospitals and insurance companies.'[13]

Though not constrained by such institutional demands in the UK, clinical psychologists in the *compliant*[14] position perform psychometric assessment thereby giving the diagnostic system a scientific gloss. This can range from agreeing that someone 'has' post-traumatic stress to confirming that a person's IQ is less than 70.

The first two chapters have recorded something of the history of the profession's ongoing involvement in psychometric assessment. Such praxis invariably leads to a label, rarely the kind of 'mark' esteemed by the general public. Thus people can be described as deviant in a huge number of ways. Here, I shall focus on two aspects of such deviance: ADHD and depression.

It can been argued that describing a child as suffering from attention deficit hyperactivity disorder brings necessary services to the child in the form of medication and other 'help'. Equally, much-needed financial benefits (in the form of Disability Living Allowance for Children) may follow a diagnosis, parents will be excused blame for their child's conduct on the basis that the child is 'ill', teachers may receive additional classroom support and so on. There has been a decrease in the numbers of children designated as having 'special education needs'. In 2011–2012, 1.62 million (19.8 per cent) of children between the ages of 5 and 19 were labelled SEN. In 2012–2013, the number was 1.55 million (18.7 per cent).[15]

In such a well-balanced – and apparently mutually beneficial – system it can be difficult to remember that the child is being given toxic and experimental drugs that 'work' by effectively overdosing his metabolism. There are increasing claims that children who are difficult to manage have a neurodevelopmental disorder. The phrase 'neuro-developmental disorder' is one aspect of a lexicon designed to simultaneously obscure meaning and give power to 'those that know' – in this case so-called child experts. In fact we have no idea how any given individual is meant to develop neurologically, nor can we readily know that a person is neurologically disordered from casual behavioural observation. Yet ADHD is frequently diagnosed through such observation before confirmation is sought from a psychometric assessment. Psychiatrists, clinical psychologists and other professionals then *infer* a neurological problem. This is perfectly in step with child psychiatrists who then prescribe medication in order to suppress the conduct. Drugs such as Ritalin become access drugs for very similar illegal stimulants like speed (amphetamine) and cocaine and the very existence of that first diagnosis points to a future 'career' in human services for the growing child. In an age of ferocious drug company marketing it is no accident that the diagnosis of ADHD has risen a hundredfold in the UK in the last 20 years.[16]

Authoritative assertions abound from clinical psychologists. These form part of the rhetoric of professions which allows statements to appear true when they can only ever be opinion. Murray and colleagues, for example, state, in *Clinical Psychology Forum,* 'There is broad support for the current medical definition of ADHD, and its sub-types among the general medical community'.[17] They cite *medical* and psychiatric *journal* articles from 1998 and 1996 in support of their statement.[18] But what is meant by 'broad support'? Moreover, in what sense is work from 15 years previously 'current?' Let us assume that some medical and related professions support a medical definition. It is tempting to conclude, 'They would, wouldn't they?' The clinical psychologist authors continue, 'ADHD can be debilitating, impacting negatively on educational achievement, social behaviour, and family life.' There is no acknowledgement of the circularity of their position – we diagnose ADHD by observing behaviour and then claim that behaviour is *caused* by ADHD. This is an example of a category error common in mainstream psychiatry. A condition – depression, schizophrenia, Asperger's syndrome[19] – is *inferred* from someone's conduct and then that same conduct is seen as arising from the inferred condition. It is like saying that chairs and tables (specific examples of a category) are furniture (the category) but also, somehow, *caused* by furniture. For categories such as ADHD, depression and so on, any meaning of the observable conduct is obscured by a nonsensical confusion of category and cause. Such statements, by repetition, soon become the mainstay of professional writings and it can be difficult to enter the arena without participating in the rhetoric – an argument frequently used by authors to justify their use of diagnostic terminology.

In much the same way that the diagnosis of ADHD is on the rise, the diagnosis of depression is becoming so common that *not* being depressed will soon be considered abnormal in Western society.

Robert Spitzer, lead author of the third *Diagnostic and Statistical Manual*, a volume containing 265 disorders and published in 1980, has the following to say about how the committee approached the challenge of categorising mood disorders, 'In the absence of such evidence (for etiology [*sic*] as a classificatory device) categories are grouped together if they share important clinical-descriptive features. This includes all of the depressions and manias regardless of severity, chronicity, course, or apparent associations with precipitating stress.'[20]

The reader is referred to Jackson[21] for an extensive exploration of theories of the construction and treatment of depression and its forebear, melancholia. Jackson charts the history of the diagnosis from humoral postulants of the 5th century BCE to the publication of *DSM-III* in 1980. He notes numerous attempts by, amongst others, Samuel Johnson, Tuke, Pinel, Esquirol, Morel, Krafft-Ebing, Kraepelin, Meyer, Henry Maudsley and Freud to categorise and delineate forms of distress variously described as melancholia, involutional melancholia, insanity and psychoneurosis; 'depression' he notes as, 'a relative latecomer to the terminology for dejected states'.[22] In 1725 Blakemore writes of 'being depressed into deep Sadness and Melancholy', while in 1801 David Daniel Davis's translation of Pinel's *Treatise on Insanity,* rendered *l'abbattement* as 'depression of spirits'.

The difficulty, if not impossibility, of knowing what previous theorists meant by the term 'depression' has not deterred modern writers on the topic from diagnosing numerous historical figures with a host of disorders.[23] In a study of 291 'world-famous men', Felix Post suggests that 72 per cent of his sample of authors would be diagnosed as depressed. He posits that Balzac would be better seen as 'hypomanic', a diagnosis not included in any psychiatric nosologies until long after the author's death.[24]

Aetiology has been as debated as classification, psychological theorising being as varied as physiological explanations. For Esquirol, for example, season, climate, gender, age, idleness and scholarliness vied with 'organic lesions of the lungs' and 'displaced colons' as putative causative factors of melancholy. Potential treatments included Moral Medicine (aimed at a sympathetic lifting of the spirits), a clear sky, exercise, attention to diet, baths and coitus.

By 1980 Spitzer and his colleagues, in publishing *DSM-III*, agreed on a scheme wherein depression was classified as an affective disorder subdivided into bipolar and major depressions and further into cyclothymic, dysthymic and (again) into atypical bipolar disorders and atypical depressions. By the mid-1980s aetiological theories included loss, learned helplessness, separation anxiety, life events, cognitive distortions, genetics, endocrine changes and depletion or excess of neurotransmitters.

The *Highlights of Changes from DSM-IV-TR to DSM-5* supplement accompanying *DSM-5*[25] notes, in addition, that a 'suicide concern scale' is now included to be used 'regardless of diagnosis'. 'Intent' can only be inferred. Thus, the scale *cannot* measure suicidal intent but will reveal how concerned the assessor might be and will, no doubt, lead to diagnosis and intervention.

With the publication of *DSM-5* in 2013, the melancholia of Aristotle became 'depressive disorder' with eight variants.[26]

The assessment procedures of clinical psychologists have been, for many years, integral to the diagnosis of depression. As a probationer clinical psychologist in the late 1970s I was frequently asked to help psychiatrists in distinguishing between depression and dementia in older patients. They expected psychometric assessment to support observational and anecdotal evidence. Over the last 30 years the *Beck Depression Inventory* (the BDI or 'beady eye') has been the standard psychometric instrument for supporting the diagnosis.

For the patients of clinical psychologists who work in services for older people these assessments will have important consequences. Older people are – by far – the largest group receiving electroconvulsive therapy (ECT) in the world today, a procedure described as an 'electrical lobotomy'.[27] ECT has been described as the 'treatment of choice' for people over 65 who are deemed depressed. Clinical psychologists working in services for older people frequently offer therapeutic alternatives (the *eclectic* position) to electrocution but the *Zeitgeist* is such that the majority of persons over the age of 65 'marked' as depressed will receive drug treatment or ECT rather than kindly comfort from a Psy professional. In their daily practice clinical psychologists are hesitant to take up a position of active and public conflict with medical colleagues pursuing physically damaging ends for their patients. Indeed, like many journalists and members of the public, there are many qualifying clinical psychologists unaware that ECT – as a treatment option – still *exists* and are horrified to discover that it is the preferred treatment for many older people diagnosed as depressed. Only *one* article in the last 30 years in *Clinical Psychology Forum* has directly addressed the issue.[28]

ECT is but one example of the *physical harm* meted out to recipients of services and one which illustrates the bystander mentality of many professions allied to medicine or its sub-discipline, psychiatry. Many clinical psychologists would be surprised at the charge that they are implicated in a system which harms individuals: a cursory glance through clinical psychology journals would, however, indicate few examples of clinical psychologists speaking out against complicity in harmful services and numberless examples of authors supporting the status quo of assessment and treatment in the context of such services.

For the record

Until recently in the UK state system patients attending clinical psychology appointments were not routinely given access to personal files. Thus, incorrect factual information could easily remain unchecked for as long as files were held (even this is a grey area: various rules exist for the destruction of psychiatric and similar records but I am unaware of *anywhere* which has a system in place for acting on the destruction policy). Ironically, the collection of files on deviant individuals is one area where the gaze is at its most inefficient – records are kept, but rarely read and frequently lost; rather like CCTV cameras, it only appears that Big Brother is watching. Whatever ultimately happens to those records it is a condition of employment in the NHS that clinical psychologists record details of the patients seen and any assessments or treatment attempted. The *BPS Guidelines on Professional Practice* offer advice on the types of notes to be kept, security, confidentiality and more. In the USA, notes on diagnosis and treatment are used to form reports for insurance companies underwriting the costs.

In a series of seminars on record keeping over some 20 years I encouraged groups of clinical psychologists to discuss the advantages and disadvantages of such praxis. The latter have consistently outweighed the former even though all the participants (in the region of 500 practitioners over 15 years) kept clinical notes; frequently the justification was along the lines, 'I think I have to'. None of these practitioners knew how long such records were kept by their employers.[29]

These are not idle concerns. If assessments and accompanying diagnoses are held on record and made available to later staff who have no direct experience of the patient, those records will be used to add substance or detract from contemporary theorising about the patient's predicament. The written word has a tendency to be reified. A 10-year-old IQ assessment or *BDI* score and subsequent diagnosis may be challenged but, as a clinical psychologist may not be on hand to offer an alternative, the patient's mark will be used to justify fresh attempts to ameliorate the patient's so-called disorder. Those attempts will be the focus of the next three chapters.

Summary

We have seen that it is very difficult to know what any given clinical psychologist does in the privacy of the consulting room. The practitioner may be alone with the patient and subject to interpersonal dynamics that, like the patient, they cannot articulate or are unaware of. Recording or videoing sessions may give more of an idea of the nature of the interaction but, for the vast majority of clinical psychologists, these practices cease on qualification.

A reading of the academic literature can reveal, in generalised terms, what psychologists do but the minutiae of daily practice are disguised in the language of 'assessment' and diagnosis. In participating in such technical activities, the clinical psychologist will be enacting the role of 'scientist-practitioner' and designated expert while simultaneously avoiding the 'person' of the patient being assessed. With some notable exceptions, for example in the work of community psychologists, the context of the patient's plight goes unrecorded, however important the context appears to the assessing psychologist. The consequence of such praxis can be a lifetime written record of deviance for the patient and a variety of physical and psychological interventions harmful in the extreme. The following chapters will focus on some of those interventions.

Endnotes

1. Sachs, H. (1992). *Lectures on Conversation.* Oxford: Blackwell.

2. Smail, D. (1990). Design for a post-behaviourist clinical psychology. *Clinical Psychology Forum, 28,* 2–10.

3. See, for example, Wise, M. J. & Rapley, M. R. (2009). Cognitive behaviour therapy, psychosis and attributions of irrationality. Or, how to produce cognitions as 'faulty'. *The Journal of Critical Psychology, Counselling and Psychotherapy, 9*(4), 177–197.

4. Boyle, M. (2011). Making the world go away, and how psychology and psychiatry benefit. In M. Rapley, J. Moncrieff & J. Dillon (Eds.), *De-medicalizing Misery: Psychiatry, psychology and the human condition.* Basingstoke: Palgrave Macmillan, pp. 27–43.

5. See, for example, Pilgrim, D. (2007). The survival of psychiatric diagnoses. *Social Science & Medicine, 65*(3), 536–547 and Rogers, A. & Pilgrim, D. (2010). *A Sociology of Mental Health and Illness* (4th ed.). Maidenhead: Open University Press.

6. Johnstone, L. (2000). *Users and Abusers of Psychiatry: A critical look at psychiatric practice.* London: Routledge.

7. Harper, D. J. (1994). The professional construction of 'paranoia' and the discursive use of diagnostic criteria. *British Journal of Medical Psychology, 67*(2), 131–143.

8. Bentall, R. P. (Ed.). (1990). *Reconstructing Schizophrenia.* London: Routledge, and (2003). *Madness Explained: Psychosis and human nature.* Harmondsworth: Penguin. Bentall has also written *Doctoring the Mind* (Penguin, 2009) and is co-editor of the PCCS series, *Straight Talking Introductions to Mental Health Problems* (2009 and continuing).

9.   Smail, D. (2005) *Power, Interest and Psychology.* Ross-on-Wye: PCCS Books.

10. Holmes, G. (2010). *Psychology in the Real World: Community-based groupwork.* Ross-on-Wye: PCCS Books.

11. Bracken, P. & Thomas, P. (2010). From Szasz to Foucault: On the role of critical psychiatry. *Philosophy, Psychology and Psychiatry, 17*(3), 219–228.

12. Foucault, M. (1967). *Madness and Civilization.* London: Tavistock.

13. Leo, J. (1985). Battling over masochism. *TIME,* Dec. 2, 76.

14. Goldie, N. (1977). The division of labour among the mental health professions. In M. Stacey, M. Reid, C. Heath & R. Dingwall (Eds.), *Health and the Division of Labour.* London: Croom Helm, pp. 141–161.

15. Retrieved 25 October 2013 from https://www.gov.uk/government/policies/increasing-options-and-improving-provision-for-children-with-special-educational-needs-sen

16. Timimi, S. & Radcliffe, N. (2005). The rise and rise of ADHD. In C. Newnes & N. Radcliffe (Eds.), *Making and Breaking Children's Lives.* Ross-on-Wye: PCCS Books, pp. 63–70.

17. Murray, G. C., McKenzie, K., Brackenridge, B. & Glen, S. (2006). General practitioner knowledge about psychological approaches to ADHD. *Clinical Psychology Forum, 158,* 13–16.

18. Goldman, L. S., Genel, M., Besman, R. J. & Slanetz, P. J. (1998). Diagnosis and treatment of attention deficit/hyperactivity disorder in children and adolescents. *Journal of American Medical Association, 279,* 1100–1107 and Taylor, E., Chadwick, O., Hepinstall, E. & Danckaerts, M. (1996). Hyperactivity and conduct disorders as risk factors for adolescent development. *Journal of the American Academy of Academic Child Adolescent Psychiatry, 35,* 1213–1226.

19. It is no accident that ADHD, Asperger's, and Alzheimer's disease begin with the letter A. Diagnosticians and others with vested interests use the first letter of the alphabet for newly named conditions (coincidentally ensuring they appear first on Internet search engines).

20. Spitzer, R. L., Endicoot, J., Woodruff, R. A., Jnr. & Andreasen, N. (1977). Classification of mood disorders. In G. Usdin (Ed.), *Depression: Clinical, biological and psychological perspectives.* New York: Brunner/Mazel, p. 75.

21. Jackson S. W. (1986). *Melancholia and Depression.* New Haven, CT: Yale University Press.

22. *Ibid.,* p. 5.

23. Jamison, K. R. (1989). Mood disorders and patterns of creativity in British writers and artists. *Psychiatry, 32,* 125–134. See also Jamison, K. R. (1993). *Touched with Fire.* New York: Free Press.

24. Post, F. (1994). Creativity and psychopathology: A study of 291 world-famous men. *British Journal of Psychiatry, 165,* 22–34.

25. American Psychiatric Association (APA). (2013). *Diagnostic and Statistical Manual of Mental Disorders-5. Supplement: Highlights of Changes from DSM-IV-TR to DSM-5.* Washington, DC: American Psychiatric Association.

26. American Psychiatric Association (APA). (2013). *Diagnostic and Statistical Manual of Mental Disorders-5.* Washington, DC: American Psychiatric Association.

27. Breggin, P. R. (1998). Electroshock: Scientific, ethical, and political issues. *International Journal of Risk & Safety in Medicine, 11,* 5–40.

28. Newnes, C. (1991). ECT, the DCP and ME. *Clinical Psychology Forum, 36,* 20–24.

29. Newnes, C. (2004). Psychology and psychotherapy's potential for countering the medicalization of everything. *The Journal of Humanistic Psychology, 44*(3), 358–376.

CHAPTER 4

Problems in practice: Effectiveness and informed consent

Evidence surrounds us but not the evidence of our senses; the new evidence is the evidence of 'evidence-based practice' and 'evidence-based medicine'. Before the days of evidence-based treatments, were psychologists and psychiatrists unconcerned with anything as substantial as training or reading books and articles on which to base their practice? They presumably adorned front doors with brass plaques and started interfering with people's minds and bodies, without even a cursory glance toward Descartes to determine whether body and mind are distinguishable. Or at least so the champions of the new evidence would have us believe.

This chapter examines some of the problems in investigating the effectiveness of psychological interventions and the nature of research privileged in clinical psychology practice. I shall also explore concerns about the significant proportion of people who claim to be harmed by Psy professionals and, in the context of such concerns, question the type of informed consent possible for those entering the mental health system as patients.

The nature of psychological evidence

There is some truth in what the evidence lobby suggests. There must be some practitioners who have studied little research since qualifying. There remain unsupervised and poorly tutored professionals in psychiatry and clinical psychology, just as in other fields. The idea that practitioners of psychiatry, clinical psychology and psychotherapy pay no attention to scientific journals is, however, patently absurd. Clinical psychologists spend valuable time absorbing pseudo-scientific writings. Equally, many psychiatrists read official psychiatric texts and counsellors avidly read and write about the latest evidence for the effectiveness of their art. These journals consistently give a mechanistic view of therapy and humanity that seems to have no place for the complexity of relationships or the challenge of attempting to systematise these relationships. It is apparent that many psychiatric journals are vehicles for drug company propaganda and few attempt to grapple with the ethics and ideology of their scientism. For those who do read the latest research, there are major questions about the ways in which it is funded and the results disseminated.[1] Reported research is only a fraction of that carried out, and only the results that suit the vested interests of researchers or sponsors appear. A UK Government publication, *Effective Health Care*, in reviewing the newest so-called anti-psychotic medication concluded, 'Most relevant trials are undertaken by those with clear pecuniary interest in the results'.[2] Further, the research is of a particular, very narrow type (randomised controlled trials), some distance from what actually happens in everyday clinical practice.

There is more to life (and therapy) than the categorisation of people into diagnostic entities or personality types and the application of theoretical models of change derived from the laboratories of psychologists and pharmaceutical companies.

Some years ago, I came across an article on the desirability of moving clinical psychologist expertise into the world of the cancer sufferer. The article was brief and well referenced. These references included the *Journal of Psychosomatic Research*, the *Journal of Psychosocial Oncology*, the *British Journal of Cancer*, *Cancer Surveys*,

Social Science and Medicine, the *Journal of the Association of the Society of Clinical Oncology, Psychological Medicine* and the *British Medical Journal,* all, no doubt, prestigious examples of the scientific approach. My partner had recently received a secondary diagnosis of lung cancer. Neither she nor I sought solace or information in these journals. I didn't need to. I had already read, some 20 years before, Solzhenitsyn's *Cancer Ward.* I knew that visits to hospital would be marked by waiting alongside grey-faced, anxious people and their forlorn lovers and relatives. I knew that the wards would be terrible places where emaciated people would barely glance up as we came in and side rooms would be reserved for the middle classes and the dying. I had already known, like Solzhenitsyn's Aysa, the moment when a breast would be offered up for kissing one last time as, 'Today it was a marvel. Tomorrow it would be in the bin'.[3] And I knew all this at 15. I can't remember the authors of the article on clinical psychology and cancer but *Cancer Ward* stays with me still. As does Douglas Dunn's poem, 'Second Opinion', in which the narrator notices, with understated envy, the wedding ring of the junior doctor tasked with breaking the news of his loved one's spreading cancer.[4] Somehow, this no longer counts as evidence: lived experience, literature, poetry, the realm of our senses. One challenge for the pseudo-scientific community of psychology would be to embrace the commonplace wisdom of philosophy, literature and poetry.[5]

Psychiatry and psychology treat the mind–body divide as if it is unproblematic. As noted in the opening chapter, the psychology of Wundt upheld an introspective position wherein philosophical concerns were considered and debated. This position changed with the establishment of the experimental school and the clinic. I am not sure what proportion of clinical psychologists and other mental health professionals now read Descartes or Ryle. Neither philosophy nor literature would appear to count for much in the practice of psychiatry or psychology however keen the practitioner may be on novels and poetry in her life away from the consulting room. There is an increasing body of work exploring links between the two areas (see, for example, *Fiction's Madness*[6]) but, even here there is a tendency to re-interpret literature in terms of modernist notions of depression or madness, to the historiographer a major failing.

The criticism that Psy underestimates the truths inherent in literature is not new. In the late 19th century the wholly subjective introspection of William James epitomised psychology. Jung broke from Freud, in part, because Freud saw his respect for spirituality, an essential human concern, as pandering to neurosis. Freud himself, however, had considerable respect for the power of mythology though his interpretation of the Oedipus story inverted the original in order to comply with Freud's version of events (in the original, far from desiring his father's death, Oedipus chose to live many miles from his parents following the oracle's prediction of his fate – the meeting and subsequent slaying of his father was entirely accidental). The psychiatrist Alfred Meyer attempted to bring a philosophical approach back into the domain of an overwhelmingly biological psychiatry, and, more recently, Forsyth has argued: 'Psychologists do not study the mind, they do experiments. If psychologists were genuinely interested in the mind they would use every scrap of evidence they could lay their hands on; novels, poems, films, folklore, introspection, dreams.'[7] Russell Davis has made a similarly powerful plea on the importance of theatre for the work of mental health professionals.[8]

It is, however, as if the human condition, as explored by philosophers or novelists and other artists, is of less concern to mental health professionals who, at least in their working lives, depend on a diet of scientism. Double has noted that many psychiatrists and junior medical staff actually receive their so-called training in psychopharmacology from drug company salespeople.[9] Looking for guidance from government bodies such as the National Institute of Health and Care Excellence (NICE) is fraught with difficulty. For example, NICE continues to change its opinion on the use of drugs or approve addictive psychostimulants for children having already admitted that the diagnosis of ADHD is 'controversial'. Strikingly, a review by Jorm concludes, 'The public's view of psychotropic medication is almost uniformly negative, contrary to the views of clinicians and to evidence from RCTs.'[10] The reading lists of counselling and clinical psychology courses contain very little on pharmacology and less on the iniquities of research funding. They rarely pay lip service to the world of literature even though practitioners themselves read novels or poetry and some (for example, the personal construct therapist and clinical psychologist Don Bannister) have been successful novelists. Similarly, Miller Mair, a clinical psychologist, merged literature, psychology and the world of personal meaning in *A Poetics of Experience*.[11]

Novels have at least one considerable advantage over scientific writing; the former are presented, honestly, as fiction. The meanings and lessons derived from novelists are the personal constructions of the reader from material not masquerading as fact. This is, perhaps, less true in the cinema industry. New films are regularly heralded as being 'based on a true story'. One wonders what a Hollywood blockbuster 'based on a lie' might look like. Evidence presented in scientific journals, supported by complex statistical analyses, is meant to be the truth: if it makes no sense to the reader, then the reader is seen to be at fault. Psychology, applied or otherwise, is characterised by this type of evidence.

Evidence from experience

If we take seriously the evidence of our senses then there are paradoxes to be found at every turn: the caring psychiatrist who sees little reason to stop using ECT; the general practitioners who wouldn't take prescribed drugs themselves but write repeat prescriptions for major tranquillisers; the clinical psychologists who claim, publicly, to work as evidence-based scientist-practitioners, but in private admit that they have little evidence for anything; and the people who espouse the benefits of multidisciplinary teams but protect patients from team members they do not trust.

Contradictory and confusing experiences abound in clinical psychology. Clinical psychology trainees may discover that some psychotherapeutic techniques work quite well. More confusingly, they also discover that some patients in some mental health settings seem to feel a lot better after only one or two sessions of what the trainee had seen as a rather stumbling attempt at assessment. So much better, in fact, that the patient no longer wants appointments. What is the trainee to make of this? Analysts might suggest a 'flight into health'. The more diffident trainee might suspect that the patient actually feels no better but doesn't have the heart to say so. The scientific literature has something to say about this in terms of the dose-response curve in suggesting that the greatest impact of therapy is to be found in the first two sessions (it is frequently claimed that the first *five minutes* determine how much a patient is prepared to divulge to a new therapist). Common sense has a different slant: 'A problem shared is a problem halved'. Talk to someone twice and your problem will be reduced to a quarter and easily manageable. Smail has questioned the real benefits to be gained by such sharing, noting that it is *precisely* the 'problem halved' adage that adds undeserved substance to claims for the usefulness of counseling.[12]

Psychologists, psychotherapists and counsellors in training can be warned against consciously using personal experience in case it makes them less objective or emerges as 'countertransference' (broadly a reaction to the suffering of the patient brought on by 'unconscious identification' on the part of the therapist – one reason why analytic therapists have to undergo analysis so as to leave them a blank slate for patients' 'projections'; a challenging goal). Experience of any kind, be it childbirth or monitoring biorhythms during behavioural experiments, can only be subjective, that is, personal. There is also evidence that psychology departments have local data available that may never be published but are of some use in looking at outcome of therapy. In a survey of West Midlands clinical psychology departments in the UK, seven of ten respondents said that they regularly audited therapeutic outcome. They used a generally agreed set of standard assessments (e.g., SCL-90 and CORE) but none had published these results. This represents a huge store of unused data.[13] There is a great deal more. Clinical notes are full of material, never cross-referenced, about common factors in human misery. Clinicians notice that people taking so-called antidepressants are still depressed or people taking major tranquillisers are exhausted most of the time.

When visiting institutions for the first time staff notice the smell on wards and feel frightened. Clinical psychologists in training feel confused at ward rounds and can't follow the logic of organic theorising. Conversations with colleagues about the terrible circumstances of people's lives, the frequent remarks about a referred child's parents in the waiting room, the way a supervisor respects colleagues or upsets supervisees: this is all evidence. It all influences the way psychologists work. They are, quite literally, surrounded by evidence which, according to the public stance of the profession as a scientific corpus, is to be ignored in favour of that found in peer-reviewed journals.[14]

The right to informed consent

In the health field there is a growing rhetoric around notions of rights and responsibilities.[15] For patients of any number of different professions, information is offered which simultaneously fulfils one of the UK Government's many appeals to 'transparency' in services and, under the guise of informed consent, subtly shifts the burden of responsibility for the effects of the service onto the patient. Despite many claims on the part of mental health professionals to be 'user friendly' or 'empowering', information which might offer the means by which a more informed choice can be made is, by some margin, more readily available in the general health field; surgeons are expected to give patients information about potential unwanted effects and dangers of all surgical procedures just as pharmacists working in cancer care centres are expected to be a reliable source of information about medication and its adverse effects. In both mental health and general health services, however, the essential question from any patient – 'Will this intervention help *me*?' – is impossible to answer. Some of the reasons for this are outlined below.

'Am I so different from everybody else?'
You have arrived at the general practitioner's surgery. Having felt unwell for a week and, fearing taking time off from a prized

job (nowadays most jobs are prized), you reluctantly book an appointment with your GP who turns out to be a locum. After a few questions and some taps on your back, the doctor suggests you may have a chest infection. After a few more questions concerning allergies and your general state of health, you are prescribed medication. You tentatively ask, 'Will this work, doctor?' The reply? 'If things don't clear up in a week, come back.'

So, 10 minutes later, you have some pills which may work but you know they will take at least a week. Taking the next day off work is no longer an option. The sub-text of your question ('Will they work for *me?*') remains unaddressed. The locum can't be blamed for this; our reactions to drugs are idiopathic. The diagnosis is a hypothesis; the prescription the logical outcome of that hypothesis.

We have physical similarities – in the arrangement of internal organs and the fact these organs are protected by layers of muscle, fat and skin. Height, weight, general appearance can be measured and, via statistical analyses, normed. But any one of these supposed similarities, if subjected to scrutiny, will differ from what might be predicted from that norm and, when taken in combination, the patterns of difference rapidly become impossible to predict. If you are of average height but your lungs aren't quite aligned with each other and your skin prone to sunburn due to its colour or thickness you will be rather different from your neighbour who, at first glance, is of similar build. Add sex and diet to the equation and we begin to see the impossibility of the reified statistical average.

Then we take the tablets. Though medication is accompanied by information leaflets suggesting contra-indications with other drugs, existing medical conditions and diet (broccoli, for example, interferes with the desired effects of Warfarin), the human metabolism is invariably unique, already dependent on a host of variables not considered by the prescribing physician – everything from exercise to the built environment via genetics is said to impact on our nervous and digestive systems. So, sadly for the hopeful patient, there can be no reliable answer to the question, 'Will this work for *me?*'

You return to the surgery. After two more attempts to control your symptoms, the locum suggests your problem is stress related. Not the worry of losing your job or the frustration of your wasted consultations you are led to understand, but some hidden factor only counselling can unearth. So, you are referred to the clinical psychologist in the local community mental health team for a probable course of six sessions of therapy.

Informed consent in psychological therapy

Patients of clinical psychologists and other mental health professionals, like recipients of prescribed medicines, want to know, 'Will this help *me*?' The gold standard of evidence – meta-analysis of large-scale research studies – will not guide Psy interventions in particular local contexts. The fact, for example, that many Americans have, apparently, as shown by a meta-analysis, been helped by, say, psychoanalytic therapy, won't be of interest to a patient in Halifax who suspects her problems are more to do with her marriage than her unconscious desires and has no access to a costly psychoanalyst. That patient may be less reassured and probably confused when her therapist turns out to be an IAPT (Improving Access to Psychological Therapies) worker who has completed a short course in cognitive behaviour therapy after a previous career as a poorly paid secretary and is now supervised by a clinical psychologist.

Unlike medicine, psychotherapy does not involve the commitment to 'First do no harm'. This might be seen as fortunate for Psy professionals. The much-maligned research of Hans Eysenck established over 50 years ago that, according to measures of health and self-report, samples of patients either receiving or not receiving psychotherapy after being diagnosed as neurotic responded as follows: after two years, for both the therapy recipients and the non-therapy group 66 per cent felt better, while 33 per cent felt unchanged or worse. Eysenck, to the consternation of the then largely psychodynamic therapy industry of the UK, suggested that the two-thirds reporting improvement could be accounted for by *spontaneous remission*.[16] In other words, we have a period in adulthood (often estimated at a year) where things feel pretty bad but if we wait it out, things will improve. At worst, things won't much change – unless we visit a therapist in which case we might feel a lot worse off. This is information rarely proffered in information leaflets given to potential patients. These concerns should be regarded as a general backdrop to the specific difficulties outlined below.

Avoiding the question

In answering the question 'Can this help *me*?' clinical psychologists have a range of potential responses. Those of a psychodynamic persuasion might turn the question back to the patient utilising a theoretical justification that incorporates transference, dependency and concerns with authority or trust. A person-centred approach may, admittedly stereotypically, reply, 'So, you want to know if I can help you' – a statement, not a question but one which invites the equally rhetorical response, 'Duh!' Body therapists may invite the patient to start disrobing. Gestalt therapists may ask the patient to address the same question to a piece of furniture, 'Can you visualise in this empty chair that distrusting part of yourself?' Others may explore the discourse of 'help' or the narrative of 'distress'. A few might say, 'I don't know'. None will say, 'I'm not sure. I'm paid to be here for an hour and the manual says I have to respond in particular ways so what's the problem as far as you see it? We have an hour.'

In the fictitious example above the clinical psychologist may be hectored about the GP's failure to cure the patient's chest infection. This is a difficult scenario – the psychologist may sympathise with the patient's frustration, might even conclude there is not much more to say, but the context of the referral is important. In order to justify citing 'stress' as a cause of the patient's anxiety the referrer may have added some – from his or her point of view – relevant factors. The patient may have been recently bereaved and there may be a history of stress in the family (noting both as supposedly contributing factors immediately implies such experiences are not a feature of ordinary life). These suggestions may provoke a pursuit of biographical avenues wholly unrelated to the patient's frustration but in tune with the professional's training – family pressures and death are seen as triggers for breakdown and are a profitable source of material to mull over as there can be very few people who have experienced neither.

Medicalisation

In the UK, counsellors and, to a lesser extent, clinical psychologists and counselling psychologists, commonly use rooms in GP surgeries as their consulting rooms. The rooms have been hard-won, practice managers having identified the possibility of charging for accommodation, however temporary. For psychologists in the NHS, an exodus from psychiatric hospitals began in 1988 following the publication of the Trethowan Report the year before.[17] The report was the culmination of a government exercise which increased the training places for clinical psychologists and recommended their dispersal into the wider community. It was apparent from the start of the de-institutionalisation of psychiatric *staff* that the increase in numbers of community psychiatric nurses (CPNs – now termed community mental health nurses, CMHNs) and clinical psychologists in primary care would turn sectors of the community into forms of psychiatric ward.[18] CPNs were soon injecting patients in their homes or at surgery 'depot clinics' and psychologists, despite an apparent anti-medical stance, were embracing the autonomy offered by work in primary care facilities.

This enabled them to perfect psychometric assessment of numerous individuals and offer a bewildering variety of therapies spanning the humanistic, psychodynamic and behavioural fields. The assessments, especially of the 'personality' type, frequently used psychiatric rather than psychological jargon. Patients (called for largely political reasons 'clients') were seen in medical surroundings (pens labelled with drug company names remain commonplace) and now had diagnoses confirmed through psychometric testing before being subjected to whatever happened to be the latest therapy the psychologist had studied. This last is not a criticism of clinical psychology *per se*. Rather, learning new psychological interventions is a process embraced by Psy professionals from the onset of training, a search for a means of helping others that can be pursued throughout many Psy careers. It is a search akin to a religious search for truth and, in encapsulating an ongoing search for meaning, one which some authors see as the human lot. Slightly tongue in cheek, Kevin Sullivan, an ex-clinical psychologist and family therapist describes the hopefulness of psychotherapists in his poem, 'A Therapist and His Book'.[19]

This is it

This is the one
My new book
This one will be the answer

I've had other books
Thousands
Seemingly good in their time

But never like this one
This one is different
This one holds the key

With this book
All will fall into place
Anxiety will melt away
Therapy will flow from me
Others will just flow because of me

This is the book
… Until the next book

In failing to note the medical context and language of their praxis, clinical psychologists are probably not acting in bad faith. They may turn a blind eye to their working context or think it impolite to protest at the relentless promotion of the medical *Zeitgeist* in which they find themselves; Baker and colleagues have discussed the simple rules of conversation that bind debate and prevent conflict in medically dominated teams. This process is used to the advantage of drug company representatives who offer GPs and community mental health teams gifts. The salespeople are taught that any individual in the team who protests in these circumstances will be branded rude.[20] This is reflected beyond the confines of team meetings; British Psychological Society guidelines consistently state that clinical psychologists should not, for example, be involved in discussions about medication with their patients. Instead they are prompted to advise the patient to discuss concerns with the general practitioner. In both contexts – drug company representatives influencing teams and potential conflict in multidisciplinary teams apparently dominated by a medical discourse – politeness, the preservation of middle-class mores, is the higher-order discourse. Thus, the social rather than scientific agenda comes to determine what happens to patients.

The discipline of clinical psychology has been joined by that of counselling psychology. As discussed in Chapter 2, there has been an extraordinary increase in psychiatric diagnoses (from 112 in 1953 to 500 initially proposed for the most recent *Diagnostic and Statistical Manual*), almost matched by an increase in the available number of psychological tests. Clinical and counselling psychologists have been quick to seize on these opportunities. As previously noted, the diagnosis of attention deficit hyperactivity disorder, for example, in part aided by psychological testing of troublesome school children, has seen a rise in diagnosed individuals from 3000 in 1988 to 300,000 today.[21] Kovacova notes, '… in the UK between 1994 and 2010, prescriptions for stimulant drugs (e.g., Ritalin) to children under 16 rose from 6,000 in 1994 to an astonishing 660,000 in 2010.'[22] Those same children are seen by clinical psychologists, educational psychologists, child psychiatrists and entire teams of health professionals, most, but not all, of whom encourage them to take methylphenidate (Ritalin), see a family therapist and claim Disability Living Allowance for Children as a state benefit.

The patient or family may find themselves seen by a psychologist who not only fails to critique the medicalisation of distress but actively supports the process. Indeed, many clinical psychologists wish to have the right to prescribe medication on the basis they would be less inclined to prescribe than psychiatrists. To date clinical psychologists in two US states have gained prescription privileges though it is too early to tell whether this has made an impact on prescribing rates. Common sense would suggest that the more people there are to prescribe then the more prescriptions there will be.[23]

Counsellors too, either in private practice or employed by health trusts on behalf of GP surgeries, commonly see people already marked with a psychiatric diagnosis or taking medication for a diagnosed psychiatric disorder. As with the early days of clinical psychology's move into primary care, those counsellors are not encouraged (at least in their job descriptions) to challenge the prescribing of psychoactive medication to their patients.[24] For the non-medically trained counsellor a reverse logic can take over here – the antidepressant is 'working', ergo the patient was indeed 'depressed'. Some use the term 'treatment' for what is, essentially, a conversation. Thus counsellors and other psychological therapists implicitly support the medicalisation of the people they see. Some, perhaps, actively embrace the medical discourse. Others may 'normalise' distress by alluding to the frequency of, say, unhappiness after childbirth. But by agreeing to see the referred person in the first place they are supporting the referrer's notion that there is something *wrong* – a process Foucault analysed in terms of a praxis of identifying abnormality in order to, by default, define normality. It is ironic that counsellors will attempt to normalise a referred person's conduct when the *disciplining role* of the Psy professions (including counselling and psychotherapy) is to do the opposite.

Sexual relationships

Little considered by those entering therapy for the first time will be the common-sense view that *all* psychological therapy is seductive; if you are feeling sad and an apparently kind professional offers almost an hour to attend to your suffering, this might well be enough for you to fall for the listener – not so different from that first time when the boy/girl next door gave up half an hour to listen to you crying about how awful you found your parents.[25] You are unlikely to be told about the organisations offering help to patients who feel cheated or abused by therapy and therapists.

Schoener's work makes interesting, if a little dense, reading here. The title may be enough for some: *Psychotherapists' Sexual Involvement with Clients: Intervention and prevention.* The volume is weighty and covers sexual relationships between, amongst other pairings, therapists and patients, social workers and clients, supervisors and their supervisees, and clergy and their parishioners.[26] Examples include both consenting adults and underage children. The book title uses the term 'involvement'. This avoids the more common 'abuse'. It is arguable whether sexual involvement between consenting adults constitutes abuse though this is the preferred parlance in much of the literature. In the case of children, 'assault' – a criminal category – is more accurate; 'abuse' is at best a diluted description of the same conduct and, at worst, a distraction from the physical act; 'abuse' being more descriptive of the breach of professional trust than the sexual behaviour.

The scenario is less straightforward between adults even though, 'When I take a train, I don't expect the driver to make a pass at me. When I enter psychotherapy, I don't expect the therapist to do likewise.'[27] But, a train driver is at liberty to make a pass (it is far more likely to be the train conductor) that the passenger may turn down. Similarly, a psychologist or counsellor can make a sexual approach to a patient who is, again, at liberty to say, 'No'. A frequent argument against such a simplistic view is that the therapist is abusing his or her power, often at the expense of a vulnerable other. Mary Boyle has examined the professional use of the term 'vulnerable', highlighting the way the discourse makes vulnerability an attribute of the individual rather than a contextual phenomenon.[28] Typical cases of therapists who have been censured for sexual relationships with patients have used a similar discourse. This is understandable, perhaps, where the patient is learning disabled, a frail elderly person or a minor but less so when the patient is of the age of consent. Consent, again, is the key. For those who can neither consent nor defend themselves 'assault' or 'rape' are more accurate terms.

For adults of consenting age an essentially undermining and medicalised discourse may replace any suggestion that the relationship is based on equal power. Therapists of many different stripes can, indeed, be censured (and in the case of National Health Service employees summarily dismissed) for sexual relationships with patients (for NHS staff, the charge is 'Gross Moral Turpitude') but patients may be tarred (or re-tarred) with a variety of diagnostic brushes something along the lines, 'He (the therapist) exploited her vulnerability brought on by grief', 'She (the therapist) exploited the masochistic tendencies so typical of those with borderline personality disorder'. Purveyors of the concept of the unconscious can go further, 'The analyst was acting out his countertransference by seducing the analysand', 'The patient projected her sexuality onto the analyst who was unable to contain (the patient's) desires and suggested a more intimate therapeutic direction'. In these last two examples, it is noteworthy that neither patient nor therapist is blameworthy – it is the unbridled unconscious that is at fault (as it is, by definition, *un*conscious, it is not clear that anything could have been done to prevent the sexual relationship).

I have been involved, as an 'external expert', in two cases where patients complained that their clinical psychologists (both men) had abused their position of power by beginning sexual relationships with them. In both cases the relationships had begun after the therapy was concluded. The commonest professional reading of this is that the balance of power had been established during the therapy. In one case the psychologist had divorced his wife in order to live with the patient and, in the other, the psychologist and patient had eventually married. In *both* cases the complaint of abuse had been made more than a year after the end of the relationship, some three years after the end of therapy. For the clinical psychologists the outcome had been suspension from work and investigation by the BPS. Their careers in the National Health Service were effectively over. A familiar reading of both scenarios might suggest that the women had acted vengefully as they had both, apparently, been content to live with their ex-therapists for two years before, with the end of cohabitation, raising their concerns. Of course, my involvement was limited to discussions with the clinical psychologists; the facts about the time periods discussed are, however, a matter of record. It is no simple matter to discover what 'really happened' in these cases; it is quite possible that the two men, in discussing events with a respected male colleague, gave highly selective accounts. The fear of losing their employment would have been a major factor. What is undeniable, however, is that the cases were not obvious examples of therapeutic abuse or assault.

In summary, information pertaining to the likelihood of sexual advances from a psychologist or counsellor might prove helpful in terms of the putative patient's right to informed consent. But the issue is clouded by the ways in which professional codes re-language assault as abuse and the subtle ways in which sexual relationships between consenting adults are positioned as exploitation of the (understandably) more vulnerable patient.

An impossible profession

UK clinical psychology trainees are expected, during a three-year doctoral programme, to develop certain competencies in relation to assessment, therapy and research. The organisational context of the NHS makes it likely that most trainees will include a child and family setting as part of their work experience. For many – single, white, women in their mid-twenties – this can be something of a trial by fire. A feared question, subtly different from 'Will this help *me?*' is more rhetorical, 'Do you have children of your own?' The sub-text, immediately deduced by the trainee, is close to 'How can you – a white, young, childless, professional – know anything about my family's problems?'

We are *all* different metabolically. Social, cultural and familial differences take our idiosyncrasies to unimaginable levels of complexity. Cognitive behaviour therapy had its origins in East Coast American college students who were struggling with their exams. (CBT for exam strugglers has now been replaced in both

the USA and UK by variants on Ritalin [methylphenidate], a drug
which, for some, focuses energy on study in the way caffeine pills
did for students in the 1970s.) It seems appropriate that a therapy
rooted in arguing with oneself should have been popular amongst
bright college kids on the Eastern seaboard but how is such praxis
to translate to modern-day Britain where referrals will be from a
myriad of intellectual, economic and cultural backgrounds? The
referred family, when confronted by a slightly hesitant young
professional, is unlikely to feel much connection with the trainee
clinical psychologist; a scenario made worse if that same trainee is
attempting a CBT variant.[29]

Counsellors can be of a different ilk. Frequently older though
again often female, they may have life experiences – motherhood,
marriage, divorce, bereavement – closer to those of their patients.
They will frequently have sought counselling help themselves.
Indeed, since Freud analysed himself, all psychoanalytic training
insists on the trainee analyst undergoing a personal analysis and
a number of humanistic therapies make an assumption that the
counsellor will have undergone personal therapy. But there the
similarity ends. Many of these counsellors will have taken up
counselling later in life, perhaps switching careers or turning to the
role as an alternative to raising children who have left home. They
may have their counselling salary as their only source of income
or already feel financially secure as a result of a previous well-paid
career or that of a careerist spouse. Some will have been interested
by humanist therapy before embarking on the CBT path, some
may have undertaken 'personal development' programmes and
some may see themselves as part of a long tradition of *healers*. The
position taken by the latter group may include the notion that
their mere presence in the same room as the patient will bring
relief.[30]

If patients are concerned that the therapist is just too different
in background to understand their struggles, might they be
encouraged to know that the therapist has survived certain life
tribulations? This may be where Freud's statement that therapy is
an impossible profession comes into its own. Surveys and statistics
from the Royal College of General Practitioners indicate that

many GPs struggle to control their nicotine or alcohol intake while others struggle to avoid the temptation of readily available opiate drugs. Information on, say, marriage breakdown or alcohol and drug use, however, is far harder to come by than that on the GP's qualifications or athletic record. Clinical psychologists too are far removed from any demand to reveal important information about their own struggles with ordinary life. Although a therapist might think it useful to describe to a patient a situation he or she has dealt with, that same therapist may elect not to tell the patient about tax avoidance, guilt at seeing the patient privately while ostensibly employed by the NHS or the fact he is impotent or neither likes nor wants children. Revelations about the therapist's sexuality or economic instability may only be made if the therapist sees these as 'relevant'. Hiding such information is seen as therapeutic.

It is possible to deconstruct the justifications for any number of secrets clinical psychologists keep from their patients (and others) but that is not my aim here. The purpose is simpler: it might be important, for the sake of informed consent at least, for the patient to know that the psychologist considers herself at least as mad (in the most ordinary of ways) as her patients. There is an increasing literature wherein clinical psychologists admit to a host of difficulties described in terms of diagnosis. Much of this literature is only available to other clinical psychologists via publications such as *Clinical Psychology Forum*; see, for example, McCourt.[31] Many patients will already suspect there is nothing particularly notable about their therapists as exemplars of wellbeing and this may matter little to them. Some clinical psychologists in the UK, for example, have gained considerable kudos and credibility for coming out as ex-recipients of psychiatric services.[32] For some patients, however, it might seem important to know that the therapist's short-temperedness is due, in part, to a row that morning with an errant spouse or the fact they beat their youngest child with a birch twig and feel morosely guilty about it.

Does clinical psychology 'work?'

This is a simple question and one which goes beyond the patient's demand, 'Will this work *for me*?' Clinical psychology is a diverse entity; as we have seen in the opening chapters there are clinical psychologists who work with a wide range of patients, using a wide range of technical methods to assess and treat. Qualifications are equally varied and the training differs across continents and within countries – see Chapter 7 for more on the professional aspects of the discipline. Clinicians seeing patients draw from many theoretical traditions which, in their popularity at least, reflect the current cultural *Zeitgeist* whilst, as a whole, the traditions can be seen as schools of psychology and psychotherapy that continue to gather new adherents. Clinical psychologists tend to be loyal to particular therapeutic schools; the evidence base for effectiveness is so disparate that no clinical psychologist need change school as it is relatively simple to access research that contradicts any evidence that claim's one's preferred praxis is flawed. The research is scientistic rather than scientific – the resultant closure of debate within pre-ordained parameters does not allow researchers or clinical psychologists practising as therapists to take a more sociological perspective. In effect, published research follows a pattern of claim and counterclaim and it is this pattern, rather than the details of particular studies, which merits examination (see Chapter 2, in particular the work of Marshall).

To the extent that the discipline enables over 200,000 academics, clinicians, researchers and lecturers worldwide to earn a living, it can be said to 'work'. These professionals require an infrastructure for their practice which also supports the salaries of those in publishing houses, administrative staff, domestic cleaning staff and so on. Inevitably entrenched in the capitalist project, clinical psychology supports and enhances that project. It worked for me in this respect. I may not have survived the physical demands of remaining a ceiling tiler. *All* the men I worked with in the tiling gang 30 years ago are now dead, a sad reminder that Engels' point about the arduousness of labour for the post-industrial working classes is as true now as it was in the 1840s.[33] Along the way I met numerous patients and colleagues who excited me and made many friends. Materially, the profession provided me with an ample living that I doubt I could have chanced upon in another way.

As a discipline, the profession also works in the Foucauldian sense of delineating normality (by identifying *ab*normality) and disciplining the populace.[34]

A modernist reading of 'work' demands an examination of the available published evidence. As noted above and in the previous chapter, published research can support most praxis with patients. Evidence cited in literature critical of the therapeutic ambitions of clinical psychology can make uncomfortable reading for practitioners. I shall return to this theme in the next two chapters. For the purposes of this chapter, however, I shall briefly review some key studies. Again the evidence is scientistic rather than scientific; for example, Strupp and Hadley concluded that professionally accredited psychologists were no more effective than untrained university professors with no psychology background in trying to improve, via a psychological intervention, a number of areas of patient functioning.[35] Strupp and Hadley's study can easily, in decidedly modernist mode, be criticised for a small sample size (30). McCord, however, with a sample of 650 boys seen as likely to become delinquent, studied the impact of either receiving a combination of individual therapy and tutoring from licensed Psy professionals (group one) or receiving no designated help (group two). The boys in group one rated counselling as 'helpful' and the professionals rated the usual two-thirds as having benefited. Despite these findings, during a follow-up study, the counselled boys were found to be committing more serious crimes and, at a 30-year follow-up, were *more* likely to be alcoholic and unhappy in their work or diagnosed mentally ill.[36] This result echoes the conclusion from one of the pre-eminent psychotherapy researchers in the USA: a decade before McCord's research Robert Carkhuff had concluded that negative effects in long-term outpatient psychotherapy treatment were extremely common.[37]

In the Fort Bragg Demonstration Project the sample size was considerably larger than McCord's sample. Here, inpatient and outpatient psychological services were offered to over 42,000 children and adolescents for five years. Patients were assessed via self-report (most were satisfied with their treatment) and psychometric assessment during and after treatment. It is here that the results make for sobering reading. A reader in the pro-professional camp might perhaps defensively turn the accusation of scientism against the research in its reliance on psychometric data. Nonetheless, the study has been heralded as an example of one of the few research projects of its type to use a sufficiently large sample; a qualitative methodology would have proved immensely costly (as it is the study cost $80 million[38]). Tana Dineen cites the downbeat conclusions of the Fort Bragg project's authors that, '... the assumption that clinical services are in any way effective might be erroneous', and, 'although substantial evidence for the efficacy of psychotherapy under laboratory-like conditions exists, there is scant evidence of its effectiveness in real-life community settings (i.e., outside of the research setting)'.[39]

According to Stein, efficacy rates for some groups are more disappointing than newly qualified practitioners might hope. For sex offenders the rate is an astonishingly low 0.05 (i.e., one in two hundred patients don't re-offend[40]) and for children diagnosed as conduct disordered 0.17 (less than one in five experience a change in conduct in the desired direction[41]). Stein's system focuses on conduct considered undesirable by observable factors, frequently antisocial.[42] I should add that on the mysteries of concepts such as 'increased ego strength' or invalid diagnostic entities such as 'depression' Stein makes no comment. For those of a psychodynamic, medicalised persuasion there are measurable goals for both. I shall examine these ideas in Chapter 6.

An information leaflet?

Given the above, what might a reasonably informative leaflet for psychological therapy services include? A person might be surprised to discover they are likely to be psychometrically assessed, diagnosed, maintained on psychoactive drugs with no protest from the clinical psychologist or counsellor and offered a therapy either reflecting the latest interest of the therapist or a therapeutic style the therapist has maintained for many years despite little evidence of therapeutic efficacy as measured by positivistic research. Patients may find themselves seduced by the intimacy of the relationship which might lead to becoming involved in a consensual sexual relationship with the psychologist. If they have brought along their teenager in the hope of changing the adolescent's obnoxious behaviour they may discover the chances of receiving the help they wanted were very slim from the outset. If an elderly relative is assessed as depressed via a psychological test, the family may be unaware that a likely outcome is ECT. None or all of this might be experienced as helpful. The ways in which Psy professionals position themselves against the medical discourse – effectively, talk is good, drugs are bad – makes it unlikely that they will offer informed consent of the type suggested by the above analysis.

Should the potential patient know of the clinical psychologist's struggles in marriage, sexuality, weight gain or obsessive checking? Should patients be informed if the psychologist systematically lies on tax-return forms, had an appalling childhood or cannot bear the colour blue? Would the therapist even be aware of some of these things? If so, how would the psychologist know *which* facets of her life to reveal? The discourse that therapists reveal those things they consider useful to the therapeutic endeavour assumes knowledge of the way in which the patient will interpret any given revelation, a knowledge the Psy professional can only gain *post hoc*.

The right to know

What then does 'the right to know' mean in the context of clinical psychology and counselling? In offering information about medication, GPs are hampered by the idiopathic nature of the human metabolism and a firm belief in the placebo effect of saying positive things about the likely success of any prescription – a belief which flies in the face of the daily experience of talking to patients about adverse effects. Information leaflets concerning medication can be difficult to understand, overly reassuring and simultaneously reframe distress as bona fide (psychiatric) illness, for example, warning against the likelihood of developing 'depression' as a *result* of taking so-called antidepressants (see the information leaflet included with, for example, Prozac). The patient's right to know may be constrained by reading ability, the small font and wordiness of the leaflet and the sheer length of the text (to avoid litigation, leaflets can be in excess of 4,000 words). Further, the information is presented in a specialist vocabulary that can prove difficult to decipher and disheartening if one can. This ignores the selective nature of the information presented and the sources of data – from drug-company-sponsored research to infrequently recorded patient self-report.[43]

For psychological therapists, however, the demand for a right to know might be yet more problematic. We know that therapy can leave people feeling worse than before and that therapists, like any of us, are perfectly capable of exploiting relationships for financial and sexual gain. Though many will baulk at the suggestion, we also know that clinical psychology, psychotherapy and counselling are embedded in a medical discourse whereby some professionals may abhor the medicalisation of distress but even as they do so are either directly or indirectly involved in the diagnostic project. Many clinical psychologists, for example, will be working in community mental health teams where medication is the norm and electroconvulsive therapy the preferred modus operandi for their psychiatric colleagues while primary care counsellors are surrounded, in GP surgeries, by medical paraphernalia and drug company propaganda. We know that therapists suffer similar tribulations, self-doubt and fears as their patients and some are considered or consider themselves to be mad, bad or dangerous. Would all this be 'too much information' for potential patients?

Perhaps, in answer to the question, 'Will this help *me*?' the response, also reinforced by an easy-to-read information leaflet could be, 'We all change through circumstances and context. As part of your context, our meetings and whatever medication you take will be part of this change. I have no idea if the change will turn out to be for the better or worse.' It is an unlikely scenario and, given the immediate concerns of many patients, may be heard as a facetious remark, an example of modesty, an attempt at rejection, or not heard at all while the patient focuses on what the clinical psychologist is wearing. Though honest, the response is unlikely to lead to the patient rejecting the offer of help. Perhaps, paradoxically, even such denials of omnipotence would add to the essential seductiveness of the therapeutic encounter.

This seems to me an important point; people arrive distressed at a clinical psychologist's door and seem frequently inclined to take on trust the expert help on offer. It is impossible to avoid the ubiquity of psychology and, increasingly, clinical psychology. Through the auspices of the BPS press office the discipline has marketed itself to good effect. It will be a rare patient who arrives for an appointment without some idea – based on a magazine article or television news story – that psychology or counselling has something to offer. The patient *may* have read information from the particular clinical psychologist though this is rare.[44] Patients may feel harried because of a difficult journey to the appointment or ashamed of what they want to divulge. The person may be confused that, due to economic constraints, there are likely to be no more than six sessions on offer whatever the problem turns out to be. Numerous factors make it unlikely that the patient will attend to what the clinical psychologist says at the first meeting; these proximal forces seem to make impossible informed consent. The distal forces of cultural influence, economic uncertainty and a *Zeitgeist* wherein psychology is an accepted aspect of modern discourse makes hard to hear virtually *anything* the clinical psychologist might say at that meeting. Assuming the potential patient can read (estimates of illiteracy in UK adults range from 17 to 23 per cent), one possibility is to send the patient an information leaflet some weeks in advance of the appointment.

The concerns detailed in this chapter might suggest a leaflet stating that, according to the self-interested research of clinical psychologists, there is a 66 per cent chance that therapy will leave the patient feeling no worse. Conversations are likely to be reasonably soothing and positive to the extent that the patient will feel grateful and unwilling to criticise the psychologist. Long-term follow-up to see how the patient is doing after a year may well show some gains but it won't be possible to say if these are a direct result of the therapy.

The next two chapters will examine in more detail the reasons for what may appear to be a rather modest espousal of the benefits of clinical psychology intervention. Chapter 8 will look at the tentative promise of that intervention in the context of a more critical praxis.

Endnotes

1. Lexchin, J., Bero, L. A., Djulbegovic, B. & Clark, O. (2003). Pharmaceutical industry sponsorship and research outcome and quality: Systematic review. *British Medical Journal, 326,* 1167–1170.

2. NHS Centre for Reviews and Dissemination. (1999). Drug treatment for schizophrenia. *Effective Health Care 5*(6), 1–12, p.9.

3. Solzenitsyn, A. (1968). *Cancer Ward.* London: The Bodley Head, p. 425.

4. Dunn, D. (1995). Second Opinion. In *Elegies.* London: Faber and Faber.

5. There are numerous textbooks on the human condition; see, for example, Shklar, J. (1984). *Ordinary Vices.* Cambridge, MA: Harvard University Press, and Rowe, D. (1991). *Wanting Everything.* London: HarperCollins. Clinical psychologists might add to their understanding via, for example, Dickens and Zola (*Hard Times* and *Germinal,* respectively, cover class oppression pretty exhaustively). The angst, desperation and anxieties of the middle classes are described throughout Balzac's *Comedie Humaine.* Grief weeps from the final pages of Byatt's *Still Life* and madness permeates *Titus Alone* by Mervyn Peake. A meaningful reading of hallucinatory paranoia nuances the film *The Fisher King,* directed by Terry Gilliam, while the drug-induced variety saturates Waugh's *The Ordeal of Gilbert Pinfold* and *Fear and Loathing in Las Vegas* by Thompson. Hypocrisy is laid bare in Miller's *The Crucible* and love is explored in *Possession* by Antonia Byatt.

   See Byatt, A. S. (1985). *Still Life.* London: Chatto & Windus; Byatt, A. S. (1990). *Possession.* London: Chatto & Windus; Gilliam, T. (1991). *The Fisher King.* Tri-Star Productions; Miller, A. (1953/1974). *The Crucible.* Harmondsworth: Penguin Books; Peake, M. (1959/1970). *Titus Alone.* Harmondsworth: Penguin Books; Thompson, H. S. (1971/1979). *Fear and Loathing in Las Vegas.* London: Granada; Waugh, E. (1957/1972). *The Ordeal of Gilbert Pinfold.* Harmondsworth: Penguin Books.

6. Clarke, L. (2009). *Fiction's Madness.* Ross-on-Wye: PCCS Books.

7. Forsyth, R. S. (1988). *From Here to Humanity.* Nottingham: Pathway Publications, p. 23.

8. Russell Davis, D. (1992). *Scenes of Madness: A psychiatrist at the theatre.* London: Routledge.

9. Double, D. B. (2001). Can psychiatry be retrieved from a biological approach? *The Journal of Critical Psychology, Counselling and Psychotherapy, 1*(1), 27–30.

10. Jorm, A. F. (2000). Mental health literacy: Public knowledge and beliefs about mental disorders. *The British Journal of Psychiatry, 177,* 396–401.

11. Mair, M. (1989/2013). *Between Psychology and Psychotherapy: A poetics of experience.* London: Routledge.

12. Smail, D. (1996). *How to Survive without Psychotherapy.* London: Constable.

13. Stewart, L. & Newnes, C. (2000). The 'scientist-practitioner' model: Discussion and evaluation of the extent to which outcome is evaluated, the measures used and what they revealed in clinical psychology adult mental health services in the UK. (Rejected by) *The Journal of Mental Health* and available from the second author.

14. It is not at all clear how wide an evidence base clinical psychologists use in practice. It is quite possible that the evidence from experience, literature and so on is already driving clinical work. We are, however, positioned as scientist-practitioners and subscribe to appropriate journals. Some departmental bookshelves heave with books on cognitive behaviour therapy, research methodology and similar signs of scientific activity. My experience of many colleagues over the years, however, has been that the journals remain unopened and the textbooks are left to moulder. Departments may have a 1975 tome on neuropsychological assessment or another on mental health promotion in children, but neither book will have been replaced by a newer edition. A dusty collection of volumes of similar vintage is likely to look untouched as are many of the books on supervisors' shelves.

Perhaps clinical psychologists are already paying attention to the world of literature, the arts and their own experiences but feel constrained by the rhetoric of our profession from saying as much. Two *Clinical Psychology Forum* papers (Cliffe, 1994; Gurnani, 1993) have, for example, used Shakespeare as a reference point for insights into distress and therapy. A few others have name-checked popular culture in their titles (e.g., Sayal-Bennett, 1996) and two poets risked publication (Hussain, 1998; Gaussen, 1999). Two papers discuss the benefits of creative writing in therapy (Mills, 1991; Gilbert, 1995). One brave soul (Bailes, 1998) used A. A. Milne to good effect. There has been only one teaching tale (Marshall, 1993) and one paper explicitly calling for an approach to the mind that honours our artistic side (Chadwick, 1996), a call repeated in book form (Chadwick, 2001). A special issue of *Changes* (Newnes & Marzillier, 1993) included papers from clinical psychologists on *Troilus and Cressida*, Vonnegut,

Wuthering Heights and Marie Cardinal's *The Words to Say It*. John Marzillier has written on narcissism and *Dorian Gray* (1990).

Clinical Psychology Forum has included personal accounts of cancer (Crawford-Wright, 1993), AIDS (Passariello, 1988), obsessionality (McCourt, 1999), visual impairment (Pimm, 1993), procrastination (Graham White, 1994), motherhood (Wallace, 1993), retirement and resignation (Cattrall, 1988; Scott, 1993; Kirkland-Handley, 1998), the experience of head injury (Newnes, 2006), and getting older (Graham White, 2000). There has been at least one appeal for clinical psychologists to look inward rather than out (Seager, 1993) and five papers on the importance of religion and spirituality (Golding, 1993; Mills, 1997; Myers & Baker, 1998; Cunningham & Simpson, 2000; Clarke, 2001). Two articles examine the experience of cross-cultural therapy (Aitken, 1998; Patel, 1998). One paper speaks of the experience of management (Newnes, 2000) and another on the felt fraudulence of being a clinical psychologist (Mollon, 1989). An honest account of being gay clinicians almost brought the house down (Taylor, Solts, Roberts & Maddicks, 1998; Roberts, 1999). Meanwhile, a coming out piece passed without public comment (Daiches, 1998). Curiously, only one paper deals directly with why the author chose to be a psychologist in the first place (Rowe, 1992), surely something which should be publicly available from all clinicians. Lars Sjodahl (1997), Peter Chadwick (1997) and Rufus May (2000) have written of their own experience of madness, recovery and receiving psychiatric services. The experience of service users has also been usefully converted into material for use with other clients (White, 1993).

Overall, clinical psychology is not a desert when it comes to discussing personal experience and the usefulness of art and literature. These examples are, however, very much the exception; the *Forum* articles cited are taken from a total number exceeding 1500 and the majority were commissioned rather than spontaneously submitted. Thus, in *Forum* at least, less than 3 per cent of papers explicitly engage with the personal in our work and fewer still have explored how it feels to sit with or attempt to help people in distress. The proportion diminishes dramatically if this kind of writing is considered in relation to the thousands of articles published in journals requiring statistical means to determine what is evident.

Aitken, G. (1998). Reflections on working with and across differences: Race and professional differences in clinical psychology therapy encounters. *Clinical Psychology Forum, 118,* 11–17; Bailes, G. (1998). Control. *Clinical Psychology Forum, 117,* 15; Cattrall, R. (1988). Live, direct and written. *Clinical Psychology*

Forum, 15, 18–20; Chadwick, P. (1996). In search of 'Deep Music': Artistic approaches to the study of mind. *Clinical Psychology Forum, 89,* 8–11; Chadwick, P. (1997). Recovery from schizophrenia: The problem of poetic patients and scientific clinicians. *Clinical Psychology Forum, 103,* 39–43; Chadwick, P. (2001). *Personality as Art.* Ross-on-Wye: PCCS Books; Clarke, I. (2001). Psychosis and spirituality: Finding a language. *Clinical Psychology Forum, 149,* 19–22; Cliffe, M. J. (1994). Literary quotes, clinical psychology and the exact significance of Shakespeare. *Clinical Psychology Forum, 74,* 11–12; Crawford-Wright, A. (1993). The big C. *Clinical Psychology Forum, 53,* 8–9; Cunningham, G. & Simpson, J. (2000). A conversation on conflict. *Clinical Psychology Forum, 143,* 24–26; Daiches, A. (1998). Fear and cloaking in psychology. *Clinical Psychology Forum, 117,* 9; Gaussen, T. (1999). Sand, surf and SPSS: Lines written whilst completing a doctorate. *Clinical Psychology Forum 134,* 41; Gilbert, J. (1995). Clients as poets: Reflections on personal writing in the process of psychological change. *Clinical Psychology Forum, 75,* 3–5; Golding, L. (1993). On being a Jewish psychologist. *Clinical Psychology Forum, 51,* 12; Graham White, J. (1994). Procrastination: Early learning, indecision, or the art of living slowly? *Clinical Psychology Forum, 66,* 33–34; Graham White, J. (2000). Some introspections on the psychopathology of retirement and older age. *Clinical Psychology Forum, 141,* 5–7; Gurnani, P. D. (1993). Facilitating cognitive-behavioural therapy with a bit of help from Shakespeare. *Clinical Psychology Forum, 62,* 19–20; Hussain, F. A. (1998). 'The leaving' and 'Here'. *Clinical Psychology Forum, 117,* 22; Kirkland-Handley, N. (1998). Retiring from the NHS: The first 12 months. *Clinical Psychology Forum, 117,* 24–25; Marshall, R. J. (1993). The true story of a white sombrero. *Clinical Psychology Forum, 62,* 22; Marzillier, J. (1990). The picture of Dorian Gray: The narcissistic quest for immortality. *Changes: An International Journal of Psychology and Psychotherapy, 8*(3), 162–171; May, R. (2000). Routes to recovery from psychosis: The roots of a clinical psychologist. *Clinical Psychology Forum, 146,* 6–10; McCourt, J. (1999). A dilemma of disclosure. *Clinical Psychology Forum, 125,* 14–16; Mills, N. (1991). The creative writing group. *Clinical Psychology Forum, 38,* 22–24; Mills, N. (1997). E = Mc^2: Psychotherapy and spiritual healing. *Clinical Psychology Forum, 106,* 8–11; Mollon, P. (1989). Narcissus, Oedipus and the psychologist's fraudulent identity. *Clinical Psychology Forum, 23,* 7–11; Myers, J. & Baker, M. (1998). Religiously committed psychologists, talking. *Clinical Psychology Forum, 117,* 30–32; Newnes, C. (2000). Just managing. *Clinical Psychology Forum, 141,* 16–20; Newnes, C. (2006). Reflecting on recovery from head injury. *Clinical Psychology Forum, 159,* 34–40; Newnes, C. & Marzillier, J.

(1993). Ecrits Critiques. Special issue of *Changes: An International Journal of Psychology and Psychotherapy*. Hove: LEA; Passariello, N. M. (1988). Living with AIDS. *Clinical Psychology Forum, 18,* 2–5; Patel, M. (1998). Black therapists/white clients: An exploration of experiences in cross-cultural therapy. *Clinical Psychology Forum, 118,* 18–23; Pimm, T. (1993). A matter of perception: Coping with visual impairment. *Clinical Psychology Forum, 51, 27*; Roberts, B. (1999). Pride and prejudice. *Clinical Psychology Forum, 131,* 5–8; Rowe, D. (1992). Learning to spell p-s-y-c-h-o-l-o-g-y. *Clinical Psychology Forum, 50,* 6–8; Sayal-Bennett, A. (1996); 'Diamonds and rust' (with apologies to Joan Baez): The US health care experience. *Clinical Psychology Forum, 89,* 22–23; Scott, N. (1993). Resignation. *Clinical Psychology Forum, 53,* 2–4, Seager, M. (1993). The courage to be truly psychological. *Clinical Psychology Forum, 53,* 38; Sjodhal, L. (1997). The patient: A fellow-being or a package of chemicals? *Clinical Psychology Forum, 103,* 2–8; Taylor, G., Solts, B., Roberts, B. & Maddicks, R. (1998). A queer business: Gay clinicians working with gay clients. *Clinical Psychology Forum, 119,* 9–13; Wallace, G. (1993). Woman, mother, clinical psychologist – the professional juggler. *Clinical Psychology Forum, 62,* 4; White, J. (1993). Straight from the horse's mouth: A stress quotes handout. *Clinical Psychology Forum, 53,* 20–22.

15. For a discussion of the nature of the term 'responsibility' in mental health services see, Baker, E. & Newnes, C. (2005). What do we mean when we ask people to take responsibility? *Forensic Psychology Update, 80,* 23–27.

16. Eysenck, H. J. (1952). The effects of psychotherapy: An evaluation. *Journal of Consulting Psychology, 16,* 319–324.

17. DHSS (1977). *Trethowan Report:* 'The Role of Psychologists in the Health Service'. DHSS. (1977). *The Role of Psychologists in the Health Service.* Report of the Sub-Committee, Chairman: Professor W. H. Trethowan. London: HMSO.

18. Holland, S. (1992). From social abuse to social action: A neighbourhood psychotherapy and social action project for women. *Changes: An International Journal of Psychology and Psychotherapy, 10*(2), 146–153.

19. Sullivan, K. T. M. (1991). A therapist and his book. In Psychopoetry. *Changes: An International Journal of Psychology and Psychotherapy, 9*(1), 28–32.

20. Baker, E., Newnes, C. & Myatt, H. (2003). Drug companies and clinical psychology. *Ethical Human Sciences and Services, 5*(3), 247–254.

21. Timimi, S. & Radcliffe, N. (2005). The rise and rise of ADHD. In C. Newnes & N. Radcliffe (Eds.), *Making and Breaking Children's Lives.* Ross-on-Wye: PCCS Books, pp. 63–70.

22. Kovacova, K. (2013). Unpublished clinical psychology doctoral thesis. University of East London, p. 12.

23. In relation to the right to prescribe, the power of envy should not be underestimated. At seminars for clinical psychologists addressing the wish for prescription privileges Newnes and Holmes found a minority of psychologists who wanted the right to prescribe psychoactive medication on the grounds they too would be entitled to receive drug company gifts and sponsorship for conference attendance (Newnes, C. & Holmes, G. (1996). Medication: The holy water of psychiatry. *Openmind, 82,* 14–15). For a further discussion see Baker, E., Newnes, C. & Myatt, H. (2003). Drug companies and clinical psychology. *Ethical Human Sciences and Services, 5*(3), 247–254.

24. Holmes has remarked that patients frequently seek medication to achieve oblivion rather than cure. In such cases, psychotherapy without a programme of drug withdrawal will result in sessions wherein the patient has momentary emotional breakthrough only to be followed by a week or more of a return to a numbed state. See, Holmes, G. (2003). An audit: Do the people I see get better? *Clinical Psychology, 24,* 47–50.

25. Ward, M. (1991) Notes on therapy. *Changes: An International Journal of Psychology and Psychotherapy, 9*(2), 113–119.

26. Schoener, G. R., Hofstee Milgrom, J., Gonsiorek, J. C., Luepker, H. T. & Conroe, R. M. (1989). *Psychotherapists' Sexual Involvement with Clients: Intervention and prevention.* Minneapolis, MN: Walk-In Counseling Center.

27. Knowles, J. (1991). The sexualized journey. *Changes: An International Journal of Psychology and Psychotherapy, 9*(4), 248–251.

28. Boyle, M. (2003). The dangers of vulnerability. *Clinical Psychology, 24,* 27–30.

29. Some CBT-oriented therapists – and indeed the UK Government in its promotion of CBT – are unaware of Ryle's discussion of mentality and physicality. Put simply, we cannot assume that the emotional sphere (and 'the mind') operates in the same deterministic way as the object world. In the latter a billiard ball can be seen to cause another ball to move on impact. We cannot know if a thought 'causes' an action in this way. Ergo, if the mind does not operate according to deterministic principles we cannot assume that thoughts 'cause' emotions. Crucially, the emotional sphere cannot with any certainty be said to operate by rational rules. Thus, in CBT 'homework tasks', the application of logic in order to assess the accuracy of beliefs via self-monitoring and rating scales ('How many people have actually said you are ugly Mrs Smith?') may well miss the (emotional)

target altogether (Ryle, G. (1949). *The Concept of Mind*. Chicago: University of Chicago Press).

30. This can be seen to be a position taken up by researchers looking at different kinds of therapy where, repeatedly, 'the relationship' between therapist and patient is found to be more important than any specific therapeutic technique. Techniques here become a praxis enabling the therapist to sit with the patient while something else (the relationship) is fulfilling a healing function. The factors identified can be summarised as 'being with' the distressed patient. Apparently, the sheer force of the therapist's healing presence is sufficient. And this despite the fact that same therapist might be considered by colleagues and acquaintances to be an undesirable character or so sanctimonious in the healing role that conversations are avoided. The research is further complicated by a faith on the part of the researchers that self-report on the part of the patient is accurate. The distorting effect of, say, gratitude that someone has spent an hour a week listening to the patient's travails is ignored as is the possibility that the patient is intuitively comparing a cosy chat with the potential or already-experienced adverse effects of drugs or ECT. In this scenario, reports on the benefits of talking therapies are likely to be exaggerated.

31. McCourt, J. (1999). A dilemma of disclosure. *Clinical Psychology Forum, 125,* 14–16.

32. May, R. (2000). Routes to recovery from psychosis: The roots of a clinical psychologist. *Clinical Psychology Forum, 146,* 6–10.

33. Engels, F. (2012). *The Condition of the Working Class in England*. Oxford: Oxford University Press. (Original work published 1845)

34. Foucault, M. (1975). *Discipline and Punish: The birth of the prison*. New York: Random House.

35. Strupp, H. & Hadley, S. (1979). Specific versus non-specific factors in psychotherapy. *Archives of General Psychiatry, 36,* 1125–1136.

36. McCord, J. (1981). Consideration of some effects of a counselling program. In S. E. Martin, L. B. Sechest & R. Redner (Eds.), *New Directions in the Rehabilitation of Criminal Offenders*. Washington, DC: National Academy Press, pp. 394–405.

37. Carkhuff, R. R. (1969). *Helping and Human Relations: A primer for lay and professional helpers*. New York: Holt, Rinehart & Winston.

38. Bickman, L. (1996). A continuum of care: More is not always better. *American Psychologist, 51*(7), 689–701.

39. Bickman, L., Summerfelt, W. T., Firth, J. & Douglas, S. (1997). The Stark County Evaluation Project: Baseline results of a randomized experiment. In D. Northrup & C. Nixon (Eds.), *Evaluating Mental Health Services: How do programs for children 'work' in the real world?* Newbury Park, CA: Sage Publications, pp. 231–259. Quoted in Deenan, T. (1999). *Manufacturing Victims: What the psychology industry is doing to people.* London: Constable, p. 128.

40. Hagen, M. A. (1997). *Whores of the Court: The fraud of psychiatric testimony and the rape of American justice.* New York: Regan Books.

41. Stein, D. B. (2004). *Stop Medicating/Start Parenting. Real solutions for your 'problem' teenager.* Lanham, MD: Taylor Publishers.

42. Stein, D. B. (2012). *The Psychology Industry under a Microscope!* Plymouth, UK: University Press of America Inc.

43. Newnes, C. (2011). Medication, psychotherapy and the right to know. *The Journal of Critical Psychology, Counselling and Psychotherapy, 11*(3), 173–186.

44. Until recently the personal profiles of all 75 clinical psychologists and counsellors working in the Staffordshire and Shropshire Foundation Trust's Department of Psychological Therapies were available online at http://www.shropsych.org. An NHS reorganisation led to the closure of the website.

CHAPTER 5

Problems with therapy: Pathologising childhood

Some confessions are easier to make than others. If you want to see how it's done try Rousseau.[1] For the purposes of this opening section I won't lean on Rousseau or Pepys – modesty (and fear) forbids.[2] By the time I started my training placement working with children I'd been around them enough to know I didn't want my own. Instead I was living the kind of life only possible for those with a safe job and a career for life around the corner. I'd looked after my much younger brothers as a teenager but that was it in terms of contact with kids, apart from cousins and friends as a child myself. It is safe to say my first session with a referred family was terrifying. Surely it would be obvious I knew nothing? Surely my discomfort with little Johnny playing in the sandpit would be plain as day? Thank goodness I had a psychometric test to administer – the Thematic Apperception Test–Children (CAT). The CAT is one of numerous psychometric procedures shown to have negligible validity; I didn't know that at the time but it wouldn't have mattered.[3] Administering the CAT gave me something to focus on other than the boy in front of me loudly complaining his parents had left the room. The CAT was valid enough for my purposes.

This chapter looks at clinical psychology interventions with children and families. I shall discuss some of the ways in which clinical psychologists have been involved in the lives of young people designated as patients, the pervasive use of diagnosis and medication and give examples of more contextualised approaches. The next section begins by addressing an apparently simple question, 'What is a child?'

The meaning of childhood

It may seem obvious to the reader what is meant by children and childhood. Any experience of child and adolescent mental health services, however, will have revealed a degree of ambiguity. In the UK NHS, different regions and health administrative structures differ in their definitions of the points at which a child becomes an adolescent and then an adult. For some, the definitions depend on education; a child becomes an adolescent when she enters secondary education, becoming an adult when she leaves the school system. For others there are age demarcations – 'children' remain children until age 13 and are adolescents until, roughly, 20. In other words, adolescents are teenagers. For others, 'children' effectively become 'adults' if child services cannot cope; more than one patient was admitted, aged 10, to the Salop Asylum as recently as the 1970s. Beyond the confines of structuralised service definitions, for many parents their children remain 'children' all their lives. Talk to someone in his eighties on a bus about his 'kids' and you will soon discover they are in their fifties or sixties. For parents whose offspring never leave home or, due to being marked as 'disabled' have been institutionalised, the social context re-languages the child as 'lazy', 'dependent', or, in the case of those with physical disabilities or psychiatric diagnoses, 'eternally innocent' or 'tragic'. The 2012 paralympics privileged a particular version of the disability identity where young people were consistently hailed as 'courageous' in their pursuit of athletic excellence. Further, Jan Burns has written extensively on how, for potential paralympic competitors, being marked as *more* disabled is, due to the compensatory points system, a much sought-after advantage to the young athletes.[4]

Service definitions of childhood reflect wider societal ambiguities; in the UK a 10-year-old can be tried for murder, but that same child would have to wait until 16 to legally begin a sexual relationship, 17 to drive, 21 to vote, etc. In the USA, the age demarcation lines differ between states for driving, owning a gun and buying alcohol. The last example is further complicated in the UK where many stores now demand that a person buying alcohol appears to be 25 even though the legal qualification is 18. To complicate matters further, once a person has been asked for proof of age, the person at the till cannot serve him or her alcohol unless proof is available in the form of a driving licence or similar.

These fluctuations are not new: 'In 1800 the meaning of childhood was ambiguous and not universally in demand. By 1914 the uncertainty had been virtually resolved and the identity largely determined, to the satisfaction of the middle class and the respectable working class ... each new construction ... may be observed in approximate chronological order as pertaining to Rousseauian Naturalism, Romanticism, Evangelicalism, the shift from wage-earning labour to "childhood", the reclamation of the juvenile delinquent, schooling, ...'[5] Here, the perspective is limited again; though 'class' and respectability are parameters used by the author, race and religion are absent. For Jews or Hindus rituals such as the Bar Mitzvah or arranged marriage are markers where the child becomes an adult with no transitional period.

Dorothy Rowe has given me some invaluable advice. Some of her books even feature my children.[6] Confused and concerned about the point at which my first daughter should be toilet-trained, I asked Dorothy. 'She'll let you know when she's ready,' was the reply. Later, when Harriet went through a phase of wanting to sleep in our bed – usually between us – Dorothy said, 'Remember, everything in childhood is a phase.' It is an aphorism that could describe any point in someone's life, but one which relieved the worry I had at the time. It is also something parents of children showing signs of unwanted conduct might bear in mind. Too often the conduct leads to a search for expert opinion, entry into the Psy system, diagnosis and a career as a patient. Allowing change at the child's pace can be too challenging for some parents whose expectancies of the 'right' age to stop wetting the bed are as constrained as the right age for a child's Bar Mitzvah.

What about the boy?

As part of my training as a clinical psychologist I was asked to perform an IQ assessment on a boy of 11 in a (relatively) small institution for young people deemed 'subnormal'. I arrived at the front door of what was once a school and was greeted by a woman in nursing uniform. Built in the 19th century, the place was close to the centre of a market town and – for staff – convenient for buying fruit and vegetables on market day. My appointment was for 9.30. After the ubiquitous cup of tea and a discussion about the purpose of the assessment, by 10 o'clock I had failed to discover why the boy was viewed as needing an IQ test. I had been told that he 'had no future' at the institution; he was considered not really suited to the service as he was 'too able' when compared to the other residents. It was hard to imagine what life had been like for him up to that point. Abandoned by parents overwhelmed by his disabilities and the demands of five other children, he had lived there for four years. At first he had shared a dormitory with six others, four of whom spent their days in cots thrashing about and occasionally crying out. For the last two years he had spent early evenings in his own side room where staff would engage him in games of cards or play with model cars with him until 'lights out' at 8 o'clock. During the day he would sit in the 'day room' idling away the hours between breakfast and lunch. The staff liked him but thought it was time for him to 'move on'. What was my role as a probationer clinical psychologist?

The first tenet of social role valorisation (SRV) is '... vulnerable people need to hold social roles in society that are valued'.[7] For Smail, although the boy's social role might not have been valued in the sense implied by SRV, he did have a role; as a consumer and as a recipient of services. He was also a necessary factor external to the chain of justifiable employment at the institution from nursing assistants and domestic staff through to the consultant psychiatrist with medical responsibility for all the residents.[8] Less directly, he held a role for me – both in justifying my salary and in being part of my learning curve as a clinical psychologist in training. Like many other supposed consumers within the health care industry he was also in the process of being *consumed.*[9]

One potential future for the boy was homelessness. In 1989, for example, there were between 20,000–25,000 homeless children in Australia; many were wards of the state. Their reasons for being homeless in preference to living under the auspices of the social care system are not recorded.[10] Flynn and Aubry's research review concluded that many adults disabled since childhood have little community participation, few friends and mix with people equally socially devalued or caretakers.[11] Many who are reasonably physically able go on to be homeless persons. Wolfensberger has wryly commented, 'Some people have no one who will touch them that does not get paid.'[12]

The boy provides a good example of the potential for de-contextualisation when using Psy labels for conduct that might seem – to a non-professionalised observer – wholly understandable. The controversies surrounding *DSM-5* have led insurance companies in the USA to move to demands for diagnoses based on the *International Classification of Diseases-10.* Although some may regard this as a positive step, *ICD-10,* like the *Diagnostic and Statistical Manual,* requires an individually oriented diagnosis wherein difficulties are located within the assessed person rather than the environment. (It should be noted that the WHO prefers the use of the *International Classification of Functioning, Disability and Health (ICF)* as an alternative to *ICD* in classifying and demarcating disability.) For the abandoned lad who had lived for four years surrounded only by care staff and children lying in railed cots, his conduct, though explicable by reference to proximal powers, could be subsumed under *F98 Other behavioral and emotional disorders with onset usually occurring in childhood and adolescence.* Staff had also observed *F98.0 Enuresis not due to a substance or known physiological condition, F98.21 Rumination disorder of infancy* (according to staff he spent a high proportion of his day 'just thinking alone and picking at himself') and *F98.9 Unspecified behavioral and emotional disorders with onset usually occurring in childhood and adolescence.*[13] Although these labels may appear absurd in the context of the little the reader knows about the boy, there is no *a priori* reason why they cannot be applied and – as noted below – if such labels were to increase the opportunity for staff to access resources, then that is frequently sufficient justification. In discussion with the consultant psychiatrist I eventually discovered that the staff simply wanted a reason to discharge the referred lad 'for his own sake'. An assessment showing an IQ above 70 would mean he had lost his qualification for staying in the service and could be discharged; a search could begin for 'appropriate' accommodation, possibly foster care. Neither the consultant nor the nursing staff held the view that living surrounded by role models who lay in cots calling out would be 'therapeutic' for *any* of the residents. In positioning psychiatric staff as 'part of the establishment' or 'pro-psychiatry' critical practitioners ignore the fact these staff are simply doing a job. If it is a job they find uncomfortable (as most jobs are) they will employ a rhetoric of justification for their activities. I shall return to this point in the next chapter.

Diagnosing children's so-called mental health is more difficult than assessing the mental health of adults. According to the World Health Organization (WHO), childhood and adolescence are normal developmental stages, and as such, it is extremely difficult to differentiate between 'abnormal' and 'normal' behaviour patterns in children and adolescent populations.[14]

Such labelling is ubiquitous in services for children. In addition to decontextualising the labelled person's conduct, the professional has no way of knowing, despite professional references to the notion of 'norms', how unusual any conduct might be. As with the majority of diagnoses the identified behaviours justifying a label are indistinguishable from ordinary behaviour – it is familial or social discomfort which leads to a referral to Psy. (Frequently the referred person lacks the resources necessary to resist referral.) Signs indicative of ADHD, for example, include difficulty in paying attention, difficulty in concentration, difficulty in keeping things in order, being easily distracted, restless, fidgety, impatient, impulsive, etc. Dorothy Rowe has suggested these signs are better read as signs of fear.[15] Notwithstanding Rowe's interpretation it is difficult, as a parent of six children, to see *anything* remarkable about the behaviours listed. In the context of an understaffed school, being 'restless' – however understandable – can still be irritating for a harassed teacher. A referral into Psy might seem like one way of relieving classroom pressure. I shall return to the theme of referral as a relief for others surrounding the referred person in the next chapter. The next section examines clinical psychology's impact on other referred children.

Another 'disorder' beginning with the letter 'A'

As noted in Chapter 3, the Psy industry prefers diagnostic labels beginning with early letters of the alphabet in part so that they appear quickly on search engines. For children there is a new holy trinity of diagnoses – Asperger's, ADHD and autism – that might be described as the triple-A of child psychology.

Like ADHD, the rate of diagnosis of autism has continued to rise. Invented by Kanner in 1943, the term originally implied 'closed in' and had been borrowed from Bleuler although Freud had used it to described an egg-like self-sufficiency, the chick growing in its own yolk sac.[16] With the expansion of the concept to include a 'spectrum' of behaviours the term has replaced nomenclature such as 'learning disabled' for many young people. Pity, however, remains a common response, at least in the media portrayal of so-called autistic children. There are daily stories concerning the struggles of parents to accommodate the supposedly unusual needs of their autistic offspring. These tales are matched by tales of young people overcoming the adversity inherent in their condition in order to lead 'productive' lives while Hollywood has portrayed, for example, stereotypical 'idiot savants' in films such as *Rain Man*.

For many commentators, the change in nomenclature for some children from learning disabled to autistic highlighted differences between the overarching class of disability and the sub-group of autism (now seen as a distinct group). For others the change simultaneously relieved parents of blame for their child's difficulties. In the 1960s the discourse around 'blaming' parents had been taken up by those in the Psy industry committed to a genetic and organic basis for schizophrenia. Laing and Esterson's work on so-called schizophrenogenic parenting and Bateman's double-bind theory of communication between parents and their offspring were – mistakenly, in the view of many commentators – read as examples of professionals placing the blame for an individual's distress within the family, particularly parental, dynamic.[17] Subsequent research has examined what parents actually say about their role in children's distress revealing a culturally normative belief on the parents' part that they are indeed responsible and some clinical psychologists have used this narrative, in a non-blaming way, to discuss options for family change.[18] Other clinical psychologists have examined historical records of family life to demonstrate the likelihood that (assuming a deterministic theory of causation) an explanatory discourse could *only* point to parental conduct as a crucial factor, research which echoes that of Schatzman's *post hoc* analysis of Freud's theories concerning a patient he only saw once, Judge Schreber.[19,20]

In the case of autism there have been continuing moves away from a label of learning disabilities for these supposedly similar children. During the 1980s there was considerable professional debate about the possibility that these moves were encouraged by essentially middle-class parents unwilling to see their children considered learning disabled. At the time the common designation was 'mentally handicapped', now considered pejorative.[21] During my child training placement I was reading much about the role of parents in childhood distress. After various personal therapy experiences that had privileged the role of my parents in what I was happy to think of as my own madness, I had no difficulty in applying these notions of parental influence in the families encountered. The role of parental guilt is highlighted in Wolfensberger's discussion of children now described as autistic or learning disabled.[22] (Wolfensberger, himself, prefers the terminology, 'children with significant impairments'.) As a trainee committed to not labelling individual children, parental guilt seemed clear. The final submission for the – now defunct – BPS Diploma in Psychology included 10 case studies. For my 'subnormality' placement case study I submitted a review of interventions with a 10-year-old boy deemed subnormal whose mother had claimed that he spent up to two hours 'shouting and kicking' every evening. The outcome had been a delay in going to bed and some evenings his mother talked to him through the bedroom wall to 'calm him down'. Reading the report some 33 years later reveals a number of elements that would have been very familiar to Laing and Wolfensberger. The father had suffered a cerebral haemorrhage some three years before the referral and the report's recommendations are exclusively concerned with the mother's exhaustion and frustration at finding herself 'dealing with two children instead of one' and 'my husband's jealousy – he follows me round the house all day'.[23] A deconstruction of the text might now suggest an overvaluing on my part of the parental role and a privileging of intra-psychic factors (labelled 'maternal anxiety'). There is no acknowledgement that, as the Psy professional involved, I had no way of knowing if there was anything sufficiently unusual about the mother's response to justify – from a paternalistic position – my recommendations for social service involvement on her behalf. Further, the highly selective nature of the report – to be submitted for examination – illustrates the concerns outlined in the opening chapter; in effect, the author is *absent*. There is no reflective account of why, at that particular time, I wrote the submission as I did.

Children and the Psy system

A recurrent trope in articles suggesting clinical psychologist involvement with children is the notion that untreated childhood problems can lead to later difficulties.[24, 25] This view might be contrasted with that of Jackson, a psychiatrist, who suggests that, as methylphenidate (Ritalin/Adderall) is a frequent Psy response to such problems, the most likely outcome for children is addiction to similar street drugs including cocaine. Here, methylphenidate appears to act as an 'access drug' to other – frequently illegal – stimulants.[26] Simultaneously there are a number of adverse effects including palpitations, chest pain, cardiac arrest, vomiting, drowsiness, constipation, weight loss, headaches and growth retardation. Breggin goes on to list a further 31 adverse effects including, ironically, *over*activity.[27] It might be argued that exposing a young person to such risks cannot be justified by reference to a hypothesised link of current to future disorder.

Clinical psychologists have acknowledged the complexity of estimating prevalence rates for childhood disorders like ADHD and autism with no validity and little reliability.[28] They also recognise considerable overlap with expected childhood behaviours and significant difficulties in diagnosis which arise from widespread differences in 'developmental rates' for children of differing biological make-up and cultural mores. It should be noted that the concepts of 'developmental rate' or 'stages' are, themselves, culturally bound. With this considerable caveat, Rutter and colleagues suggested a prevalence rate for 'mental health problems' of 24.5 per cent for boys and 13.2 per cent for girls.[29] According to Lethem and Liekerman such problems include 'bonding problems', school refusal and truancy, aggression, temper tantrums, teasing, lying, stealing, nightmares, peer relationship difficulties and disobedience.[30] There can be few parents who have not experienced all of these challenges with their children. Foucault suggested the naming of such behaviours as 'problems' is part of the disciplining process wherein 'normality'" (actually behaviour which is useful for the maintenance of power in society) is defined by default: a child who does none of these things is not only extraordinary but of no threat to societal order.[31]

The 'benefits' of establishing wider child psychology services are detailed by Conn and Papadopoulos. In descending order these are: (1) to the clients, (2) to experienced clinical psychologists 'wishing to move up the grades … to non-specialist management roles, (3) … to the psychology service through an increasing range of resources and … to trainee clinical psychologists required to have some experience in the area.'[32] The stress placed on the advantages to the professionals involved in service expansion garners no reflexive comment from the authors and requires no further Foucauldian analysis from me.

For the child Brown-Wright and Gumley suggest the advantages of receiving an autistic label include access to mental health and paediatric departments, educational resources by way of 'statements', support groups and advocacy services. They suggest looking beyond a narrow definition and, whilst recognising that so-called autistic features prevail throughout non-clinical populations, clinicians should be on the lookout for 'very subtle yet clinically significant presentations of autism'.[33] The expansion of the criteria for the diagnosis and the structural linking of diagnosis to social, educational and Psy support thus results in more diagnosed individuals and more professionals employing justificatory rhetoric for their assessments and use of diagnostic terminology. I shall continue this theme in the next chapter.

All therapies commonly used with adult patients are used with children.[34] Stein, in a review of diagnosis-based clinical work, recommends an eclectic approach based on a unified model of psychology – the 'pyramid approach'. The model is based on a dual theory of early-life and current-life stressors; treatment implications range from dynamic and cognitive therapeutic modalities to behavioural programmes, drug regimes and 'ventilation of feelings'.[35] Whilst acknowledging the scientistic discourse around research in these approaches and cautioning against the adverse effects of medication, Stein's approach tends toward the decontextualised individualism common to the majority of therapies. His model is echoed in the work of the Cactus Clinic in Middlesbrough, UK, established by Professor Steve Baldwin in the early years of this century. Baldwin's work, rigorously researched and well received by parents and schools, included systematic nutritional investigation and recommendations. Again, the approach restricts itself to individual children and families.[36]

For some, this type of focused approached is normal praxis. The complexities of the child's world, however, might imply that the majority of child- and family-oriented interventions fail to take account of sufficient variables. Even the broader narrative and system approaches are – necessarily – constrained by relatively proximal zones of influence (siblings, parents, the extended family, schools and some members of the Psy complex). Distal influences (which include influences on the therapists themselves) are unknown or ignored. The proximal zone must also include important factors (in using a cause–effect paradigm) which remain unspoken and, perhaps, unknown to the families. In an article pre-dating some of the now familiar cyber technology-based interventions Radcliffe and Newnes discuss the possibility of encouraging families to consult with friends or influential relatives via mobile phone *during* any therapeutic encounters. In such a scenario children may well choose to call peers who the parents consider a 'bad influence' whilst the parent might call a grandparent, until then not mentioned but clearly of some significance.[37] Clinical psychologists working with children and families will frequently lose any sense of mastery of the therapeutic space. Lone therapists are invariably outnumbered, only supported by co-workers behind a two-way mirror. Stein, in attempting perhaps to support clinicians, makes a call for therapists to be familiar with 'all specific human problems'.[38] This seems a tall order. One reading of the suggestion is that Stein overvalues the positivistic frame wherein *more* (linear) knowledge is better. Again, a postmodern reading might suggest that attempting to gain such knowledge or the input of more professionals reflects the discourse of professionalism and maintains an 'us and them' position for professionals and patients. Inherent in such praxis is the belief that knowledge is divorced from the context in which it is sought (a family seeking help in a culture privileging 'experts').[39]

Imagine that you are a single parent of two children of mixed race, one of whom has started to refuse to go to school. Aged 10, she can pass as a teenager if wearing make-up and teachers have expressed concern that she might put herself in danger as well as missing classes. Her attendance has been a priority for you because knowing that she is safe for six hours a day enables you to go to paid employment. Your mother, a born-again Christian from Brazil, consistently criticises your parenting and your daughter's other parent refuses to contribute to the family income. Your ex-partner does, however, visit on a regular basis to watch television with you and stay until the early hours for (mutually enjoyable) sex. You feel unable to tell anyone about your partner's visits and have never told anyone that you find helping your daughter with her homework impossible because you can barely read. Your daughter is referred to a clinical psychologist and you are asked to the interview to provide some background.

A clinical psychologist, however receptive, would be hard-pressed to have an open discussion with a parent in such a scenario. There are certain features which may be representative of numerous such referrals – teachers' concern, a child experimenting with her sexuality and culture-bound notions of attractiveness, financial worries, guilt, personal secrets and shame. The proximal pressures (financial and legal concerns around school attendance) are clear. The distal power of the mother's own upbringing, culture and religion are not immediately apparent though may be discussed at some point. The immediate influence of the ex-partner's visits or the mother's difficulties in reading, however, may never be raised. For many years the UK's Division of Clinical Psychology has promoted 'psychological formulation' in favour of traditional psychometric and diagnosis-based assessments. This requires the mutual identification between psychologist and patients of problems to be addressed. This ethos echoes Stein's call for an encyclopaedic knowledge of human problems on the part of the psychologist; it is a considerable challenge for a clinical psychologist to identify factors with the most significant weighting in a context where referred parents may find it difficult to articulate cultural influences and understandably withhold information as in the above example.

In summary, children entering the Psy system are likely to be assessed and diagnosed (judged and labelled). For many children and adolescents in the UK the clinical psychology approach is represented by a relatively new praxis, problem formulation. There are as many therapies for children and families as for individual adults. The (more apparent) complexity of referred families makes a family or 'systemic' therapy approach more likely. As noted in Chapter 1 (and to be reconsidered in Chapter 7), the gender and age bias of the profession of clinical psychology in the UK makes it likely that parents of referred children will be interviewed by white, female clinical psychologists in their late twenties who are not themselves parents. This may be problematic if the assessing psychologist hopes for an open discussion concerning important factors in the family's distress.

Clinical psychology and the wider system in child work

Like any profession, clinical psychology makes claims about its potential benefits for the public good. In the UK a perceived shortage of practitioners has been a factor in position papers by the Division of Clinical Psychology, for example, urging employers to use clinicians as supervisors of other staff, trainers and consultants. As Director of Psychological Therapies I was responsible for writing job descriptions encompassing a roughly equal mix of direct clinical work, training, supervision and research. As noted in Chapter 1, individual clinical psychologists prefer meeting patients and supervision to other roles. Research tends not to support supervision as having much impact on therapy outcome. Similarly the evidence base for the effectiveness of consultancy is poor. Clinical psychologists have nonetheless consistently broadened their horizons to include the wider field of health maintenance and improvement specifically targeting children and young people. In a review of primary prevention programmes aimed at decreasing alcohol consumption and smoking, for example, Aldridge cites Bandura: 'We have the knowledge and the means to bring benefit to many … to accomplish this calls for a broader vision of how psychology can serve people, and a fundamental change in the uses to which our knowledge is put'.[40] Bandura was either unaware of or ignored Beloff's claim less than a decade before – cited in Chapter 1 – that psychology had yet to establish a *single* fact about human behaviour.[41] Aldridge's proposal was for clinical psychologists to 'draw on many models in order to prevent children taking up the smoking habit.'[42] Her suggestions reflected the anti-smoking *Zeitgeist*; she could not have been aware of Snowdon's historical analysis some 20 years later of the role of government and tobacco companies in both promoting *and* regulating smoking, his critique of the concept of passive smoking and his deconstruction of the evidence base used to justify public smoking bans throughout the world.[43] Nor could she have foreseen the dramatic impact of legal constraints on smokers, to be sure a form of behavioural intervention but not one requiring educative programmes by clinical psychologists.

Children may be the future but they are not likely to be the future of clinical psychology. Indeed, they are barely the present. Since the introduction of the tiering system in the NHS it is teachers who increasingly act as the first point of referral to psychology, usually educational psychology. Child and adolescent mental health services have several 'tiers', from 1–4; the higher the number, the more specialist the service, ultimately residential. Teachers are part of Tier 1. But those teachers no longer need the intricacies of psychometric testing to confirm diagnoses. Many teaching staff in the UK now *make* diagnoses. The language of Psy has so permeated the classroom that primary school teachers call children autistic or suggest ADHD as the 'cause' of a child's restlessness with no reference to Psy professionals or, indeed, textbooks. There is no need, daily newspapers, television, radio and the Internet are a constant source of Psy-determined knowledge. For many teachers it is 'obvious' that a struggling child is hyperactive or deserves to be marked as Asperger's. The school systems are often the primary referral source for children's mental health; in the United States, 96 to 98 per cent of all referrals for psychiatric diagnoses come directly from the public school system as teachers and administrators routinely refer children that do not conform to school standards for psychiatric evaluation.[44] Simple economics are sometimes behind this – in the UK a child designated Special Educational Needs will bring much needed additional resources to the classroom in the form of additional teaching help, computers, etc. Since 1991, individual schools in the USA have received federal monies for each child labelled with a physical, behavioural or learning disability. Paralleling this macro-economic change psychiatric diagnoses have increased exponentially in America where schools profit from psychiatric labelling of children and adolescents.[45]

In Western Australia, *governmental* interventions have reversed a trend of increasing diagnosis of ADHD and medication of children by 60 per cent from a high of around 18,000 children in 2000 to 6,000 in 2009. Over that decade there was a simultaneous 50 per cent reduction in teenage amphetamine abuse rates, lending support to Jackson's concerns noted earlier in this chapter regarding methylphenidate as an 'access' or 'gateway' drug.[46]

In recognition of broader societal changes and the need to embrace a political discourse, some projects involving clinical psychologists have incorporated a wide range of allies in attempting community-based interventions with children and families. 'Imagine Chicago' began in September 1992 with a design team consisting of educators, corporate and media executives, philanthropists, community organisers, youth developers, economists, religious leaders and social service providers under the direction of Bliss Browne, a mother of three, Episcopal priest and former Division Head of the First National Bank of Chicago. Their aim, via 'appreciative' enquiry with distantiated youth and gang leaders in one of the most violent and rundown areas of the city was to create an environment that might enable young people to thrive rather than go on to a life of crime and incarceration. Over 20 years later many of the goals have been achieved and the project has expanded to embrace similar enterprises in other cities.[47, 48]

In Birmingham, UK, the Family Well-being Project is co-ordinated by Carl Harris, a social science and philosophy graduate with two children, who qualified as a clinical psychologist in the mid-1990s. The project has analysed micro-neighbourhood referral patterns to find any common features of neighbourhoods more likely to have high proportions of those deemed 'problem' families. Allies include teachers, local residents, police, substance abuse workers, general practitioners and other health and social service workers. The project focuses on three council estates with a population of 10,000 and has been supported from the outset by a New Deal for Communities government programme which provided £50 million over 10 years. At one point, with support from the BPS Community Psychology Network (now a BPS section) the project hosted a visit from Professor Bernardo

Jiminez-Dominguez of the University of Guadalajara, a specialist in community psychology. His analysis revealed an arrangement of oppressive building design and lack of green areas for play, obvious to local residents but without the necessary imprint of the Gaze.[49] Subsequent plans for new housing have avoided this type of design and referrals to specialist services have dropped significantly.[50]

In summary, clinical psychology is finding its influence over diagnosis and treatment of children waning as families themselves and those seeking benefits ranging from Disability Living Allowance for Children (DLA benefits for those over 16 are now termed Personal Independence Payments) to direct intervention by health and social service use the Internet and other resources to *self*-diagnose.[51] Children's conduct is regularly re-languaged as disordered. Diagnosis by tier one practitioners – for example, teachers – is now also the norm. Despite these developments psychologists and powerful allies are working alongside families to enhance the living conditions of children.

Endnotes

1. Rousseau, J.-J. (1931). *Confessions.* London: Everyman's Library. (Original work published in two parts: 1782, 1789)

2. Tomalin, C. (2012). *Samuel Pepys: The unequalled self.* Harmondsworth: Penguin Viking.

3. Stein, D. B. (2012). *The Psychology Industry Under the Microscope!* Plymouth, UK: University Press of America Inc.

4. Burns, J. (2013). Won't get fooled again: Psychology and the Paralympics. Presented at University of East London Conference, 'I Can See for Miles – The future of Psy', a celebratory conference in memory of Professor Mark Rapley. Saturday, 13 April 2013.

5. Hendrick, H. (1997). Constructions and reconstructions of British childhood: An interpretative study, 1900 to the present. In A. James & A. Prout (Eds.), *Constructing and Reconstructing Childhood: Contemporary issues in the sociological study of childhood.* London: Routledge Falmer, pp. 33–60, p. 35.

6. Rowe, D. (2007). *My Dearest Enemy, My Dangerous Friend: Making and breaking sibling bonds.* London: Routledge.

7.   Wolfensberger, W. (2003). *The Future of Children with Significant Impairments: What parents fear and want, and what they and others may be able to do about it*. Syracuse, NY: Training Institute for Human Service Planning, Leadership and Change Agentry (Syracuse University), p. 43.

8.   Smail, D. (2001). *The Nature of Unhappiness*. London: Robinson.

9.   Newnes, H. (2010). A warning unheeded: Consumerism in *The House of Mirth and Nana*. *The Journal of Critical Psychology, Counselling and Psychotherapy, 10*(2), 111–118.

10. *The Age* (Australia), 7 March 1989.

11. Flynn, R. J. & Aubry, T. D. (1999). Integration of persons with developmental or psychiatric disabilities. In R. J. Flynn & R. A. Lemay (Eds.), *A Quarter Century of Normalization and Social Role Valorization: Evolution and impact*. Ottawa: University of Ottawa Press, pp. 271–316.

12. Wolfensberger, W. (2003). *The Future of Children with Significant Impairments: What parents fear and want, and what they and others may be able to do about it*. Syracuse, NY: Training Institute for Human Service Planning, Leadership and Change Agentry (Syracuse University), p. 17.

13. Retrieved 15 May 2013 from http://www.icd10data.com/

14. Breggin, P. (2002). *The Ritalin Fact Book*. Cambridge, MA: Perseus Publishing.

15. Rowe, D. (2005). ADHD: Adults' fear of frightened children. In C. Newnes & N. Radcliffe (Eds.), *Making and Breaking Children's Lives*. Ross-on-Wye: PCCS Books, pp. 71–74.

16. Kanner, L. (1943). Autistic disturbances of affective contact. *Nervous Child, 2*, 217–250.

17. Bateson, G., Jackson, D. D., Haley, J. & Weakland, J. (1956). Toward a theory of schizophrenia. *Behavioral Science 1*, 251–264 and Laing, R. D. & Esterson, A. (1964). *Sanity, Madness and the Family*. London: Penguin Books.

18. Dallos, R. (2013). Don't blame the parents: Blame versus responsibility in families and family therapy. *Clinical Psychology Forum, 243*, 34–42. See also Coulter, C. & Rapley, M. (2011). 'I'm just, you know, Joe Bloggs.' In M. Rapley, J. Moncrieff & J. Dillon (Eds.), *De-medicalizing Misery*. Basingstoke: Palgrave Macmillan, pp. 158–173.

19. Johnstone, L. (1999). Do families cause 'schizophrenia'? Revisiting a taboo subject. *Changes: An International Journal of Psychology and Psychotherapy, 17*(2), 77–90.

20. Schatzman, M. (1974). *Soul Murder: Persecution in the family.* Harmondsworth: Penguin.

21. A post-structuralist reading of labelling such disablement as an individual matter might suggest that we language others as disabled in part to avoid our responsibility for their societal context. So-called handicaps are created by a *handicapping* society that remains focused on the able-bodied in everything from the provision of public conveniences to warning notices and buses poorly equipped for more than one wheelchair user.

22. Wolfensberger, W. (2003). *The Future of Children with Significant Impairments: What parents fear and want, and what they and others may be able to do about it.* Syracuse, NY: Training Institute for Human Service Planning, Leadership and Change Agentry (Syracuse University).

23. Newnes, C. (1980). M.W. (10 years of age). Assessment for alternative placement and treatment of a boy presenting with behaviour problems. Case 2 in part submission for BPS Diploma in Clinical Psychology. Unpublished thesis.

24. Saxe, L., Cross, T. & Silverman, N. (1988). Children's mental health: The gap between what we know and what we do. *American Psychologist, 43,* 800–807.

25. A recent study at the University of Bristol similarly concluded that signs of 'depression' in children aged between 0–10 when their fathers left home were likely to resurface when the children entered their teens. Rather than voice the familiar warnings about the need for intervention to avoid problems as adults, the authors emphasised that it does not necessarily follow that a teenage girl who experiences depression as a teenager will continue to be affected. See Culpin, I., Heron, J. E., Araya, R., Melotti, R. & Joinson, C. J. (2013). Father absence and depressive symptoms in adolescence: Findings from a UK cohort. *Psychological Medicine, 14,* 1–12.

26. Jackson, G. (2005). Cybernetic children: How technologies change and constrain the developing mind. In C. Newnes & N. Radcliffe (Eds.), *Making and Breaking Children's Lives.* Ross-on-Wye: PCCS Books, pp. 90–104.

27. Breggin, P. (2008) What psychologists and therapists need to know about ADHD and stimulants. *Journal of Critical Psychology, Counselling and Psychotherapy, 8*(4), 210–219.

28. The following letter, sent to numerous US newspapers, is an example of an increasingly common phenomenon in voicing the concerns of some clinical psychologists:

To Whom It May Concern

Dear Sirs:

It has come to my attention that Doctor S must defend his decision to treat a child diagnosed with ADD/ADHD without drugs and according to his own psychosocial precepts.

I have long advanced a similar position taken by Dr S and first developed by Dr Thomas Szasz that ADHD, along with every other so-called diagnosis in the *Diagnostic and Statistical Manual of Mental Disorders, IV-TR (DSM)* are not true medical conditions but moral labels stripped of their moral connotations.

I argue the following:

1) The diagnosis of ADHD is based purely on the behavior of the child and judgments of behavior cannot *logically* be other than moral or ethical in nature. Therefore, it is logically impossible to diagnose ADHD as the so-called diagnosis is merely a bad name given to the child or the offending behavior in question.

2) As a consequence of using a moral label as if it literally was a medical condition there can be no clear criteria to make the diagnosis of ADHD. Therefore, all of the *DSM* descriptions of the so-called symptoms of the medical disorder or disease read as follows: 'Often fails to give close attention to details ..., often has difficulty sustaining attention ..., often does not seem to listen ...' (pp. 83–84). What is often to one observer is not often to another. As a result agreements as to diagnosis, or what bad name to call the child are notoriously unreliable making any standard of diagnosis impossible.

3) There is absolutely no clear evidence that ADD/ADHD or any other 'diagnosis' in the *DSM* has any etiological relationship to any known physiological or anatomical problems in the human brain. The *DSM* clearly states that there are no laboratory tests of any kind available to prove that ADHD has any clear relationship with any known physiological problems. A recent news release from the American Psychiatric Association (Friday, September 26, 2003 8:49 AM) reads as follows: 'Brain science has not advanced to the point where clinicians can point readily to discernible pathologic lesions or genetic markers that in and of themselves serve as reliable or predictive biomarkers of a given mental disorder or mental disorders as a group. ... mental disorders will *likely* be proven

to represent disorders of intercellular communication; or of disrupted neural circuitry' (emphasis added).

4) Unless and until it is proven that a) such neuro-physiological problems exist and b) that such neuro-physiological problems play a causative role in the patterns of unwanted, unexplained behavior 'diagnosed as ADD/ADHD' established scientific logic and procedure demand that the scientific, medical and academic communities hold in abeyance any firm claims that ADD/ADHD is a medical condition and the province of trained and licensed medical personnel.

5) If ADD/ADHD is not a disease and has no discernible anatomical or physiological etiological factors, then the drugs used to treat ADD/ADHD, namely powerful stimulants that are otherwise illegal to sell or use by ordinary citizens, cannot *logically* be called medicines. They are simply drugs. If parents want to drug their children I suppose it is their choice but I consider it misleading, unscientific, immoral and unethical for any professional from any discipline to advise or prescribe to their fellow citizens drugs under the false claim that they are medicines. I take this position with those who consult with me professionally as well as provide them evidence that these stimulant drugs are of dubious value, are potentially addictive and destructive to those taking them. (I will not develop the latter thesis in this letter.)

It is perfectly clear that any claims that ADD/ADHD exists as a real disorder rather than as a moral label are based on faith and not science. We can only surmise what political and economic motives are behind the demands that children be diagnosed and treated with powerful stimulant drugs rather than sensible, time honored forms of support and discipline advocated by myself and Dr. S.

I hope that the Health Providers' Board will consider wisely its scientific and political move against Dr. S. They are setting a chilling precedent to all those who oppose the current climate in the mental health field that seeks to cut off debate concerning the validity of ADD/ADHD as a diagnosis or treatable medical condition or to help children and families seeking to achieve better in school with means other than the use of potentially dangerous chemicals.

Laurence Simon, PhD, New York Certified Psychologist,
Professor of Psychology, CUNY.

29. Rutter, M., Cox, A., Tupling, C., Berger, M. & Yule, W. (1975). Attainment and adjustment in two geographical areas: I. *British Journal of Psychiatry, 126*, 493–509.

30. Lethem, J. & Liekerman, H. (1989). Service development: Estimating needs for clinical psychology services for children. *Clinical Psychology Forum, 24*, 11–14.

31. Foucault, M. (1979). *Discipline and Punish.* Harmondsworth: Penguin.

32. Conn, P. & Papadopoulos, R. (1989). Services for children and young people. *Clinical Psychology Forum,* 21, 2–6.

33. Brown-Wright, L. & Gumley, D. (2007). Diagnosing autism: Can it make a difference? *Clinical Psychology Forum, 173,* 26–28, p. 27.

34. For critiques of this enterprise the reader is referred to Armstrong, L. (1993). *And They Call It Help: The psychiatric policing of America's children.* Wokingham: Addison-Wesley Publishing Co. and Dineen, T. (1999). *Manufacturing Victims: What the psychology industry is doing to people.* London: Constable.

35. Stein, D. B. (2012). *The Psychology Industry Under the Microscope!* Plymouth, UK: University Press of America Inc.

36. Retrieved 16 July 2013 from http://news.bbc.co.uk/1/hi/england/2792009.stm

37. Radcliffe, N. & Newnes, C. (2005). Welcome to the future of liberal family therapy working. *Clinical Psychology, 47,* 33–35.

38. Stein, D. B. (2012). *The Psychology Industry Under the Microscope!* Plymouth, UK: University Press of America Inc.

39. Schwartz and Lees note the complexity of identifying vested interest and other influences in espousing children's 'needs' (itself a political term) and conclude, '… our thoughts are that this is a huge area'. Schwartz, A. L. & Lees, J. (1994). Children and young people: An area of need. *Clinical Psychology Forum, 71,* 30–36, p. 35.

40. Bandura, A. (1984). On paradigms and recycled ideologies. In S. Rachman (Ed.), *Contributions to Medical Psychology: Volume 3.* Oxford: Pergamon Press. Cited in Aldridge, J. (1988). Primary prevention in medicine with children. In F. Watts (Ed.), *New Developments in Clinical Psychology: Volume 2.* Chichester: Wiley in association with BPS Books, pp. 158–171, p. 165.

41. Beloff, J. (1973). *Psychological Sciences.* London: Staples.

42. Aldridge, J. (1988). Primary prevention in medicine with children. In F. Watts (Ed.), *New Developments in Clinical Psychology: Volume 2.* Chichester: Wiley in association with BPS Books, pp. 158–171.

43. Snowdon, C. (2009). *Velvet Glove, Iron Fist: A history of anti-smoking.* Ripon: Little Dice.

44. Baughman, F. (2006). *The ADHD Fraud: How psychiatry makes patients of normal children.* Oxford: Trafford Press.

45. Stolzer, J. M. (2010). The medicalization of boyhood. *The Journal of Critical Psychology, Counselling, and Psychotherapy, 2,* 187–196.

46. Whitely, M. (2011). Lessons from Western Australia: The world's first ADHD hotspot to experience a massive downturn in child prescribing rates. *The Journal of Critical Psychology, Counselling and Psychotherapy, 11*(2), 103–114. For Jackson's concerns about methylphenidate as an 'access drug', see Jackson, G. (2005). Cybernetic children: How technologies change and constrain the developing mind. In C. Newnes & N. Radcliffe (Eds.), *Making and Breaking Children's Lives.* Ross-on-Wye: PCCS Books, pp. 90–104.

47. Browne, B. W. (2005). Imagine Chicago: Cultivating hope and imagination. In C. Newnes & N. Radcliffe (Eds.), *Making and Breaking Children's Lives.* Ross-on-Wye: PCCS Books, pp. 151–167.

48. http://www.imaginechicago.org

49. Foucault, M. (1979). *Discipline and Punish.* Harmondsworth: Penguin.

50. Harris, C. (2005). The Family Well-being Project: Providing psychology services for children and families in a community regeneration context. In C. Newnes & N. Radcliffe (Eds.), *Making and Breaking Children's Lives.* Ross-on-Wye: PCCS Books, pp. 138–150.

51. Such diagnosis is now available in app form. Retrieved 8 January 2014 from http://www.healthline.com/health-slideshow/top-adhd-android-iphone-apps

CHAPTER 6

Problems with practice:
Pathologising adults

In part this chapter is about – and within – context. It began on the back seat of the 501 from Ellesmere to Shrewsbury, a bus that stops anywhere on request but doesn't run after 6 o'clock on weekday evenings and never on Sundays. The pen – a black biro bearing the insignia Papermate – was borrowed from an adjacent student assiduously studying for an A-level exam later that day. The Shropshire countryside flashes past; 15 fellow passengers sit mostly in silence for once spared the blare of radio preferred by some drivers.

Where we write is frequently unrecorded (for an exposition of where Steinbeck preferred to construct his novels – a six-sided shed – see the introduction to *The Grapes of Wrath*[1]). Where clinical psychologists see patients is rarely described. My most recent office had some comfortable chairs, two large windows and shelves laden with over 1,000 books of which, unknown to most patients as few asked, I'd read about 50 cover to cover and skimmed another three hundred or so. There was a desk, paintings, sometimes flowers and always plants. Alongside the desk a large grey filing cabinet sat incongruously, one side adorned with photographs, tickets to festivals and assorted memorabilia. In a career spanning 30 plus years I had seen people in various offices, GP surgeries and their own homes ranging from one-bedroom maisonettes on scary housing estates to, by comparison, palatial four-bedroom houses with gardens front and back. Meeting venues had included buses, cars, supermarkets, a memorably dilapidated hospice and numerous hospitals. Little is published about where clinical psychologists see patients, the smell of rooms, noise from corridors, the complications of booking shared venues. A patient's perspective is provided by Deborah Cheney whose heart sank a little when awaiting appointments. The waiting room was unkempt and uncared for, the magazines frayed and the plants neither watered nor thrown out for the full two years she saw the clinical psychologist (for whose attention Cheney expresses immense gratitude).[2]

Still less is known about what therapists of any persuasion actually do. As noted in the opening chapters, written accounts favour generic terms – CBT, interpretation, psychological formulation. We don't read much about the minutiae of encounters – the way patients react to particular environments, the way therapists surround themselves with comforting objects.[3] With the exception of some analytic authors we don't read much about how therapists are reacting to their ever-changing worlds – changes in style justified by recent reading or changes in tolerance in the context of worries about how impossibly crowded that day's appointment diary seems. I have given patients rides to bus stops on rainy days, walked with them while enjoying a cigarillo, given money, books – even an old NHS heater past its sell-by date. At first this all seemed rather daring, even risky, certainly way beyond my early analytic training and – to an analyst – no doubt saturated in countertransference. By necessity then this chapter is largely about what clinical psychologists say they do with adult patients, either via publication or in supervision. The professional context of obfuscation is paramount – reality almost entirely absent.

Adults in services

Focusing on informed consent, Chapter 4 looked at difficulties in clinical psychology and psychotherapeutic practice. The last chapter expanded this theme with an emphasis on the position of children in the Psy complex. In examining the practice of clinical psychology and psychotherapy with adults this chapter will also pursue the notion of 'consent'. I shall site current praxis in a historical overview of – largely – institutionalised psychological endeavour.

The term 'adult' is, in itself, a matter for debate in the psychological literature. For potential recipients of services the definition used by service providers will determine which services the person is entitled to receive. Financial pressures on services, whether reimbursed by insurance companies or funded by the government, create concomitant pressures on service providers to be as selective as possible. An adult may be defined in terms of certain rights and responsibilities (for example, the right to hold a driving licence), age (in some UK health administrative areas the transfer to adult mental health services is attained by those aged 17 'who are not in full education'. For others, 19 is the boundary mark) or 'not' being in receipt of a related service (for example, services for people with learning disabilities). The term is an administrative marker with only broad similarities to the ways it is used outside the health care system. Sometimes referred to as 'Elderly Services', services for older people may have an age cut-off at 65 or 70, depending on local funding. A concentration on 'dementia' for these services is one outcome of the requirement to target available resources. In a system consistently under-resourced, managers will be directed to ask staff to see only those who fall within strict demographic definitions. An 'adult', having perhaps been assessed for suitability for psychotherapy, may not receive that therapy because he or she has been assessed as learning disabled and is now aged over 65. Psychotherapy is increasingly available to learning disabled people and Psy professionals will ignore age limitations on occasion.[4] For many, new contracts of employment in the NHS based on 'targets' of numbers seen challenge this laissez-faire approach. Changes in service definition also mean that people previously outside the net are now caught; 'Older People Services' are increasingly re-titled 'Dementia Services' so that clinical psychologists working with 'adults' are no longer restrained by an upper age limit.

For the sake of this chapter, 'adult' could be loosely defined as any person with a legal right to make a choice about entering into a treatment contract with a Psy professional. This definition would exclude those psychiatric patients under compulsory treatment orders. Szasz has argued that anyone is at risk of compulsion as the options to refuse medication or even go for a walk unattended exist in a context where compulsion is a continuing threat.[5] The next sections briefly explore Psy as one aspect of institutions in which adults might find themselves. Here, institution may mean a building or administrative structure. In both contexts informed consent is regularly assumed rather than affirmed. The section begins with observations on the nature of 'the asylum' as buildings and their concomitant policies and procedures form the historical origins of much current praxis beyond the hospital.

'Victorian asylums were dreadful'

By common consent institutions built as asylums in the 19th century were dreadful and 'asylum' was not really on the agenda. Some private hospitals (for example, Ticehurst House Asylum in Sussex[6]) were considered places of refuge for the rich. Those built as public lunatic asylums in the middle of the century were overcrowded and rapidly became places for the medical profession to experiment on the inmates using drugs of varying toxicity, spinning cures, straitjackets and the like.[7] A modernist reading would suggest that we have progressed in the last century and a half. We now offer so-called community and primary health care, smaller residential centres for those deemed mad and dangerous and specialist units for those diagnosed with eating disorders, dementia and other Psy labels. As Allderidge has noted, however, the provision of small, purpose-built specialist centres for those deemed mad is actually something of a return to much earlier practice. Henry Maudsley's proposal, in 1907, for a small facility was, '... in fact recycling a model which had previously been used at the end of the 14th century'. Bethel Hospital in Norwich, built in 1713, still only housed 27 inmates 17 years later.[8]

Between around 400 CE and 1300 CE about 100,000 hospices catering for up to 12 dependent people each were established in Europe.[9] The hospices were used as places of refuge for those without the resources to look after themselves, often due to physical difficulties. Foucault, amongst others, has written extensively on the rise of the convent as a place of healing and a place to hide the unruly.[10] Some religious houses, for example Fontevrault Abbey in the Loire, were, by later standards, liberal with equality of gender and a laissez-faire approach to the more dependent novitiates, some of whom were battered women.[11] Others gradually became dominated by medical staff who preferred physical intervention over simple labour and prayer. Elsewhere, workhouses started incarcerating a high proportion of mad inmates. Private madhouses, increasingly run by medical superintendents, were built in England in the late 17th and 18th centuries. *Why* the asylum movement began then is hard to establish: Andrew Scull's contention that the expansion was one consequence of industrial capitalism is difficult to support given that the social effects of capitalism (displaced families, disrupted family life, increasing employment for women and unemployment for men, the sheer obnoxiousness of polluted cities, etc.) were not felt until the mid-19th century.[12] County asylums proliferated in the years 1800 to 1900; Lincoln, Warwick, Leavesden and Lancashire were typical – imposing, built well away from centres of commerce or residential areas and with adjacent agricultural holdings to allow a regime of work and fresh air. By the 1880s near London there were, 'vast, utilitarian pauper lunatic asylums at Hanwell and Colney Hatch'. Banstead and Claybury hospitals were soon added and by 1894 the five asylums managed by London County Council's Commissioners in Lunacy provided 11,668 beds, a figure that rose to over 19,000 by 1910.[13] The USA had close to 150 equally large (and frequently unkempt) institutions.[14] Italy had many, some based in 14th century buildings. Two, Macerata and Turin, were directed by the reformer Morselli, the progenitor of the term 'clinical' psychiatry and a firm advocate of physical work over the common praxis of blood-letting, coercion and restraint.[15]

Mechanical restraint for madness became a centre of controversy for alienists and psychiatrists in the USA and Britain in the 19th century. In part this was due to the successes at the York Retreat, successes based entirely on a *non*-medical model of cure; insanity was to be held at bay via 'moral treatment'. Instead of being faced with purgatives and straitjackets, it was claimed that inmates at the Retreat were given work (frequently in the gardens), varied amusements and discipline.[16] The Quaker origins of the Retreat encouraged the formation of regular discussion groups wherein patients reflected on the reasons for being incarcerated, effectively a forerunner of group psychotherapy. Although Foucault has criticised the regime at the Retreat for the way in which the treatment emphasised *internal* discipline (in effect, the patients became their own gaolers), the system seemed to show that a medical ethos was unnecessary in treating the insane. One outcome was the way in which medical superintendents now began to champion non-restraint and hard work for patients.

A series of Acts of Parliament in Britain in the 19th century had seen medical domination reach its apogee in the creation of public lunatic asylums. The 1845 Lunacy and County Asylums Acts in Britain mandated the construction of county asylums, to be regulated by the National Lunacy Commission. Economic necessity soon led to savings based on scale rather than efficiency or cure. The West Riding Asylum, for example, had opened in 1818 to 150 patients. Eighty years later it held 1,469.[17]

Opening over 160 years ago on the 28th March 1845 and designed to accommodate 60 mad people, Shelton Hospital, then the Salop County Lunatic Asylum, welcomed 120 patients. As in most other similar asylums, overcrowding led to the necessity of calming the residents. Bromides were introduced in 1857 and paraldehyde in 1882. Three years later the population stood at 800. Patients worked on the local farm, many leading productive lives notwithstanding the risks inherent in being housed with so many others. Between 1905 and 1915, for example, the close proximity of so many people resulted in the deaths of 167 inmates from tuberculosis, 27 more died from dysentery and 28 from an outbreak of influenza at the end of the First World War. By 1938 there were 1,000 patients, the population peaking in 1946 at 1,100. Overcrowding was already a major factor when considering a patient's discharge.

The hospital had been one of the first in the UK to use ECT and insulin coma therapy (in 1942) and when chlorpromazine was declared a breakthrough for those diagnosed with schizophrenia, this new technology was embraced. Chlorpromazine, as a major tranquilliser, had the effect of reducing any protest from patients at the overcrowded conditions – an effect to be valued whatever the therapeutic intent behind the prescription.

In 1965 a fire on Beech ward killed 24 women patients, an event still remembered by some senior staff (at least in the form of myth) and one which continues to be offered as evidence of the need for extremely detailed fire procedures to this day.[18]

The history of Shelton Hospital is similar to that of many psychiatric institutions in the UK and USA, some of which continue to expand the number of residents. Others, using as justification the requirement for 'providers' to make profits in an ostensibly 'national' health service, are divided into specialist 'units' and services transferred to community centres. The closed nature of these institutions, despite regular visits from official reviewers such as Mental Health Commissioners, can make examination of the day-to-day life of patients difficult for the outside observer. The introduction of Patients' Councils in the 1990s and government schemes for greater transparency or institutionalised advocacy such as the Patient Advice and Liaison Service (PALS) have had limited success in opening the institution to a more public gaze.[19] The treatments offered to patients remain under the direction of a member of Psy – usually a psychiatrist.

For those hoping to practise Psy via the tenets of social role valorisation, the history of institutional response to those that society finds disturbing forms the context for 'wounds' suffered by stigmatised individuals and groups.[20] The next section will examine these wounds in more detail, explicating clinical psychology's role in aiding the process and potential for resisting it. I shall then highlight one – rarely mentioned except by activists – example of psychiatric treatment, electroconvulsive therapy (ECT), which exemplifies the wounding process. The practice exists in a context of the essentially hidden nature of what occurs behind the doors of the psychiatric clinic.

The 'wounds'

According to Wolfensberger, the 'wounds' begin with *rejection or exclusion* by those closest to the identified patient. In general medicine such exclusion might be life-saving, for example, if the person is moved to a highly sterile place of safety due to vulnerability to infection. But, for many, the rejection occurs because the person is different in some way from expected physical or social norms. Clinical psychologists may assess people and agree they need to go to a 'specialist unit' for those with learning disabilities or a diagnosis of anorexia nervosa. In the markedly psychometric phase of the profession's development such assessments were a predominant feature of daily clinical work. The continuing closure of large psychiatric hospitals has resulted in the development of smaller, specialised units where assessments leading to exclusion from mainstream society are maintained. Though these units are generally less isolated than in the past (many 19th century psychiatric hospitals were built many miles from centres of urban population), individuals still find themselves *congregated* with strangers whose main similarity is that they are also unwanted, unpopular, difficult to live with or *marked* (diagnosed) by a Psy professional, frequently a clinical psychologist. Within the NHS some clinical psychologists have maintained praxis where a medical diagnosis is either ignored in favour of a patient's exposition of her difficulties or, favouring Goldie's 'eclectic' stance, an adjunctive therapy or problem formulation approach is suggested.[21] Others, trained in the use of psychometric protocols, have confirmed or changed diagnoses. This is a more common approach in, for example, the preparation of court reports. As noted in Chapter 1, for clinical psychologists dependent on reimbursement of fees by insurance companies, diagnosis is ubiquitous. From 2015 the insurance company standard manual for diagnosis will be *ICD-11*, a volume no less flawed than the much maligned *DSM*. American clinical psychologists are expected to use *ICD-11* thereby marking patients with labels having no validity or reliability.[22]

The places where people are congregated bear little relation to ordinary homes. The necessary rules around safety make, for example, fire doors ubiquitous and for many older, more frail, people pushing open a heavy fire door is impossible; they are trapped for the best of intentions. As one ex-patient and carer at Shelton Hospital has remarked, '... there is nothing *normal* about these places'.[23] There are numerous psychological theories of human development clinical psychologists are exposed to both in their first psychology degree and in later reading and post-doctoral work. From a perspective of proximal power the idea of 'peer pressure' is well established in public and professional discourse. If the notion is valid then congregating people with other people who act in ways seen as mad or self-destructive should not be condoned by members of the profession. Advertisements in publications such as the *BPS Appointments* for clinical psychology positions, however, continue to promote the 'excellence' and exclusivity of unitary diagnostic units.

Once so *distantiated* the person is likely to be moved again, frequently as a result of changes in local circumstances (for example, something as simple as redecoration of the unit or something more dramatic such as unit closure due to financial pressures). The person, having already suffered *disruption to relationships* that are frequently valued (close relatives, local friends, etc.[24]) now loses relationships with new-found companions. Although Wolfensberger, in seeing rejection and exclusion as the first phase in social devaluation, tends to downplay the often aversive nature of local and family relationships in peoples' lives, especially those who are already implicated in the patient's distress, it is a common feature of institutional life that people *do* find some degree of solidarity with others who are institutionalised – moves within the institution or hurried discharge break up these new alliances.

Any person finding themselves in the hands of the social or health care system soon *lacks control and concomitant sense of security*. The Byzantine nature and sheer *size* of the psychiatric and social care system means that loss of notes, mistakes in note-keeping or the tiredness of busy care staff may lead to patients being *confused with others*. If labelled via a clinical psychology assessment the labels themselves are likely to be confusing to both patients and staff; ignoring for a moment the lack of reliability and validity of psychiatric nomenclature it is a rare member of Psy who can adequately explain the difference between 'schizophrenia,' 'schizotypy,' and 'schizoid' personality 'disorder'. Despite rhetoric from assessors that their assessments, and hence services, are 'needs-led' the bestowal of such labels says little in terms of patient need. More psychotherapeutically inclined clinical psychologists might make clinical notes including assessments of 'ego-strength' or 'insight'; it is impossible to know what the patient or other professionals reading the notes make of such jargon. Further, as I have outlined in previous chapters, notes – frequently now a computerised record – will be kept for many years.[25] An interesting exercise for a clinical psychologist reviewing her own professional development might be to look at random sets of notes on patients that she has taken at, say, two year intervals. Some may find little change, others may be surprised at the apparent ease they have adopted new jargon, others will observe how an early ease with medicalisation of distress has changed to a focus on specific conduct. A further challenge might be to follow up the random sample and discover if the patients found the notes helpful. As I have suggested in earlier chapters, notes are one way in which clinical psychologists place a professional distance between themselves and patients. They also fulfil one aspect of 'the gaze'.[26]

Patients in the system, confused by forms or neglected by busy Psy professionals who should be organising state benefits on their behalf, soon become *financially worse off*. They can be *blamed* for 'resisting' therapy and will be *subject to case conferences*, often attended by staff they have never seen before and won't see again. Clinical psychologists in the NHS remain under pressure to see as many patients as possible; the idea that someone who is persistently late for appointments is 'resisting' helps make it easier to discharge the patient. The nature of professional justification and the long life of the psychiatric record may mean that a reputation for 'resistance' (no bad thing for liberation psychology) will be one of the marks the patient receives. A combination of cost and policies encouraging societal inclusion of diagnosed individuals has led to a new generation of psychiatric inpatient facilities, generally more liberal in approach while, in the main, still requiring diagnosis before admission. Some environments eschew diagnosis and encourage a less formal atmosphere where residents can escape the pressures of their ordinary lives. The emphasis here is on safety and companionship rather than treatment; the Wokingham MIND Crisis House and the Soteria House in Bradford, for example, have support from local statutory services. The Berlin Runaway House enjoys a similar degree of freedom. I shall offer a brief analysis of these projects in Chapter 8.

For those at risk of societal devaluation then, a wide range of 'wounds' may result from treatment by human services in their present form. The next section will look in more detail at one such wound – harm suffered by those receiving ECT.

ECT: a diversion or an example of a 'wound' behind closed doors?

In the days when I regularly received phone calls from journalists asking for quotes about the state of Psy I would usually say, 'You're asking the wrong questions. You should be writing about ECT.' Invariably, the response would come, 'They don't still do that do they?' But they do. Campaigns against most, if not all, Psy treatments have existed for well over a century – from the Alleged Lunatics Friends Society of the mid-19th century to POPAN today (see Chapter 1). There are several websites devoted to critiquing ECT.[27] One of those criticisms is the public invisibility of the practice. Focusing here on a specific and relatively little-used technique may appear to be a diversion. I should suggest that ECT might be viewed as representative of much that occurs within the Psy complex: the technique has harmed millions; it is based on suspect and ever-changing theoretical assumptions; research is scientistic and carried out exclusively by those with vested interests in the results; it is most commonly used on those with little power who have been marked, frequently via psychometric assessment, in the context of coercion and lack of consent; and – importantly – clinical psychologists are largely silent on the topic. For Erwin Staub, they would be classed as 'bystanders' in the face of harm perpetrated on patients in the same system within which they work.[28]

During ECT an electric current is passed briefly through the brain, via electrodes applied to the scalp, to induce generalised seizure activity. The person receiving the treatment is anaesthetised; muscle relaxants are given to prevent spasms. Melinda James, an ECT survivor, notes, 'The drug they give to avoid bones breaking is NOT a muscle relaxant. It is a muscle paralyser. It paralyses all the muscles. You cannot blink your eyes, you cannot breathe. I know because one time or maybe more (I only remember one) they did not give me enough of the anaesthetic, and I was not asleep. I could not tell them I was fully conscious — could not move, could not blink my eyes. I saw the doctor leaning over me with the electrodes. Then I was knocked out by the shock. Fully conscious, but paralysed. It felt like someone had bashed my head in with a hammer.'[29] ECT is recommended to be given twice a week up to a maximum of six weeks. Repeated treatments induce molecular and cellular changes in the brain, characterised by Peter Breggin as, 'brain damage'.[30]

The story of Cerletti finding the inspiration for ECT in a slaughter house in Rome in 1938 is well known. Less well known, perhaps, is that he was searching for the cure to schizophrenia. For some years a Hungarian psychiatrist, Julius Nyírő, had promoted a theory that schizophrenia could not co-exist with epilepsy. Ergo, if epilepsy could be induced in someone diagnosed with schizophrenia, the schizophrenia would be cured. Ladislas von Meduna claimed dramatic success with a catatonic schizophrenic after injecting camphor (used as a stimulant for centuries in China and Japan) to induce convulsions. He quickly changed to using the synthetic metrazol and shock treatment began.[31] Bini and Cerletti are credited with the move from chemically to electrically induced convulsions. It would be kind to describe Cerletti's discovery, diagnosis and subsequent electrocution of a vagrant as 'haphazard'. The 'patient's' subsequent avowal that he was cured might be taken as a sign that he was aware of one technique for dealing with oppressive force – *appear* to do what the powerful want. Some 60 years later at a local seminar Viv Lindow, an ECT survivor and researcher, explained to a group of psychiatrists that the way to avoid further shocks and get out of psychiatric hospital is to say you feel better *however you feel*.[32] It is a technique clinical psychologists working as psychotherapists might bear in mind when claiming successful therapeutic outcome on the basis of patient report.

To the surprise of many the practice remains a core treatment in psychiatry, especially for elderly people. Its reputation as alternatively 'life-saving' and 'barbaric' ensures that the public remains largely ignorant of its popularity. It is a treatment hidden behind the closed doors of modern asylums, one well known to the staff and rarely publicised despite at least one psychiatric journal being entirely devoted to the practice.

The ECT suite was originally in the entrance corridor of the Warneford Hospital in Oxford. For many years it was disguised to visitors by an illuminated sign reading 'Dentist' when in use. A colleague, on first moving to St George's Hospital in Stafford, found her office located alongside the ECT suite and was regularly interrupted by the dimming of her office lights due to fluctuations in electricity when the suite was in use. The medical superintendent and his colleagues at Shelton Hospital in the late 1950s had sufficient faith in the practice to give each other shocks and there is a – possibly – apocryphal tale of a local farmer who bypassed the need for psychiatric authority by giving himself rather haphazard electric shocks via the battery of his tractor.

Electroshock – as it was then known – was introduced into the USA soon after Meduna's first publication on the topic in 1935. By 1940 ECT was the preferred way to create the desired seizures and 43 per cent of US mental institutions were using it. Between 100,000 and 200,000 patients now undergo ECT in the United States annually. This is only an estimate, however, as only four states (Colorado, California, Texas and Massachusetts) require reporting on ECT statistics.

The American Psychiatric Association claims that 1 in 200 ECT patients suffer memory loss. Figures from California suggest a proportion closer to 1 in 5. Reporting of adverse effects ('complications') is limited to non-fatal cardiac arrests or arrhythmias requiring resuscitation, fractures, apnoea persisting 20 minutes or more after initiation of treatment, memory loss reported by the patient extending more than three months following the completed course and deaths which occur during or within the first 24 hours after a treatment. Between 1989 and 1994 (1993 figures were unavailable) over 12,000 people received ECT, 445 (3.6%) of whom were involuntary patients and 364 (3%) received ECT without consent. About half were over 65 years old, 21 (1.7%) were under 18, and 68 per cent were female. More than a fifth of all patients had serious complications. The most often reported complication (19.7% of all patients and 93.6% of all complications) was extended memory loss lasting longer than three months.[33]

Between September 1993 and April 1995 15,240 ECT administrations in Texas hospitals have been subjected to a review. Almost all of the patients (88.1%) were white, five were less than 18 years of age and 70.3 per cent were women. Eight patients died within 14 days of a treatment, three of whom killed themselves. The researchers conclude, 'Our data support the common finding that ECT is generally safe and effective.'[34]

Use of ECT at the Father Muller Medical College Hospital, Mangalore, over the ten-year period 2002 to 2011 peaked at 2.14 per cent of inpatients in 2006. Usage returned to an average of 1 per cent. About half the patients were being treated for schizophrenia, a much higher proportion than in Western countries.

A major difference between use of ECT in India and its use elsewhere is the number of treatments patients receive. During the Mangalore study 189 patients received just 638 treatments, a mean of between 3 and 4 treatments per patient as opposed to 12 in the UK and US.[35] In some African countries practice is limited by anaesthetic resources, so that unmodified ECT is used in Nigeria; the risks to the patient of broken bones or dislocation are considerably heightened.

Effectively banned in Italy, Austria, Germany and Switzerland for some years, ECT is now returning throughout these countries. Peter Lehmann, a publisher and founder of the European Network of Users and Survivors of Psychiatry, claims that Uwe Peters, recently appointed to the ethical council of the German Society for Psychiatry, Psychotherapy and Neurology, is responsible for the resurgence of ECT in Germany.[36] In his *Dictionary of Psychiatry and Medical Psychology* Peters defines ECT as: Production of a generalised epileptic seizure as treatment procedure. Technology: With the help of a convulsor an alternating current from 70 to 100V and about 150mA is passed through the head of the anaesthetised and muscle relaxed patient for 1 to 9 seconds. With the release of seizure the treatment is finished.[37]

ECT is forbidden in Slovenia though a small number of patients are referred outside to Zagreb, Croatia where the procedure is still used. Slovenian authorities claim only 3 to 12 patients are referred each year.

In Greece a 2007 survey found 137 people were given ECT (Greece has a population of about 11.3 million), a rate of 0.001 per cent of the population. Schizophrenia was the most common diagnosis. In Turkey one hospital (Bakirkoy Research and Training Hospital for Psychiatric and Neurological Diseases in Istanbul) accounted for 3,490 ECT patients from 2008–2010, the majority with a diagnosis of mania or schizophrenia.[38]

Finding reliable data on the practice in the UK is difficult and reveals widely varying use between NHS administrative regions. ECT data were routinely collected by the National Health Service until 1991, when specific ECT reporting was replaced by Hospital Episode Statistics, considered to significantly under-report ECT activity.

In a survey conducted that year two authorities, Mid-Staffordshire and Herefordshire, used very little while others in the same West Midlands region gave ECT to more than one in ten psychiatric admissions. Typically about two-thirds of recipients were women. In Great Yarmouth and Waveney less than one in a hundred admissions were electroshocked; in the adjacent East Suffolk one in five admissions received ECT.[39]

ECT standards and practice vary remarkably, not only between different countries but also within them and even within individual centres, for example, there is an 18-fold difference in use of ECT between 11 general adult psychiatric teams within a single Edinburgh teaching hospital. During 2000–2001 the Mental Health Act Commission reported that there were substantial departures from best policy, practice or training in a fifth of 230 ECT facilities they surveyed in England and Wales.[40]

To attempt to improve quality control of ECT administration, the Royal Colleges of Psychiatrists, Anaesthetists and Nursing launched the ECT Accreditation Service (ECTAS) in May 2003. ECTAS surveyed mental health trusts that had used ECT between September 2004 and February 2006. The protocol included a questionnaire for recipients of whom 72 per cent said that ECT had been helpful, 20 per cent that it had had no effect, five per cent that they would not want it again and 14 per cent that it had changed or saved their lives.[41]

The use of electroconvulsive therapy (ECT) was assessed in 56 clinics over three months in England in 2006 (private clinics were excluded). Compared with 1999 and 2002 the number of clinics providing ECT and the number of patients receiving ECT had declined (down to an estimated 1,276) of whom a higher proportion (30%) received ECT as involuntary patients under the Mental Health Act.[42]

In England the Care Quality Commission (CQC) report on monitoring the Mental Health Act in England. The report gives statistics on the use of ECT with patients sectioned under the Act, i.e., patients considered incapable of making an informed decision and treated without their consent. The CQC has a panel of psychiatrists (second opinion appointed doctors or SOADs) who give their approval for treatment. SOADs seldom withhold approval.

In 2009/2010, over a quarter of trusts had no reports of ECT, although they had made requests to the CQC for a SOAD visit to approve ECT for non-consenting patients. Amongst the trusts that reported *no* ECT were some with the highest rates of SOAD requests: Greater Manchester West (41 SOAD requests), Leicestershire (33), North Essex (59), Northumberland, Tyne and Wear (39), South London and Maudsley (45), and West London (38).

By contrast two trusts made requests where ECT administration followed. As noted above SOAD permission is rarely denied – it is possible that these data are more accurate. Cornwall made 12 SOAD requests followed by 451 ECT administrations and Kent and Medway made 43 requests followed by 547 ECT administrations.[43]

Overall in 2011/2012 there were 1006 completed SOAD visits, a slight increase (about 3%) from the previous year, i.e., approximately 1,000 people were given ECT without consent. Over 85 per cent of these were women.[44]

In Wales the estimated annual rate fell from 3.9 to 2.2 patients per 100,000 between 1990 and 1996.[45] In Scotland, according to the Scottish ECT Accreditation Network, 418 patients received ECT in 2010. The commonest 'indication for treatment' was the failure of prescribed antidepressants (63%). SEAN reported that 75 per cent of patients 'showed an improvement' after a course of ECT (on average 8 treatments). Two thirds of recipients were women.[46]

The consistent over-representation of women receiving ECT has frequently been 'explained' in terms of higher numbers of women being diagnosed as depressed. As I have tried to show, however, in many countries those diagnosed with schizophrenia make up the highest proportion of recipients, a finding wholly consistent with Nyírő's original speculations concerning an antagonistic relationship between schizophrenia and epilepsy. A second explanatory discourse emphasises the relative longer lives of women. As ECT is more frequently given to older people there are more women in the target group. Other tentative hypotheses might include a more general antagonism to women from the male dominated Psy complex or, more radically, the possibility that 'depression' is identified in a group who are actually exhausted by their multiple societal roles and who have less support for their travails.[47] Women entrants to the profession of clinical psychology outnumber men by a factor of nine to one (see next chapter); a possible role for the profession is a collaborative venture with survivor groups to protest the use of ECT against their sex.

The Regulation and Quality Improvement Authority report on the administration of ECT by the five Health and Social Care Trusts (HSC) in Northern Ireland shows that in the year of record, 2010/2011, 168 patients received ECT. During the 2011/12 year, 147 patients underwent the procedure, a drop in the rate of 9 per 100,000 to 8 per 100,000. Again, women were in the majority (68%) with an age range of 22 to 95. Of the treatments 69 per cent were 'voluntary' (see Szasz[48]). Of the detained patients, 19 per cent were able to give valid consent to ECT, with 81 per cent of the detained patients requiring a second doctor's opinion. The Western Health and Social Care Trust recorded the highest number of patients receiving ECT (14 per 100,000) while the South Eastern Health and Social Care Trust had the lowest rate at 4 per 100,000.[49]

My aim in craving the reader's indulgence by giving such a detailed account of the numbers of people still undergoing a procedure the majority may believe has been long extinct has been two-fold. First to provide material for practitioner clinical psychologists to use in an evidence base informing them of the hazards to people treated in the system in which they work – some UK academic psychologists already use similar data in collaborative campaigns.[50] Second, to give some rough guide to well-known concerns of ECT recipients in terms of the harm that ECT can do and the idiosyncratic nature of its use – a preference to use it with women and older people and, despite government regulation, a lack of monitoring which might emphasise the inconsistency across NHS areas of administration.

Some noted figures have received ECT, amongst them authors Linda Andre, director of the Committee for Truth in Psychiatry, Janet Frame, Ernest Hemingway, Robert M. Persig and Sylvia Plath; actors Judy Garland, Vivien Leigh, Gene Tierney and Carrie Fisher; musicians Bud Powell, Vladimir Horowitz, David Helfgott, Michelle Shocked, Tammy Wynette,

Townes van Zandt, Peter Green and Lou Reed. Dick Cavett, the American television talk show host, Yves Saint-Laurent and Edie Sedgwick were all recipients.[51] Ted Chabasinski, an American attorney and psychiatric survivor activist first received ECT aged six. The ahistorical tendency of some psychiatric historians to retrospectively diagnose famous folk as depressed would suggest that Churchill (who diagnosed himself with the 'Black Dog' of depression) might have been a candidate. A 1994 study of famous *men* concludes, '… *certain* pathological personality characteristics, as well as tendencies towards depression and alcoholism, are causally linked to *some kinds* of valuable creativity' (my italics).[52] It seems possible Churchill would have been spared; few, if any, psychiatric historians suggest that someone should *become* a depressed alcoholic in order to increase creativity though this is a perfectly logical conclusion from the association.

A treatment whose efficacy is predicated on the destruction of healthy brain tissue might be seen as a risk worth taking for a suicidal patient or for a family asked to give consent for the treatment of a child or elderly relative. The website of MIND (a UK mental health charity) claims that ECT is only given if a patient is diagnosed with 'severe, life-threatening depression' or has not responded to medication or talking treatments. Mania and catatonia are claimed to respond as is 'postnatal depression' on the basis that ECT works quickly thus increasing the opportunity for mother and baby bonding. Patients can explicitly request ECT on the grounds it has helped before.[53]

Although ECT is claimed to be an evidence-based treatment, research in the field is on the decrease. A review of research articles on ECT between 1992 and 2001 revealed 117 articles, of which 10 per cent were randomised controlled trials. The majority of articles were North American (47%) and from the UK (14%).[54] *The Journal of ECT*, founded as *Convulsive Therapy* in 1985 by Max Fink, continues to publish the majority of studies. Given the likely adverse effects of ECT, the conclusions of a review commissioned by the National Institute for Health and Care Excellence (NICE) seem important. They say, 'In people with depression, real ECT is *probably* more effective than *sham* ECT but stimulus parameters have an important influence on efficacy; low dose unilateral ECT is no more effective than sham ECT. ECT is probably more effective than pharmacotherapy in the short term but the evidence on which this assertion is based was of variable quality' (my italics) [55].

In summary, a combination of the closed nature of institutions, lack of power or choice on the patient's part, a privileging of technical over humane procedures in Psy and the authority of the Psy professional with medical responsibility means that certain patients are quite likely to undergo ECT. A historical analysis would perhaps suggest that a variety of factors maintain the practice. These might include clinical preference, changing theoretical justifications, paralleled by a failure to acknowledge adverse effects from memory loss to death, and a certain desperation on the part of psychiatrists to change patients, often women, that they don't understand. A lack of public knowledge and the unwillingness of non-medical practitioners to speak out about its use maintain the invisibility of the procedure. Brain damage resulting from ECT might be regarded as one of the 'wounds' suffered by those at most risk of devaluation by society – the mad, the odd and those without the physical or material resources to resist, frequently elderly people.[56]

The idiopathic nature of an individual's physical make-up and metabolism makes any medical procedure something of an experiment. ECT is no exception. Effectively, every ECT treatment is an experiment.

The complexity of relationships between people and the context they find themselves in makes each meeting a unique event. Meetings between clinical psychologists can also be regarded as a form of experiment. In the next section I look in more detail at what clinical psychologists *claim* to do with patients.

Psychological intervention

One of Freud's injunctions was that the therapist should *never* take at face value what the patient first described as the problem.

All initial utterances were defensive, examples of transference. Only through months of 'evenly suspended attention' from the analyst and speaking unfettered by the ego could the patient begin to approach those areas of experience previously censored by social mores internalised by the patient.[57] Paul Salkovskis, doyen of cognitive behaviour therapy in the 1980s, once said something similar to me – in effect, patients would only trust a therapist with intimate revelations after months of sitting together in the consulting room. Clinical psychologists using psychological formulation and under employer pressure to 'assess' as quickly as possible might regard these ideas as nonsensical, as would numerous service survivors fed up with the arrogant authority of members of Big Psy claiming to know best. For Racker, psychological formulation would have been a combination of ill-considered countertransference (untouched by so-called reflective practice) and 'manic interpretation'.[58] For others, surprised at the range of variables a clinical psychologist is meant to understand and incorporate, the process is perhaps hubristic, for the profession of clinical psychology in the UK, the current big thing.

Psychiatric patients, those in 'homes' for older people, young people in 'adolescent units' and learning disabled people in supported accommodation will all be *invaded without consent* (most often via injections of drugs to pacify them) and *referred without consent*. The first port of call for many people in distress is the general practitioner. Busy GPs will refer people to local psychology departments without mentioning the referral, as they see 'mental health' as having negative connotations for many of their patients. But even if the person is aware of the referral, few National Health Service Departments of Clinical Psychology have easily accessible public information about their staff and services (fewer still have *any* information about their success rates). One example was www.shropsych.org, a public information system for Shropshire's Department of Psychological Therapies. The website was closed a few years after the department came under the auspices of a new NHS Trust.

Clinical psychologists have entered the profession to help others. Chapters 1 and 2 covered this ambition in detail. It continues to be an aim that finds its focus in therapy rather than research. To this end clinical psychologists in the USA and UK will undergo further training and supervision in specific therapies. These therapies have their own formal qualifications and professional bodies. A clinical psychologist can find herself a member of the DCP, the BPS, and for NHS employment purposes, under the umbrella of the Health and Care Professions Council. The Association for Family Therapy will welcome her if she completes the approved training as will the British Association for Behavioural and Counselling Psychology and many similar enterprises. The organisations control particular qualifications and may, as in the case of the British Psychoanalytic Association, expect continuing personal therapy. The organisations have codes of practice and may have ethical statements concerning the nature of therapy or financial and other types of exploitation. An uncritical account of such codes would suggest that potential patients might be confident that accredited Psy professionals are unlikely to exploit them in the ways referred to in Chapter 4.

The opening chapter discussed how clinical psychologists acting as psychotherapists can undergo further training in any of hundreds of different therapies. These have been variously criticised as being harmful, based on specious theorising by corrupt founders in the field or wholly constrained by modernist notions of 'the individual' which fail to take social context into account. The theoretical underpinnings of many therapies are particularly open to critique – concepts such as 'ego strength' or 'faulty cognitions' are inferences based on observed conduct judged by social mores or the self-report of patients who are expected to be able to reveal their thoughts in much the same way they might be able to describe a piece of furniture. This privileging of thoughts neglects the complexity of interaction between feelings, body and context in which people are situated.[59]

In the UK, the Division of Clinical Psychology suggests that clinical psychology doctoral courses, in response to governmental promotion of CBT, now train practitioners in CBT and at least one other therapeutic modality. This is something of a bold endeavour as few, if any, courses offer enough teaching or supervised experience in, for example, psychodynamic or family therapy. In general, clinical psychologists in training are loath to enter therapy themselves for the kind of training many analytic and humanist traditions demand. Instead, those that are inclined towards individual therapies will take post-qualification courses. An outcome of this process is that clinical psychologists may take a total of six or seven years before regarding themselves as therapeutically competent. They will *still* fail to research the success or otherwise of their interventions and, in the context of the NHS, will be employed solely to offer short-term interventions seeing the maximum number of patients in the shortest time possible – a process dictated by local and national targets and contracts rather than informed choice of patients.

The notion of 'clinical need' is a professionally determined construct – rather like the 'need' for a car to be serviced every six or ten thousand miles – it is a concept that is consistently used to justify clinical psychology therapy contacts exceeding the approved number (frequently 12–18 hourly sessions). Therapy relationships, like any relationships, are uniquely contextualised by the process of power and external circumstances. These forces mean that the suggestion that an adult patient who had been assaulted in childhood 'needs' more 'intense therapy' than a person who has only recently experienced some mildly fearful moments while in a bus queue becomes a self-serving suggestion – made for the best intentions – on the therapist's part. Clinical psychologists can blame a lack of progress from the patient's perspective on 'not enough therapy' or 'not enough of the right kind of therapy'. This process might be seen as preserving the illusion that individual therapy can magically transform individuals whose very real difficulties lie in the context of the lives they are constrained to lead rather than a failure of will on their part.[60]

The concept of 'will' like that of the self (see Chapter 2) is one which pervades, as an unstated subtext, the world of therapy. Colin Feltham has proposed that a rather vague substrate of philosophising around free will and determinism divides the broadly CBT schools and the humanist tradition. He suggests that, in general, counsellors err on the side of free will while *not* being able to say what they mean by the expression.[61] For clinical psychologists working within a CBT or other deterministic frame, their role becomes one of persuading patients that their distress is 'caused' by various thoughts, circumstances, life events and ways of thinking about these events. The rhetoric of a shared construction of meaning of the patient's difficulties disguises the potential for a psychological discourse to dominate the interaction. Patients are not seen to 'choose' distress but are seen as being able to 'choose' to alter their thought patterns or external circumstances in order to alleviate distress. They are also seen as 'choosing' to enter therapy contracts with clinical psychologists who, with rare exceptions, do not publish the results of their therapeutic endeavours but instead justify their approach with reference to scientistic research of the type outlined in Chapter 2. In any case, as previously noted, clinical psychologists are 'eclectic' in their therapeutic style and can justify anything they do in terms of numerous theories.

This is, by necessity, a generalisation – the unobserved nature of therapeutic work means we don't *know* what any given clinical psychologist is actually doing with any given patient in therapy sessions, nor do we know whether clinical psychologists are consistent across patients or across time.

How might an NHS therapy session be imagined by people who read the kinds of promotional material familiar to those with responsibility for purchasing services and managers who don't see patients? A clinical psychologist, happily married and relaxed after cycling to work, greets a patient, also relaxed after a brief wait in a cheerful waiting room. The patient is on time, smiling and holding her completed 'thought diary', one feature of the CBT that has already seen her making great strides to her stated therapeutic goal of being confident to return to paid employment. The psychologist's room is warm, book-lined and quiet. After 20 minutes of talk focused on her latest successes, the clinical psychologist suggests the session might finish a little early as progress seems unhindered and there doesn't seem much more to talk about. As part of the initial problem formulation she had considered adding some psychodynamic interpretations to explicate some of the origins of the patient's troubles in terms of her relationship with her father and men in general but these seem redundant in the face of ongoing therapeutic success. As the patient leaves she reassures the psychologist that she knows the forthcoming week's 'homework' tasks and has the full support of her partner in their completion. She thanks the psychologist and leaves with a spring in her step.

Or, perhaps: the clinical psychologist shares a room with two other mental health professionals, one of whom has left unwashed coffee cups on the floor. She is late for the appointment as the office accommodation is in a busy part of town with no reserved parking. She is a single mum who has recently joined an Internet dating agency and is considering working for a new NHS employer in order to better afford her rent. She is concerned that the patient has been late to several recent sessions and seems tired during their talks. She has wondered if the medication is adding to the patient's tiredness but hasn't had the time to discuss this possibility with either the patient or prescribing general practitioner. The patient is late again offering the clinical psychologist the opportunity to catch up on some administration – she has been told that unless details of contacts with patients are properly recorded she may lose pay. Unsure whether NHS employers can legally instate employment contracts *post hoc* she has done her best to comply and is quite grateful the patient is so late. When the patient arrives she immediately bursts into tears and apologises for failing to complete her thought diary yet again.

Searching for reasons (meaning)

For both Anselm and Spinoza reason was the ultimate expression of G-d's grace. To be able to think and reason through one's experience was living proof of G-d. For Sartre, the unreflected life was pointless – to reflect on one's place in the order of things and how one may find oneself at any given point *was* the point. To conclude one acted *because* of a selfish need, though not a position encouraged by society, was to be in good faith.

Reason has been subtly replaced by *reasons*; we suggest we do this or that due to various external or supposedly internal movers. Meanwhile, to acknowledge one acts selfishly is considered a bad thing. These are two of the concerns that, for me, create intractable complications for clinical psychologists attempting to use the profession's stated approach with patients – psychological formulation.

Lucy Johnstone and Rudi Dallos list the 'essential features' of such praxis. For them *all* formulations: summarise the service user's core problems; suggest how the service user's difficulties may relate to one another by drawing on psychological theories and principles; aim to explain, on the basis of psychological theory, the development and maintenance of the service user's difficulties, at this time and in these situations; indicate a plan of intervention; and are open to revision and re-formulation.[62] This is a considerable challenge. What are 'core' problems? Is a lack of material resources more important than thinking in particular ways about, say, not being a good-enough parent? This seems more essentially a religious question, answered by Jesus in terms of the lilies of the field or by Buddhists who abjure desire. For a clinical psychology interview to establish 'core' problems seems to demand a great deal of an hour or two's 'assessment'. The essential features, however, suggest this question can be addressed by reference to psychological theory. The theory is meant to explain development *and* maintenance of the targeted problem. As I discussed in Chapter 2 there are numerous theories, some tautological, many based on untestable hypotheses involving unobservable abstractions (for example, the simplistic notion that thoughts dictate feelings). A clinical psychologist agreeing a formulation based on these theories could be accused of abandoning the role of scientist-practitioner in favour of a role as rhetorician.

I should guess that few clinical psychologists will read *The Core Purpose and Philosophy of the Profession* produced by the DCP. For those that do, it could be a dispiriting experience. This slim volume suggests that, for the profession in the UK,

Psychological formulation is the summation and integration of the knowledge that is acquired by this assessment process that may involve psychological, biological and systemic factors and procedures. The formulation will draw on psychological theory and research to provide a framework for describing a client's problem or needs, how it developed and is being maintained. Because of their particular training in the relationship of theory to practice, clinical psychologists will be able to draw on a number of models (bio-psycho-social) to meet needs or support decision making and so a formulation may comprise a number of provisional hypotheses. This provides the foundation from which actions may derive ... Psychological intervention, if considered appropriate, is based upon the formulation. [63]

Again, if taken as reflecting the profession's position, these are considerable demands – an assessment will lead to knowledge about a person's psychology, biology and system context. Psychological theory is privileged as an explanatory discourse as it can easily be argued that we *all* have 'psychological' theories about our situation (perhaps not readily referenced but easily translated into a mainstream theoretical model if pressed); the process described. Psychological formulation, as a formal praxis, requires, however, an expert. It is thus likely to be the clinical psychologist's formulation that is privileged in any judgement concerning the patient's predicament. The privileging of the dominant professional discourse is elucidated in the work of conversational analysts but it might be summarised as, 'Quiet dear, the professor is talking'. The psychologist is positioned as constructing shared explanations with any given patient. Conversational analysis aims to reveal the way a *professional* explanation is frequently the one that emerges in meetings between patients and Psy professionals. There is no way of knowing if the patient actually believes any given explanation but patients know well how to *appear* to be in agreement with the more powerful other. [64]

The *Core Purpose* document deploys the language of 'needs' rather than wants – again a professionalised term and one which *requires* professional input. It might be suggested that to respond to what a patient says she wants (for example, 'I want my children to keep quiet in the evening') without using the professional rhetoric of 'need' places the clinical psychologist in a position more on a par with the patient's friends than an expert role. Admittedly the substitution of 'need' for 'want' is part of common speech (children often seem to 'need' an extra hour in front of the telly, the shop assistant 'needs' a bottle of lager after a long working day and so on). In the context of formal documents of this type, however, the substitution of 'want' for 'need' would downplay the position of the professional. Again, no hierarchy of need is suggested; what is the clinical psychologist to do if the person, as in the example given in Chapter 5, is too ashamed of a particular difficulty (reading, in the example) to name it? Even at the simple level of description of problems, the assessment will not reveal some important (and potentially easily soluble) difficulties.

A second official document, *The DCP Guidelines on Formulation*, stresses that the quality of a formulation is dependent on the quality of the assessment. Additionally clinical psychologists are, 'expected to be competent to use a range of procedures such as psychometric tests, risk assessments and structured interviewing'. Information may also be gathered from, 'relatives and carers, other professionals, diaries, medical notes, observation, feedback from homework tasks, and so on'. The formulations should also be 'informed by the most recent evidence, as summarised in NICE guidelines, Cochrane reviews and scientific journals'.

In the section entitled 'A partial formulation and a full formulation', the guidelines acknowledge that all formulations are partial and dynamic, some formulations are seen as necessarily more comprehensive and detailed than others. A coursework assignment, for example, may be 'several paragraphs long and focus on a complex set of difficulties in the context of a person's whole life story'. A qualified psychologist 'may find that simple diagrammatic formulations (e.g., demonstrating how automatic thoughts lead to anxiety which leads to avoidance) are often more suitable for routine clinical practice'.

Overall,

> ... best practice clinical psychology formulation and formulating is person-specific not problem-specific, draws from a range of models and causal

factors, integrates, not just lists, the various possible causal factors through an understanding of their personal meaning to the service user, includes a cultural perspective and understanding of the service user's presentation and distress, [and] … is clear who are the stakeholders in any given situation and starts from a critical awareness of the wider societal context of formulation. [65]

In summarising potential elements for an information booklet aiding informed consent for patients seeing clinical psychologists, Chapter 4 concludes 'A person might be surprised to discover they are likely to be psychometrically assessed, diagnosed, maintained on psychoactive drugs with no protest from the clinical psychologist or counsellor and offered a therapy either reflecting the latest interest of the therapist or a therapeutic style the therapist has maintained for many years despite little evidence of therapeutic efficacy as measured by positivistic research.' I should tentatively suggest that these elements are not exclusive to individual therapies. They also seem to be factors in the psychological formulation approach. The latter seems more ambitious to me, becoming a 'person management' model rather than psychological model *per se*. In other words, psychological formulation is not itself a psychological formulation – rather it is a way for the DCP to publicly present clinical psychologists as extremely wide-ranging in their approach. In addition to the paragraph above an information leaflet for psychological formulation might have to include statements that the psychologist will take virtually all possible factors into account, including culture, in a session lasting a couple of hours. The leaflet might add that there is little, if any, research supporting psychological formulation over a more direct therapy approach in terms of its benefits to patients.

The benefits of psychological formulation have been studied in the context of multidisciplinary teamwork. The authors cite several studies urging psychological formulation within teams in order to counteract the medical *Zeitgeist* and dominance of diagnosis.[66] They refer to the DCP document's list of seventeen advantages to the team including raising staff morale and 'generating new ways of thinking'.[67] The paper assumes a knowledge of formulation amongst their readership (despite the research finding that many members of multidisciplinary teams see formulation as the business of the clinical psychologist), an assumption evidenced by the absence of any definition of the practice. There is no acknowledgement that formulation, as a psychological knowledge, is, like any such knowledges, '... from a critical standpoint potentially problematic and potentially to be contested regarding: how they are constructed and legitimised; whose interests they serve; how they can be resisted or subverted'.[68]

Clinical psychologists are not alone in using psychological formulation. Psychiatrists and other professionals claim the praxis as a skill. There is a ubiquity of the psychological discourse for conduct – sometimes referred to as 'pop psychology'. Non-professionals can offer explanations for hooliganism, creativity, temper tantrums and artistic endeavour based on *ad hoc* psychological formulation that may include such constructions as culture, parenting, 'normal child development' and crowd behaviour. I should argue that laying claim to psychological formulation as a praxis is a professional move. It is not – indeed cannot – be based on evidence that the praxis is better for the patient than other practices. It might be argued that the immediate appeal to clinical psychologists is, again, the status gained by appearing to offer a more sophisticated analysis than medical or nursing colleagues. I shall return to this theme in the next chapter.

A brief psychological formulation of psychological formulation

Clinical psychologists are encouraged to be reflexive. Psychological theory tends to lack reflexivity. An example might be the behavioural theory of intermittent reinforcement. Put simply this states that the best reinforcer is one that reinforces behaviour through intermittent reward. Ergo, a clinical psychologist will continue to practise an intermittent reinforcement schedule if it works occasionally. Praxis rewarded all the time will be dropped. Applied to a particular form of therapy the theory would suggest that a therapist continues with the favoured therapeutic style because *it doesn't work that often.*

Reflexively applying psychological formulation to psychological formulation itself might be regarded as an academic exercise. I hope the reader will bear with me. A summary of the user's core problems might be: the profession of clinical psychology continues to herald new technologies as breakthroughs (termed 'paradigm shifts') particularly in relation to the looming ubiquity of psychiatry. Simultaneously the profession is wedded to scientism in its efforts to remain within the paradigm of science. These difficulties relate directly to one another in that psychiatry too claims scientific credibility privileging the language of science and 'evidence' over a more grounded and self-questioning philosophical approach (clearly many psychiatrists, for example, Jung and Laing attempted to ground their approach in a more philosophical discourse). Mary Boyle, a clinical psychologist, has argued that both professions are 'insecure' (a psychological theory) and for clinical psychologists it might be suggested that the promotion of problem formulation is another example of a relatively young profession trying to break away from the (psychiatric) parent.[69] Perhaps a Freudian theorist would argue this is an oedipal position, a Kleinian envy, or a systems theorist an example of maintaining homeostasis (the struggle against psychiatry) via a gradual metamorphosis (slowly shifting positions within a developing socio-professional *Zeitgeist*). The problem developed in clinical psychology's formative years (see Chapter 1), torn between the 'bad breast' of medical domination and the 'good breast' of science, both projections which obtain today. A more Smailian approach might be to suggest that the problem is maintained via proximal power; for individual clinical psychologists faced by challenges from non-psychologist colleagues to justify therapeutic conduct, presenting a 'psychological formulation' has the advantage of sounding both wise and complex. Distally, influences on the profession include increasing pressure to justify relatively high salaries and the cultural significance of maintaining an eclectic position through changing adherence to 'new' praxis.

Clinical psychologists may be trained psychoanalytically. Those who attempt to incorporate the influence of transference in their psychological formulation (a potential weakness in the model for some commentators[70]) should necessarily take account of countertransference (the influence, frequently seen as unconscious) of the patient on the psychologist. If we take Racker seriously, then psychological formulation is a *result* of countertransference.[71] Rather than attempt it, the psychoanalytically inclined psychologist should adopt Freud's 'evenly suspended attention'.

Maintaining the institution

During my career as a therapist, researcher, clinical psychologist and director of services I spent little time *intending* to hurt people. When patients said they felt better, I had no difficulty ending therapy and didn't chase patients who had come for only one session. As a manager I ensured that the majority of the psychologists and other Psy staff in the department had individual and relatively private offices. The two psychotherapy centres had been modernised and provided free drinks and Internet access in comfortable waiting rooms. The history and nature of Psy institutions outlined earlier in this chapter might however suggest that my role was one of simply modernising the clinic – the gaze and the essential power differentials between patients and 'experts' remained unaltered. My stories to staff and patients about my bullied Jewish childhood and birth on a council estate can be seen as ploys to establish working class (and oppressed) credentials amongst a group of predominantly working class staff and patients. I was – sometimes – consciously using 'referent power' to gain influence (see Chapter 2), while the comfort of the waiting rooms can be seen as environments designed to seduce patients who, given the role of psychology and counselling in maintaining the status quo, should have maintained their wariness rather than submitting to the gaze.

This kind of deconstruction can go on *ad infinitum*. When patients say, 'Thanks for the help Doc, I feel better', that should be evidence enough. For the majority of clinical psychologists it probably is. Examining our role in the context of institutions, wounds, the nature of free will and hubristic statements from the

Division of Clinical Psychology is, I suspect for the majority, just a little *too* reflexive. The next chapter continues the process in relation to the profession as profession.

Endnotes

1. Steinbeck, J. (1995). *The Grapes of Wrath* (Foreword by Elaine Steinbeck). London: Arrow Books. (Original work published 1939)

2. Cheney, D. (2008). Room for thought. *Journal of Critical Psychology, Counselling and Psychotherapy, 8*(2), 98–102.

3. Newnes, C. (1998). 'What we don't much write about.' *Clinical Psychology Forum, 117,* 35–36.

4. Bender, M. (1993). The unoffered chair: The history of therapeutic disdain towards people with a learning difficulty. *Clinical Psychology Forum, 54,* 7–12.

5. Szasz, T. (2007). *Coercion as Cure: A critical history of psychiatry.* London: Transaction Publishers; and Szasz, T. (1994). *Cruel Compassion: Psychiatric control of society's unwanted.* Chichester: John Wiley & Sons.

6. Turner, T. H. (1992). A diagnostic analysis of the Casebooks of Ticehurst House Asylum, 1845–1890. *Psychological Medicine, Monograph Supplement, 21,* 3–70; and Turner, T. H. (1990). Rich and mad in Victorian England. In R. M. Murray & T. H. Turner (Eds.), *Lectures on the History of Psychiatry: The Squibb series.* London: Gaskell/Royal College of Psychiatrists, pp. 170–193.

7. See, for example, Busfield, J. (1986). *Managing Madness: Changing ideas and practice.* London: Hutchinson; Bynum, W. F., Porter, R. & Shepherd, M. (1988). *The Anatomy of Madness: Essays in the history of psychiatry, Volume III: The asylum and its psychiatry.* London: Routledge; Hunter, R. & Macalpine, I. (1974). *Psychiatry for the Poor.* London: Dawsons; Ignatieff, M. (1978). *A Just Measure of Pain.* London: Macmillan; Scull, A. T. (1979). *Museums of Madness.* London: Allen Lane; Scull, A. T. (Ed.). (1981). *Madhouses, Mad-Doctors and Madmen: The social history of psychiatry in the Victorian era.* London: Athlone Press.

8. Allderidge, P. (1990). Hospitals, madhouses and asylums: Cycles in the care of the insane. In R. M. Murray & T. H. Turner (Eds.), *Lectures on the History of Psychiatry: The Squibb series.* London: Gaskell/Royal College of Psychiatrists, pp. 28–46, p. 45.

9. Kealey, E. J. (1981). *Medieval Medicus: A social history of Anglo-Norman medicine.* Baltimore, MD: Johns Hopkins University Press.

10. Foucault, M. (1972). *Histoire de la Folie à l'Âge Classique*. Paris: Gallimard.

11. Melot, M. (1971). *L'Abbaye de Fontevrault*. Paris: Jacques Lanore.

12. MacDonald, M. (1990). Insanity and the realities of history in early modern England. In R. M. Murray & T. H. Turner (Eds.), *Lectures on the History of Psychiatry: The Squibb series*. London: Gaskell/Royal College of Psychiatrists, pp. 60–81.

13. Cochrane, D. (1988). 'Humane, economical and medically wise': The LCC as administrators of Victorian lunacy policy. In W. F. Bynum, R. Porter & M. Shepherd (Eds.), *The Anatomy of Madness: Essays in the history of psychiatry, Volume III: The asylum and its psychiatry*. London: Routledge, pp. 247–272, p. 247.

14. An 1880 census of the use of restraint and seclusion in American asylums surveyed 139 public and private facilities. Tomes, N. (1988). The great restraint controversy: A comparative perspective on Anglo-American psychiatry in the nineteenth century. In W. F. Bynum, R. Porter & M. Shepherd (Eds.), *The Anatomy of Madness: Essays in the history of psychiatry, Volume III: The asylum and its psychiatry*. London: Routledge, pp. 190–225, p. 204.

15. Guarnieri, P. (1988). Between soma and psyche: Morselli and psychiatry in late-nineteenth-century Italy. In W. F. Bynum, R. Porter & M. Shepherd (Eds.), *The Anatomy of Madness: Essays in the history of psychiatry, Volume III: The asylum and its psychiatry*. London: Routledge, pp. 102–124.

16. Allderidge, P. (1990). Hospitals, madhouses and asylums: Cycles in the care of the insane. In R. M. Murray & T. H. Turner (Eds.), *Lectures on the History of Psychiatry: The Squibb series*. London: Gaskell/Royal College of Psychiatrists, pp. 28–46. Ann Digby has shown that the regime at the Retreat *did* include restraining chairs, straps and straitwaistcoats despite a public profile of firm but kind discipline. Digby, A. (1985). *Madness, Morality and Medicine: A study of the York Retreat, 1796–1914*. Cambridge: Cambridge University Press, pp. 78–82.

17. Russell, R. (1988). The lunacy profession and its staff in the second half of the nineteenth century, with special reference to the West Riding Lunatic Asylum. In W. F. Bynum, R. Porter & M. Shepherd (Eds.), *The Anatomy of Madness: Essays in the history of psychiatry, Volume III: The asylum and its psychiatry*. London: Routledge, pp. 297–315.

18. Newnes, C. (1995). *One hundred and forty-five years of madness: Salop County Lunatic Asylum, 1845–1990*. Unpublished PhD thesis: Keele University.

19. See, for example, Newnes, C. & Shalan D. (1997). Fear and loathing in Patients' Council visitors. *Clinical Psychology Forum, 110,* 10–12; and Williams, A., Harris, K.

& Newnes, C. (1994). The Patients' Council: Shelton Hospital. *Clinical Psychology Forum, 73,* 30–32.

20. Wolfensberger, W. (1998). *A Brief Introduction to Social Role Valorization: A high-order concept for addressing the plight of societally devalued people and for structuring human services* (3rd ed.). Syracuse, NY: Training Institute for Human Service Planning, Leadership and Change Agentry (Syracuse University).

21. Goldie, N. (1977). The division of labour among the mental health professions. In M. Stacey, M. Reid, C. Heath & R. Dingwall (Eds.), *Health and the Division of Labour.* London: Croom Helm, pp. 141–161.

22. See, for example, Boyle, M. (1999). Diagnosis. In C. Newnes, G. Holmes & C. Dunn (Eds.), *This is Madness: A critical look at psychiatry and the future of mental health services.* Ross-on-Wye: PCCS Books, pp. 75–90.

23. Bucknall, O. & Holmes, G. (2001). Relatives and carers. In C. Newnes, G. Holmes & C. Dunn (Eds.), *This is Madness Too: Critical perspectives on mental health services.* Ross-on-Wye: PCCS Books, pp. 127–134.

24. Goodwin, I., Holmes, G., Newnes, C. & Waltho, D. (1999). A qualitative analysis of the views of inpatient mental health service users. *Journal of Mental Health, 8*(1), 43–54.

25. Newnes, C. (1995). On note taking. *Clinical Psychology Forum, 80,* 31–36.

26. Foucault, M. (1975). *Discipline and Punish: The birth of the prison.* New York: Random House.

27. See, for example, http://intcamp.wordpress.com/ban-ect/ and http://camhjournal.com/2012/04/24/2004-a-campaign-against-direct-ect/ Retrieved 30 May 2013.

28. Staub, E. (1989). *The Roots of Evil: The origins of genocide and other group violence.* New York: Cambridge University Press. For examples of clinical psychologists speaking out via publication see, Baldwin, S. & Jones, Y. (1990). ECT, children and clinical psychologists: A shock to the system? *Clinical Psychology Forum, 25,* 2–4; Johnstone, L. (1999). Adverse psychological effects of ECT. *Journal of Mental Health, 8*(1), 69–85; Johnstone, L. (2002). *Users and abusers of psychiatry: A critical look at psychiatric practice* (2nd ed.). London: Routledge.

29. Retrieved 30 May 2013 from http://ectstatistics.wordpress.com/2013/05/20/75-years-of-electroconvulsive-therapy/

30. Breggin, P. (1991). *Toxic Psychiatry: Why therapy, empathy and love must replace the drugs, electroshock, and biochemical theories of the 'new psychiatry'.* New York: St. Martin's Press.

31. Valenstein, E. (1986). *Great and Desperate Cures: The rise and decline of psychosurgery and other radical treatments for mental illness.* New York: Basic Books.

32. Lindow, V. (1993). *Thinking about ECT.* Shropshire Institute of Mental Health seminar series 'Alternatives to Psychiatry': Shropshire Mental Health Authority. See also, Lindow, V. (1999). Survivor-controlled alternatives to psychiatric services. In C. Newnes, G. Holmes & C. Dunn (Eds.), *This is Madness: A critical look at psychiatry and the future of mental health services.* Ross-on-Wye: PCCS Books, pp. 211–226.

33. Retrieved 30 May 2013 from http://www.ect.org/resources/california.html

34. Reid, W. H., Keller, S., Leatherman, M. & Mason, M. (1998). ECT in Texas: 19 months of mandatory reporting. *Journal of Clinical Psychiatry, Jan, 59*(1), 8–13, p. 13.

35. Aruna, G. & Yadiyal, M. B. (2013). Is electroconvulsive therapy fading into oblivion? – a study of ten-year trends. *Online Journal of Health and Allied Sciences, 12*(1), 3. Retrieved 30 May 2013 from http://www.ojhas.org/issue45/2013-1-3.html

36. See, for example, Lehmann, P. (2010). Medicalization and irresponsibility. *Journal of Critical Psychology, Counselling and Psychotherapy, 10*(4), 209–218.

37. Peters, U. H. (1997). *Wörterbuch der Psychiatrie und medizinischen Psychologie.* Augsburg: Bechtermünz Verlag.

38. Retrieved 30 May 2013 from http://ectstatistics.wordpress.com/2013/03/18/ect-in-greece-and-turkey/

39. Newnes, C. D. (1991). ECT, the DCP and ME. *Clinical Psychology Forum, 36,* 20–4.

40. Eranti, S. & McLoughlin, D. M. (2003). Electroconvulsive therapy – state of the art. *British Journal of Psychiatry, 182,* 8–9.

41. *Ibid.*

42. Bickerton, D., Worrall, A. & Chaplin, R. (2009). Trends in the administration of electroconvulsive therapy in England. *The Psychiatrist, 33,* 61–63.

43. Retrieved 30 May 2013 from, http://ectstatistics.wordpress.com/2011/08/14/ect-is-the-hospital-episode-statistics/

44. Retrieved 30 May 2013 from http://ectstatistics.wordpress.com/2013/01/30/ect-without-consent-in-england-201112/

45. Eranti, S. & McLoughlin, D. M. (2003). Electroconvulsive therapy – state of the art. *British Journal of Psychiatry, 182,* 8–9.

46. SEAN. (2011). *Scottish ECT Accreditation Network Annual Report 2011. A summary of ECT in Scotland for 2010.* Edinburgh: Scottish ECT Accreditation Network.

47. Burstow, B. (2006). Electroshock as a form of violence against women. *Violence Against Women, 12*(4), 372–392.

48. Szasz, T. (2007). *Coercion as Cure: A critical history of psychiatry.* London: Transaction Publishers.

49. Retrieved 30 May 2013 from http://www.rqia.org.uk/cms_resources/G_Electroconvulsive_Therapy_Report_FINAL%20WEB%20final%20v6%200.pdf

50. The North West Right to Refuse Electroshock Campaign. Retrieved 4 June 2013 from www.discourseunit.com/ppr_downloads/ppr_rre.doc

51. Retrieved 1 June 2013 from http://www.ect.org/famous-shock-patients/

52. Post, F. (1994). Creativity and psychopathology: A study of 291 world-famous men. *British Journal of Psychiatry, 165,* 22–34.

53. Making sense of electroconvulsive therapy (ECT) http://www.mind.org.uk/mental_health_a-z/8027_electroconvulsive_therapy_ect

54. Eranti, S. & McLoughlin, D. M. (2003). Electroconvulsive therapy – state of the art. *British Journal of Psychiatry, 182,* 8–9.

55. Greenhalgh, J., Knight, C., Hind, D., Beverley, C. & Walters, S. (2005). Clinical and cost-effectiveness of electroconvulsive therapy for depressive illness, schizophrenia, catatonia and mania: Systematic reviews and economic modelling studies. *Health Technology Assessment, Mar, 9*(9), 1–156, iii–iv, p. 9.

56. Despite the evidence outlined here, the RQIA for Northern Ireland still claims, 'Electroconvulsive therapy is an important and necessary form of treatment for some of the most severe psychiatric conditions and is, in many instances, a life-saving treatment. It is medically safe and has good efficacy.' *The Regulation and Quality Improvement Authority Report on the Administration of Electroconvulsive Therapy in Northern Ireland* October 2012. Available at http://www.rqia.org.uk/cms_resources/G_Electroconvulsive_Therapy_Report_FINAL%20WEB%20final%20v6%200.pdf

57. Freud, S. (1912). The dynamics of transference. *The Complete Works, Standard Edition, Vol. 12.* London: The Hogarth Press.

58. Racker, H. (1968). *Transference and Counter-transference.* London: The Hogarth Press.

59. Cromby, J. (2006). Reconstructing the person. *Clinical Psychology Forum, 162,* 13–16.

60. Smail, D. (1995). Power and the origins of unhappiness: Working with individuals. *Journal of Community and Applied Social Psychology, 5,* 347–356.

61. Feltham, C. (2013). *Counselling and Counselling Psychology: A critical examination.* Ross-on-Wye: PCCS Books.

62. Johnstone, L. & Dallos, R. (2006). Introduction to formulation. In L. Johnstone & R. Dallos (Eds.), *Formulation in Psychology and Psychotherapy: Making sense of people's problems.* London: Routledge, pp. 1–16.

63. Division of Clinical Psychology. (2010). *The Core Purpose and Philosophy of the Profession.* Leicester: British Psychological Society. Retrieved 30 May 2013 from http://goo.gl/RXi8K

64. Rapley, M. & Antaki, C. (1996). A conversation analysis of the 'acquiescence' of people with learning disabilities. *Journal of Community and Applied Social Psychology, 6,* 207–227.

65. Division of Clinical Psychology. (2011). *Good Practice Guidelines on the Use of Psychological Formulation.* Leicester: British Psychological Society.

66. Hood, N., Johnstone, L. & Christofides, S. (2013). The hidden solution? Staff experiences, views and understanding of the use of psychological formulation in multi-disciplinary teams. *Journal of Critical Psychology, Counselling and Psychotherapy, 13*(2), 107–116.

67. Division of Clinical Psychology. (2011). *Good Practice Guidelines on the Use of Psychological Formulation.* Leicester: British Psychological Society, p. 9.

68. Fryer, D. & Easpaig, B. N. G. (2013). Critical analysology: The critical theorising of analysis. *Journal of Critical Psychology, Counselling and Psychotherapy, 13*(2), 67–72.

One admittedly brusque way of critiquing formulation might run along the lines, 'It's a privileged white person's view of what makes people tick – a view based on minimal reading , not much training in diverse psychotherapeutic approaches and one that maintains the expert role in token resistance to diagnosis.' Positioning themselves as critics of 'the system' clinical psychologists espousing formulation could be challenged – *pace* Fryer and Easpaig – to *subvert* the practice.

69. Boyle, M. (2011). Making the world go away, and how psychology and psychiatry benefit. In M. Rapley, J. Moncrieff & J. Dillon (Eds.), *De-medicalizing Misery: Psychiatry, psychology and the human condition.* Basingstoke: Palgrave Macmillan, pp. 27–43.

70. Johnstone, L. (2006). Controversies and debates about formulation. In L. Johnstone

& R. Dallos (Eds.), *Formulation in Psychology and Psychotherapy: Making sense of people's problems.* London: Routledge, pp. 208–236.

71. Racker, H. (1968). *Transference and Counter-transference.* London: The Hogarth Press.

CHAPTER 7

Clinical psychology as a profession

As a child I didn't come across many professionals; my family didn't mix much with people where wage earners had guaranteed incomes. I remember the smell of the GP's surgery and copies of *Women's Weekly* in the dentist's waiting room. The dentist turned out to be less professional than my parents had hoped – he was struck off 20 years after performing unnecessary dental work on numerous children's teeth, including mine. If the reader finds a mildly antagonistic attitude to the profession of clinical psychology here, perhaps my position can be tracked back to an oral fixation brought on by a need to bite professionals.[1]

This chapter focuses on the profession of clinical psychology. In the UK concerns from British Psychological Society's (BPS) Division of Clinical Psychology (DCP) members about the profession's public profile or internal rules and procedures are frequently met with the response, 'But you members *are* the profession'. As in any professional body, however, it is the officers who work tirelessly in producing guidelines, organising conferences, overseeing training and other tasks too daunting for ordinary members. I shall attempt a broadly deconstructive commentary on professional praxis by reference to the archive of the BPS – the official papers, minutes, public statements and other ephemera. This is not a neutral endeavour but nor is it an attack on those who attend the numerous committee meetings or author the documents in the public domain. No longer shelved by their recipients these are now available 24/7 on the web. I should be surprised if many are read – the nature of professional discourse would suggest they are not produced for that purpose. What follows is a critical reading of some key texts, all relatively recent and all produced as professional documents. The reader has no access to *how* they were produced – who said what, whose opinions were privileged and what a conversational analyst might have made of the talk that became text.

The profession of clinical psychology

As editor of *Clinical Psychology Forum* (*CPF*) I had been a 'participant observer' on the DCP National Committee for some 21 years at the point where retirement became inevitable. Working as a ceiling tiler seemed a long way back. In those 21 years I had struggled to gain committee approval for the establishment of a *CPF* collective rather than editorial board and was roundly censured for publishing an article of my own questioning the DCP role in relation to electroconvulsive therapy (ECT). I had observed at first hand the machinations of a professional body comprised of highly intellectually able clinical psychologists immersed in a kind of professional exasperation that psychiatrists, as represented by the Royal College of Psychiatrists, continued to have prestige, power and resources (frequently sponsored by drug companies) that left clinical psychologists in the shade. Despite their supposed understanding of people, committee members were repeatedly taken aback by the ease with which the Royal College made public statements. These could range from well-publicised concerns about dramatic rises in the incidence of mental illness to the need for consultant psychiatrists to lead community mental health teams or be the automatic choice as directors of NHS departments of psychological therapy. The members of the committee understood rational argument perfectly well. Though held back (according to private conversations between committee members) by the need as dictated by the BPS to present itself as a scientific body and registered charity rather than trade union, they produced well-argued position papers on innumerable aspects (qualifications, employment structures, supervision) of working as a clinical psychologist. To me they seemed hampered by a lack of appreciation of how *power* operates at the level of policy making. Simply stating one's authority or right to lead remains anathema to many clinical psychologists, perhaps as Mollon has argued, due to an ongoing sense of fraudulent self; clinical psychologists know their science is actually scientism and their therapeutic praxis not as well-founded in experience and training as those who practise psychotherapy.[2]

In the US, the American Psychological Association (APA) seems to have had less difficulty aligning itself with power. One reason for the success (in professional terms) of *DSM-IV* was the APA's insistence that psychologists should have a formal place at the design stage. Concerns and protests concerning *DSM-5* (see Chapter 3) are part of a – deceptively – anti-psychiatric shift; psychologists now contribute to *ICD* revisions as it is *ICD* that has been formally embraced by insurers (as noted below, the *codes* in both systems have been aligned for many years). A more striking alignment with power might be the involvement of APA members in interrogations at Guantanamo Bay.[3]

In the following sections I shall attempt an analysis of internal aspects of professional clinical psychology via an examination of training praxis and the profession's approach to diversity. This is followed by a reading of the ways in which the profession is positioned in relation to external aspects of Psy. Here, I focus on the – rapidly diminishing – importance and influence clinical psychology holds in the context of the wider world of diagnosis and therapy. Again, this reading is grounded in publications from the BPS and DCP. As an aside, it might be of interest for the reader to know that this is the *first time* I have read *any* of these documents cover to cover in a career which latterly involved 19 years as director of an NHS department of psychological therapies. I suspect I am not alone.

Training – positioning the DCP

In the US there are 120 APA-accredited clinical psychology doctoral programmes. A survey of 115 courses showed considerable variation in the core course subjects (all US states also insist on annual continuing education to maintain licensure). Despite the weak validity of projective tests, *all* of the programmes teach the Rorschach and most the Thematic Apperception Test as core topics. Similarly 98 of the courses include psychometric assessment as a core subject while 94 offer psychopathology. An observer might find it more accurate to describe as core subject matter *only* psychometry and psychopathology given the inconsistent presence of other topics; research methods are taught on 79 courses, ethics on 75, theory and philosophy on 30 and community psychology on seven. No courses offer critical psychology as either a core topic or elective course. Understandably, perhaps, the latter show even more variety. Elective modules on different courses include, 'Design of the mind' (two programmes) and social influence (two). Speciality courses offered include 'Ethnic and minority issues in psychology/diversity' (49), group psychotherapy (32) and family therapy (44). One doctoral programme still offers a speciality course in the MMPI.[4] In summary, a patient of a clinical psychologist in, say, New York may on moving to, say, Michigan be hard pressed to find a clinical psychologist with *any* of the same basic training other than competence using the Rorschach. The previous psychologist may be reasonably well versed in minority issues (though cultural norms and *languages* differ considerably from state to state) while the new clinician has some experience of group psychotherapy but not CBT, the New York psychologist's preferred modality.

In the UK the DCP maintains a position as a profession of 'scientist-practitioners'. Typically BPS documents and websites promote the discipline along the following lines: 'Psychology is the scientific study of human mind and behaviour: how we think, feel, act and interact individually and in groups.' To underline the scientific nature of the enterprise, we find, 'Psychology is a science and psychologists study human behaviour by observing, measuring and testing, then arriving at conclusions that are rooted in sound scientific methodology.'[5]

There are 30 clinical psychology doctoral courses in the UK. I helped found one (Staffordshire and Keele), was secretary of another (Oxford) and have conducted seminars on another 15 on topics as diverse as 'Groups and Group Analysis', 'Avoiding Harm in Clinical Psychology' and 'How to Get Published'. It might be suggested that a scientist-practitioner profession would, through a thorough scientific analysis of the aim and outcomes of training, create training centres teaching core topics in a consistent manner. Both the range of subjects taught and the teaching methods would be subject to empirical study to ensure consistency with best-practice principles. An anecdotal account of the nature of current courses would propose that, rather than reflecting a scientific discourse, clinical psychology training centres reflect the interests of the course organiser. In the 1970s courses had reputations as, for example, 'research oriented', 'psychodynamic' or 'behavioural' – these orientations were seen as the preferred approach of the different course directors. For almost 50 years that influence stemmed in large part from the Institute of Psychiatry. In 2000 there were 31 courses of which a third were run by graduates of the Institute. The Institute itself had never been headed by an outsider since its inception in 1946. Leeds and Liverpool had, over the years, produced 11 course directors between them.[6] The influence of the Institute of Psychiatry seems to be waning: by 2013, a Bangor University graduate was head of the Institute of Psychiatry. In turn, the Bangor programme was directed by an Institute graduate, one of only three course directors to have graduated there.

Details of all 30 current courses are available through the university clearing house.[7] In addition to general subheadings regarding 'application', 'equal opportunities', 'current staff' and similar topics, there are outlines of the academic programmes. The Institute of Psychiatry at King's College London, for example, offers trainees core teaching in, 'Adult mental health (including anxiety, depression and psychosis), Psychology and psychiatry of childhood and adolescence, Neuropsychological theory and practice, Clinical psychology as applied to intellectual disability, Mental health of older adults, Clinical health psychology, Forensic psychology, Psychological therapy (with strong emphasis on CBT, family therapy and mindfulness-based therapies), Research methods, Professional, legal and ethical issues and Race, equality and diversity'.[8]

Manchester offers, '… core clinical areas (encompassing common presentations and core clinical skills/issues in adult, child, older adult and learning disability services); therapeutic approaches (e.g., cognitive therapy, psychodynamic interpersonal therapy, systemic and family therapy); specialist areas (e.g. health psychology, forensic); research methods and statistics; and trainee presentations (e.g., case presentations and seminars)'.[9]

In the first year (all courses are three years) the Staffordshire and Keele course outline includes modules for, 'Personal & Professional Issues, Psychological Models 1: Understanding People's Experiences, Society & Context 1: Working with Systems and Context, Research Methods for Clinical Psychology and Assessing Psychological Processes – Neuropsychological Assessment and Rehabilitation'.[10]

Edinburgh informs prospective applicants, 'Our curriculum is designed to cover core competencies in CBT and other psychological therapies, such as Interpersonal Psychotherapy (IPT), Behavioural Family Therapy (BFT) and Acceptance and Commitment Therapy (ACT) as well as other psychological therapies. The emphasis of clinical training is on a variety of models as befits the current state of clinical psychology, the scientist-practitioner model and the reflective-practitioner model'.[11]

At Bangor first-year teaching focuses on adult mental health, older adults, health psychology and neuro-psychology. Year Two covers child and adolescent mental health and learning disabilities. In the first year there is a focus on Mindfulness, with a gradual shift of emphasis to Dialectical Behavioural Therapy (DBT) in Year Two, and Acceptance and Commitment Therapy (ACT) in the final year.[12]

These course outlines are only broadly similar. Within and between each course there remains considerable variation. For first- and second-year trainees topics are frequently taught by core university staff using didactic presentational styles, videos and small group discussion. All the courses aim to enable trainees to *do* something with patients. For my fellow probationer clinical psychologists and me, the routine of assessment preserved a distance between patients and the expert clinician. Technical procedures such as administering tests of 'intelligence' or 'depression' serve a disciplinary function whilst aiding relatively young clinical psychologists to sit with people under the gaze. Variations in the type and frequency of supervision make it likely that the tests will be administered differently with every patient thus nullifying claims to 'objectivity'. Similarly there is wide scope for variation within general topics such as, for example, 'health psychology' or 'adult mental health'. Therapies are presented differently by different tutors. Inevitably, these will then be enacted differently by individual trainees under the (occasional) gaze of equally idiosyncratic supervisors. This is not a criticism of clinical psychology *per se* but could be regarded as a criticism of the profession's public stance of being a 'science' akin to, say, pharmacy.

Diversity and the DCP

For medicine and veterinary science there has been, over the last 20 years, a major change in the gender balance of practitioners. Women are now in the majority in both fields. In Scotland female general practitioners outnumber men.[13] In the UK, the profession of clinical psychology has attracted mostly white applicants for training. Since 2000 the proportion being accepted on courses has been from 89 to 93 per cent, of whom about 85 per cent are women.[14] A summary of the position concludes, 'Unfortunately the make up of clinical psychology trainees frequently does not reflect the population demographics of the communities within which training courses are located or serve.'[15] The qualifiers 'unfortunately' and 'frequently' reveal an aspirational subtext, as if the make-up of clinical psychology trainees should be reflecting community demographics. 'Communities' differ from locality to locality, street to street. As the average age of first-year trainees is around 28 and some 90 per cent are not parents there would be no possibility of matching local demographics. The cited document is predominantly concerned with ethnicity. Here, the profession, unlike medicine and veterinary science, has consistently failed to change its ethnic profile. Strategies to increase diversity have been put forward since at least 1989.[16] Since 1998, courses have rejected the possibility of changing selection criteria to increase diversity in favour of developing teaching materials to 'raise awareness' of cultural diversity.[17] In 2000 the DCP formed a Special Interest Group in Race and Culture Issues as part of this process.

A comparison may be made with the state of the profession in the US. Graduate programmes in psychology were originally closed to women and members of ethnic minority groups. Between 1879 and 1920 10,000 doctorates were awarded in psychology; eleven of these went to Black students. In the following half century (to 1966) of 3,767 doctorates awarded, eight went to African-Americans.[18] Following the formation of associations of Black, Hispanic, American Indian and Asian American psychologists in the 1960s and subsequent decade, the American Psychological Association created a Board of Ethnic Minority Affairs in 1980. By 1986 there was a Division-Society for the Psychological Study of Ethnic Minority Issues. Numbers of Black and minority ethnic psychologists increased. The percentages remain small. In 1986 there were 16,519 clinical psychologists with PhDs in the US; 505 were Hispanics, American Indians and African-Americans (a total of 3 per cent). For the African Americans involved (159), this was, however, a 20-fold increase over the previous 60 years.[19]

Three years later the proportion of Black and minority ethnic students being awarded PhDs in clinical psychology had risen to 10 per cent of the total. This may reflect changes in access for education amongst Black and minority communities and policy changes on the part of the APA.[20]

In the UK, DCP-sponsored strategies to increase the proportion of trainees from Black and ethnic minority backgrounds have borne little fruit. Since the initial report in 1989 cited above there have been regular surveys and projects.[21] The most recent concludes that in relation to psychology and diversity, '… the road to hell was paved with good intentions'.[22] A BPS 'action plan' was drawn up but not monitored. A further BPS Professional Practice Board action plan was not implemented. In fact it was superseded by the Equalities Policy of the BPS. There has also been a 'diffusion of responsibility' across three DCP subgroups (the Group of Trainers, the Special Interest Group in Race and Culture and the Managers' Faculty).[23] *Clinical Psychology and Diversity: Progress and Continuing Challenges* reveals that in the 10 years 1994–2004 the average acceptance rate for applicants to training from 'non-white' backgrounds was 6.2 per cent. The last four years of the time period reviewed saw an average acceptance rate of 8 per cent. Between 2004 and 2009 this figure increased to 9.6 per cent, a rise the authors describe as, 'extremely disappointing'.[24]

In email exchanges with me in June 2013 Graham Turpin, co-author of the 2010 report said, 'I'm not certain that much has changed – no DCP initiatives as far as I'm aware'. Nimisha Patel, winner of a British Medical Association prize for her co-authored training pack on raising diversity issues in clinical psychology training, confirmed Turpin's view. She also withdrew from a conference on the issue set for September commenting, 'Some "big" white names on the podium will champion "BME issues" on our behalf and say what the profession is (apparently) doing' (personal communication).

It is tempting to analyse the lack of substantive change in the area of diversity in terms of the usual suspects; institutionalised racism, a changing political and governmental context which leaves all but the most administratively well-resourced professions unable to respond quickly enough to policy change at national level, the amount of BPS work taken on by a relatively small number of members who mostly have full-time (academic) employment and the slowness of large bureaucracies enmeshed in other large bureaucracies. It is equally possible to suggest that the *goal* of achieving a supposedly 'more representative workforce' is misguided; the historical Eurocentricity of clinical psychology theory and praxis discussed in previous chapters (a concern repeatedly raised by groups such as the DCP Special Interest Group in Race and Culture) creates too great a challenge if attempting to make such praxis 'fit' a more diverse population. Perhaps, as Mays and Albee have commented when discussing psychotherapy, clinical psychology is something for white middle-class professionals to be delivered by white middle-class professionals.[25] Whether or not the reader concurs with such a position, the lack of change since 1989 would suggest that the profession has been unable to achieve its stated goals, though *reiterating* those goals is now part of professional praxis. The profession is faced with a paradox. Wedded to a philosophy of individualism, yet expecting that theories, research and psychological therapies can be generalised, it might conclude, *pace* Sartre that 'Hell is other people' because *everyone* is different. It is a position the profession resists.

Clinical psychology services

Concerns within the profession about diversity would, if acted upon, ultimately have a direct effect on clinical psychology services. The pace of change and distal forces operating on the NHS make it very difficult for the profession to have a great impact on service provision either in structure or delivery.[26] Despite this, *as* a profession, it is incumbent on the DCP to issue documents about the organisation of clinical psychology and related services. *Guidelines for Clinical Psychology Services* was published in 2011. It references 13 BPS publications dated 2002 to 2010, 14 Department of Health papers from 2004 to 2010, five DCP publications (2001 to 2010) and three 'standards' papers from the Health Care Professions Council from 2008 and 2009.[27] To paraphrase Frank Zappa when speaking of music journalism, 'These are pieces written by people who generally can't write for those who don't read.'

As a psychological therapies director for over 20 years I only looked at documents of this type if asked by senior managers to write a report or if a service development might be funded (at most a four-yearly event). In adding a professional gloss to such reports the BPS papers were invaluable though in a context where professional self-interest was endemic the various recipients of these reports quickly scanned the pages for reference to costs.

The aspirations of the guidelines are for psychologists to have an impact on services in five areas. To achieve this, clinical psychologists are supposed to have read *all* the relevant referenced documents. Whilst *simultaneously* working as clinicians, practitioners are to have an impact on policies, law and statute, quality control and research and development. Despite the younger age of a predominantly white, female profession relative to other professions, clinical psychologists should, 'seek to develop their role ... through process consultancy at systems level, peer consultation and supervision, leadership ...'. The authors note that in providing consultancy and systems improvement, like leadership, 'the competence and confidence of clinical psychologists cannot be assumed'. [28]

One example of such 'consultation' was a local NHS management meeting discussion of the use of email shortly before I retired in 2007. The managers included senior trust nurses, medical staff, community managers, service user representatives – perhaps 20 people in all. The poor response to an email directive sent by the director of mental health services the previous Friday had been so varied I asked those at the meeting how those present usually dealt with emails (at that point I was receiving over 60 a day). Three managers said they never read emails, another had no access to a computer on Fridays, a fifth said she deleted all emails on Fridays to leave the weekend clear, another *only* read and responded to Friday email correspondence, several denied all knowledge of receiving the directive. This discussion provoked some amusement and was *formally* minuted along the lines, 'A full discussion confirmed that all managers would, in future, read and respond to similar email directives'. As is, I think, typical of such discussions, my intervention resulted in no change in management praxis – nor did the director monitor the outcome.

The organisational context of clinical psychologists in the NHS means that members of the profession daily face similar discussions, sometimes at clinical team meetings or case conferences, frequently at management meetings. The aspiration to influence as embodied in the guidelines should be read as part of the professional discourse rather than a realistic aim. The selective use of such guidance documents *does* result in limited change on occasion – any positive impact on service recipients is, however, unknown.

Companies pay lobbyists to change laws. Laws and government policies are in constant flux. To *predict* a policy through influencing its development would be immensely useful to citizens and professions alike. For the profession of clinical psychology, *following* changes in health and social care policies has been the norm. For some this will have been a frustrating, apparently fruitless endeavour. For over 20 years the BPS lobbied for compulsory registration and regulation of psychology in the NHS. Letters in *Clinical Psychology Forum* and conversations at DCP committee meetings attest to the belief that registration was 'just around the corner', usually less than two years away. The Society introduced voluntary registration as a gesture of good will; many members, including most of the clinical psychologists in my department, didn't register. The Society could not have predicted that it was to be subsumed under the Health Care Professions Council (HCPC). Since 2010 registration with the HCPC has, indeed, been compulsory and the BPS increasingly sidelined.

Another interpretation of the guidance might therefore suggest it was produced as an attempt to bolster the waning influence of the BPS itself. Under the heading, 'Professional Responsibility', clinical psychologists are urged to be ' … aware of the standards of proficiency and ethical conduct set out by the HPC regulatory body'. A footnote adds, '*NB: The British Psychological Society and the Division of Clinical Psychology continue to act as the major professional body for clinical psychologists serving to support, promote, advise and help guide the direction of the profession.*'[29] As clinical psychologists employed in the NHS are *only* required to register with the HCPC, the subtext of this and similar guidance documents might be positioned as an attempt to shore up the influence (and falling membership) of the BPS.

The public face of clinical psychology

Psychology has a prominent public place, clinical psychology less so. For many, a psychological discourse has replaced a broadly moral discourse. The media portray ordinary members of the public as 'mad or bad' while celebrity culture tends to embrace a 'mad or tragic' vocabulary. Rather than describing people as 'weak', overwhelmed', or 'frightened' editorial policy prefers the pseudo-scientific vocabulary of 'depressed' or 'anxious'. It is a discourse evident in ordinary conversation between members of the public or in journalism; no longer do people go up and down – they are 'suffering from bipolar disorder'. For those with resources, especially those facing court proceedings or potential public vilification, their conduct will be construed as 'caused by an underlying disorder', something over which they have little control, itself 'caused' by faulty genetics, disordered brain biochemistry, 'difficult' childhood, oppressive circumstances or a combination of all four. The 'solution' put forward is likely to be psychiatric drugs or counselling, for the 'lucky' few, to be provided in private clinics. The discourse is maintained via the media, courts, the Internet and any of us using medical jargon, particularly Psy 'experts'. It is a discourse frequently critiqued from within the Psy community and by recipients, many of whom attempt to reclaim ordinary language.[30] Since the first – 19th century – formal classificatory systems of distress, there have been critics of efforts by the medical and psychological communities to claim expertise in the mysteries of the human condition through their colonisation of language. The *invention* of experiences labelled illnesses by Psy experts has also been subject to forceful criticism.[31]

In this final section, I hope to offer something of a deconstruction of two attempts by the British Psychological Society to enter the public forum of disputation concerning psychiatric terminology. To me, one possible reading of the BPS position displays internal contradictions while its publication may have been prompted by the waning power of the profession noted above. I shall briefly address the question, 'Why now?' In doing so, I hope to explicate some of the factors involved in the wide dissemination of the BPS and DCP position.

The official diagnostic system in the United States is based on the *International Classification of Diseases and Related Health Problems* (*ICD*) of the World Health Organization (WHO). The *ICD* is the global standard in diagnostic classification for health reporting and clinical applications, for mental disorders as well as for all other medical diagnoses. Originally constructed as a system for classifying causes of death, the *ICD* has been a disease classification system for over half a century. All WHO member countries, including the USA, are required by international treaty to collect and report health statistics to the WHO using the *ICD* as a framework.

Like the preceding conferences (which began in 1898) the Fifth International Conference for the Revision of the International List of Causes of Death had been convened by the Government of France. It was held in Paris in October 1938. The Conference approved three lists: a detailed list of 200 titles, an intermediate list of 87 titles and an abridged list of 44 titles. The lists were amended according to the most current medical practice and research, particularly in chapters on infectious and parasitic diseases, puerperal conditions and accidents. Contents, number, and the numbering of the items were largely unaltered. A list of causes of stillbirth was also drawn up and approved by the Conference.[32] The *Seventh Revision of the International Classification of Diseases* was held in Paris under the auspices of WHO in February 1955.

When *ICD-9-CM* (9th revision, Clinical Modification) was released in 1979, it was seen as a purely administrative and statistical tool, with little direct relevance to US practitioners. Subsequent federal regulations required physicians to use *ICD-9-CM* codes on Medicare claims. In 1996 the Health Insurance Portability and Accountability Act (HIPAA) required the use of *ICD-9-CM* codes on all electronic transactions for billing and reimbursement. Since 1996 any clinical psychologist submitting claims for billing and reimbursement or using diagnostic codes in the *DSM* is actually using the *ICD*. Because the current *ICD-10-CM* is an official activity of a US government agency, there is an explicit and public process involving notices, review periods, and public hearings in order for health systems, professional groups, and other interested parties to propose any changes. As part of the *ICD-10-CM* development process, the National Centre for Health Statistics (NCHS) froze changes to the *ICD-10-CM* in October, 2011, to allow time for refinement of health information systems and for training of health professionals and other users. During that time the American Psychiatric Association and organised US psychology made proposals to bring *ICD-10-CM* more in line with proposals for *DSM-5*.[33] From 2013 US psychologists were required to use *ICD-10-CM* for all third-party billing and reporting.[34] The *DSM* had been effectively replaced by a system also based on a descriptive, criteria-based approach to diagnosis. Diagnostic reliability has marginally improved particularly in research settings, where explicit diagnostic criteria can be applied through lengthy, complex, and costly standardised diagnostic interviews.[35] There is no evidence of a corresponding improvement in diagnostic reliability in everyday clinical practice. As noted in previous chapters a half century of research has failed to demonstrate that the prevailing nosology for mental disorders is based on valid disease entities.[36]

Despite the downgrading of *DSM*'s relevance in relation to *ICD* the proposed publication of *DSM-5* engendered numerous criticisms: by the British Psychological Society,[37] the Australian Psychological Society, and an online petition supported by over 50 mental health associations.[38] Critics from within psychiatry included the chair of the *DSM-IV* taskforce Allen Frances.[39] The context changed once *ICD* was formally embraced by insurers. The criticisms form part of a much-trod path of critique. I shall use the BPS response and a later Statement as illustrations of professionalising rather than critical praxis. The response was prepared by a group including the Chair of the Division of Clinical Psychology, two fellow committee members and four ordinary members of the DCP. The critical *psychiatry* background of some of these authors is well established. One has post-graduate qualifications and a considerable bibliography in the fields of clinical psychology, psychotherapy and sociology; he has been a foremost critic of the professional ambitions of clinical psychology.[40] Another, an ex-director of a clinical psychology doctorate programme, was one of the first clinical psychologists in the UK to outline, in book form, the abuse inherent in psychiatric practice.[41] Two others have repeatedly exposed the solipsistic theorising around madness.[42, 43] Similarly two are contributing authors to the two volumes of *De-medicalizing Misery*, lucid exposés of the scientism of psychiatry.[44]

It is as *psychologists* that these authors' expertise is utilised. As Smail, however, has suggested, it may not be possible to separate action from the vested interest of the actor, perhaps especially when that actor is an authorised professional.[45]

The introduction to the response begins; 'The British Psychological Society thanks the American Psychiatric Association (APA) for the opportunity to respond to the DSM-5 Development.'

A critical reading would see it as fitting that UK psychology, as represented by the BPS, 'thanks' the APA. Thomas Szasz would have seen this kind of gesture as one profession supporting – whilst naming certain reservations – another in a system used to undermine citizen agency through designation of illness.[46] The position is mirrored in the work of Peter Breggin.[47] Both psychiatrists, the work of Szasz and Breggin remains something of a rear-guard attempt to undermine the psychiatric project.[48] Jeffrey Masson, ex-director of the Freud Archive, goes further in his comparison of psychiatric practice with assault; assault is not something society should try to refine but something which is already illegal, a fate he sees as psychiatry's just desserts.[49] Wolfensberger's concept of 'death-making' has been used to suggest that psychiatric praxis is *designed* to kill body, spirit or both and should be banned.[50] As a fellow profession, clinical psychology would not position itself as 'extremist' in this way. The language of professions is geared towards a measured critique. Individual clinical psychologists – including the majority responsible for the BPS response – might align themselves with politicised praxis closer in spirit, if not deed, to ideas espoused by Szasz and others. UK clinical psychologists are less likely to position themselves as politically aligned with these US critics; Szasz and Breggin are essentially libertarians and Wolfensberger an ardent Christian (typical criticisms of Masson have been explored in Chapter 2). Practising as professionals or academics, individual UK clinical psychologists associated with critique might prefer to be positioned as on the political left and inclined towards a rejection of American writings. The rejection of US diagnostic systems such as *DSM* seems misplaced given the global reliance on *ICD* discussed above. Rejection based on the idea that psychiatric praxis is bound by American and capitalist values fails to take account of the way in which US psychiatry and psychology are, in large part, a refinement of *European* ideology re-exported throughout the world.[51]

An alternative statement from an organisation promoting individualism and the application of genuine scientific endeavour might read, 'The British Psychological Society rejects all nosologies of human conduct as unscientific and, in the case of *DSM-5*, rejects a technological praxis which will further the interests of psychiatric practitioners, the pharmacological industry and state control.' As noted earlier, professional statements form part of a *polite* discourse. Statements seen as strident jeopardise the Society's position as a politically neutral 'Learned Body' with charitable status. One can only conjecture that, given their publication record, a conversational analyst observing the debates amongst the authors of the response would have proposed the brief statement suggested above as a summary of their discussions.

After the introductory section the BPS response begins: 'The Society is concerned that clients and the general public are negatively affected by the continued and continuous medicalisation of their natural and normal responses to their experiences; responses which undoubtedly have distressing consequences which demand helping responses, but which do not reflect illnesses so much as normal individual variation.'[52]

'The Society' has around 50,000 members. The language used is both impersonal and a rhetorical device implying consensus amongst the members of 'The Society' (there is no note in the BPS response to the effect that the views expressed are only the views of the named authors). No mention is made of the considerable numbers of member psychologists in organisational, clinical and counselling specialisms who use diagnoses in their practice and design or use questionnaires to *aid* the diagnostic endeavours of psychiatric or other colleagues. These clinical psychologists publish journal articles and books suggesting psychological 'treatments' for virtually all diagnosed conditions, medical and psychiatric.

The history of the profession of clinical psychology in the UK can be approached using Goldie's schema outlining three possible positions taken up by non-medical professions in a context where medicine is the dominant discourse.[53] According to Goldie, professions and individual professionals move between the three positions depending on context and their professional development. Non-medical professions, relative to medicine, can be positioned as *compliant, eclectic* or *radically opposed.*

Compliance might be summarised as taking care not to rock the medical boat. In the UK since clinical psychology's establishment as a profession under the 1948 National Assistance Act, compliance has been a consistently held position. An example is the use of psychometric assessment procedures for many assumed ills – from the tests for 'Schizophrenogenic Thought Disorder' of the 1960s via the Beck Depression Inventory to the many different tests for so-called attention deficit hyperactivity disorder of today. As noted on page 64, in the United States, where the majority of health care is paid for via private insurance, insurance companies *insist* on psychometric assessment and subsequent psychiatric labelling before agreeing to fund treatment. The point was not lost on Spitzer and his colleagues when revising *DSM-III*: *Time* magazine reported from the first of their meetings that the most important thing, '... is that *DSM-III* is of crucial importance to the profession [because] ... its diagnoses are generally recognized by the courts, hospitals and insurance companies'.[54]

Though not constrained by such institutional demands in the UK, clinical psychologists in the *compliant* position perform psychometric assessment thereby giving the diagnostic system a scientific gloss. This can range from agreeing that someone 'has' post-traumatic stress to confirming that a person's IQ is less than 70.

Eclecticism is positioned as a collaborative endeavour offering an alternative to the diagnostic and physical interventions of psychiatry and psychology. Psychotherapy and counselling professionals offering therapy as an adjunct to medication for diagnosed individuals can be described as *eclectic*. In such praxis the clinical psychologist offering therapy neither directly challenges the diagnosis ('What do you *mean* by the term schizophrenia?') nor the use of medication ('Have you tested for the brain-biochemical imbalance you say is producing this person's feelings of overwhelm?'). Instead, the clinical psychologist offers psychotherapy to the patient and reports progress to the referring physician or psychiatrist. Such practice has been predominant in clinical psychology in the UK for over 50 years from the behavioural therapies of the Maudsley Hospital under Eysenck, via the psychoanalytic approach of the Tavistock Clinic, through to current privileging of cognitive behaviour therapy and postmodern narrative approaches.

Radical opposition is a polarised fight or flight modality. Here, non-medical professions and individual professionals might take up a public opposition to the dominant medical discourse or attempt to leave the conflict zone. From the fight pole can be found the work of some critical clinical psychologists, for example, those authors who actively challenge the medical paradigm by facilitating alternative, normative means of – frequently – local and community rather than professional aid.[55]

Individual practitioners, depending on context, might claim a position not easily identifiable to an observer. For example, a newly qualified practitioner may challenge a consultant psychiatrist's proposed diagnosis or treatment. The clinical psychologist may assume herself to be in at the fight pole of the fight-or-flight position. From a critical perspective, however, as a professional attending the case conference the clinical psychologist implicitly supports a medical discourse wherein patients are designated 'cases' by powerful others. Thus, for Goldie, the majority of the profession would be positioned as either compliant or eclectic. The Division of Clinical Psychology had, until recently, adopted a public stance which consistently failed to challenge a medical discourse. The profession's journals (for example, *The Journal of Clinical Psychology* and *Clinical Psychology and Psychotherapy*) have supported psychiatric diagnostic nosologies and professional/

patient dichotomies. This essentially medical discourse is almost ubiquitous in practitioner-oriented publications; in a recent *British Journal of Clinical Psychology* for example, reference is made to work comparing 'psychotic-like phenomena in clinical and non-clinical populations'.[56] In a profession frequently claiming human experience to be on a *continuum* it is self-contradictory to position some experience ('phenomena') as 'psychotic-like'. As Rosario has noted, since the mid-19th century Psy professionals have first claimed madness to be *different* from normal conduct before finding examples of that madness in virtually anyone even using the *literary* work of, for example, Zola to diagnose the author.[57] The use of the phrase 'psychotic-like' implies both the existence of 'psychosis' and the authors' expertise in separating psychosis from normality.

In summary, using Goldie's classification of professional conduct, clinical psychology moves, broadly, between the compliant and eclectic positions.

The BPS response continues:

> The putative diagnoses presented in DSM-5 are clearly based largely on social norms, with 'symptoms' that all rely on subjective judgements, with little confirmatory physical 'signs' or evidence of biological causation. The criteria are not value-free, but rather reflect current normative social expectations ... psychiatric diagnoses are plagued by problems of reliability, validity, prognostic value, and co-morbidity. Diagnostic categories do not predict response to medication or other interventions whereas more specific formulations or symptom clusters might (Moncrieff, 2007).[58]

The authors of the BPS response were aware that psychiatric diagnoses always have depended on 'subjective judgements', which have few, if any, 'confirmatory physical "signs" or evidence of biological causation'. It is hard to imagine any criteria that would be 'value-free', or reflecting something other than 'current normative social expectations'. The notion of 'biological causation' seems a red herring here. Though suggesting biological causation legitimises the use of physical treatment and as Moncrieff, amongst others, suggests, embeds psychiatry in the world of 'real' medicine, confusion is maintained about the essential difference between 'cause' and 'reasons'.[59] Human beings are not billiard balls – human agency must include the notion of reason as one aspect of conduct.[60] Intoxication or brain injury, for example, may 'cause' a person to experience colours, sounds and touch in unfamiliar ways. Those ways, however, are particular to the person in any given time, context and phase of physical development; A does not simply lead to B. Exploring the 'reasons' any given individual acts in particular ways necessitates a shared explanatory discourse that may involve concepts such as 'beliefs', 'desires', family context and so on. To say someone hears voices 'because' they have disordered brain biochemistry is to say nothing about why that person hears particular voices saying things at certain times. To suggest, as the voice hearer herself might, that the voices 'caused' her to act in socially undesirable ways is to ignore the concepts of 'reason' and 'choice' altogether. Psychology and psychologists, though perhaps eschewing ideas about physical 'causes' for certain human actions are, necessarily, limited to a social-context-bound discourse of 'reasons'. This forms the basis of psychological formulation discussed in the previous chapter. This form of explanation requires a shared discourse involving the idea that a person is *capable* of giving sufficient reasons for personal action through access via some kind of inner speech to the essential movers of conduct or that, through attending to what the person says or does, a professional can construct sufficient reasons for that conduct. For both professional and patient, the supposed absence of 'choice' can appear advantageous.[61] Psy professionals invoke the need to offer 'compassion' to those claiming to suffer through no fault of their own; their interventions, whether physical *or* psychological are thereby legitimised by recourse to normative (Judeo-Christian) morality. There continue to be many interventions, from electroshock to counselling, justified in the name of compassion.[62,63]

Compassion is a value-laden concept. Responding to the proposed *DSM-5* was value laden. Nor can the statement be seen beyond 'current normative expectations' for the profession. Though accurate, the suggestion that diagnoses depend on social norms cannot be regarded as critical unless, as in the case of UK clinical psychology, there is an ongoing attempt, by aligning with the natural sciences, to position psychologists as objective observers and recorders of human conduct. Such objectivity is supposedly achieved via the use of psychometric tests and 'evidence-based' therapeutic technologies. Underlining this position, the fourth paragraph of the introduction to the response reads, 'The Society is committed to providing and disseminating evidence-based expertise …'.[64] In a context where expertise, particularly, *scientific* expertise is valued, it seems non-reflexive for psychologists to criticise diagnostic praxis as value laden when the values and methodologies of science are the means by which much of the ensuing criticism is pursued.

The response's proposal that 'more specific formulations or symptom clusters' might 'predict response to medication or other interventions' was unlikely to disconcert those who see the *DSM* enterprise as a helpful diagnostic tool. As noted above, 'formulations' are popular in clinical psychology and appear in the response document as one of the newer emblems of the profession. The authors accept *a priori* that someone using *DSM* would have a *reason* for formulating someone's conduct; once the professional gaze is turned on an individual, that individual will be scanned for oddness, whether through 'formulation' or the examination of – by definition problematic – 'symptom' clusters. In promoting one of its recent shibboleths ('formulation') and not criticising the pseudo-medical praxis inherent in the language of 'symptoms' the response positions psychology within a Psy discourse (Goldie's *compliance* position); indeed, this section ends, 'We therefore believe that alternatives to diagnostic frameworks exist, should be preferred, and should be developed with as much investment of resource and effort as has been expended on revising *DSM-IV*. The Society would be happy to help in such an exercise.'[65] There may be a tongue-in-cheek element to this comment; how 'The Society' might have enjoyed being funded to promote its preferred praxis, although of course, as employees of the NHS, UK clinical psychologists are being funded though the public purse to do exactly that. The problem remains that individual psychologists would need to *justify* seeing particular individuals for 'formulation' and, at present, the rhetoric of justification is limited to, 'Because the individual or those close to her are suffering'. The individual is then thrown back on some kind of *assessment* of that suffering as – to the professional – it is self-evident that suffering is a measure of need. Science, the framework giving psychology its authority, is not necessary to such rhetoric and has nothing to say about *why* someone's feelings or displays of madness are worthy of more attention and resources than another's.

A final example from this initial section summarises the paradoxical position in which clinical psychology finds itself. As a prelude to specific criticisms the response continues:

> Personality disorder and psychoses are particularly troublesome as they are not adequately normed on the general population. This problem – as well as threatening the validity of the approach – has significant implications … social factors are minimised, and the continuum with normality is ignored … people who describe normal forms of distress like feeling bereaved after three months, or traumatised by military conflict for more than a month, will meet diagnostic criteria.[66]

Within the discipline of psychology 'personality' is a much-contested concept. Many psychologists, particularly those working in the clinical and occupational arenas, have utilised tests of so-called personality – a construct rather than an entity. Concepts such as *introversion* have entered the public domain. *Leadership* and *diligence* can, apparently, be measured by those employed in human resources departments and it is psychometric procedures which legitimise the expertise of those offering advice to employers. Tests for depression, obsessionality and schizophrenia are available online for those wishing to self-assess.[67] Personality is neither a stable nor, by definition, a measurable, construct; the *act* of completing a personality questionnaire changes the person to some extent while reinforcing the idea that such assessment is a valid enterprise. The notion is better seen as a working hypothesis often, though not always, helping social intercourse. The response positions 'personality' as unproblematic while not noting that the concept of personality *disorder* must be nonsensical.[68]

Neglecting to address the problematic nature of the personality or personality *disorder* constructs, the response authors revert to a mainstay of psychological praxis – the establishment of 'norms'. This was not a problem for those pursuing descriptive psychopathology from the mid-19th to the mid-20th centuries. In the absence of identifiable brain disease (except in clear cases like Huntington's disease – previously called Huntington's chorea), practitioners based praxis on the degree of social disturbance or personal distress expressed by the individual. The quoted paragraph above also, by default, suggests that responses such as bereavement can be normed. If responses – according to the individualising philosophy of psychology – are idiopathic, then, for some, still feeling bereaved 'after three months' will be construed as abnormal. It is not, however, abnormality which defines the Psy enterprise but undesirability and, for some, virtually any experience of distress will be undesirable. The need to, say, maintain one's employment after a bereavement might make unexpected expressions of loss inconvenient. Here, the promise of medication or support would be accepted if the ostensible price were a psychiatric label.

For the authors of the BPS response, medical diagnosis, as part of the medicalisation of madness project, 'negatively effects' the public. One advantage of receiving a psychiatric diagnosis in the UK, however, is the entitlement to Personal Independence Payment and other state financial benefits. For some, a diagnosis is a person's 'get out of jail free card'.[69] The iatrogenic effects of receiving medication justified via psychiatric diagnoses are, nonetheless, likely to be undesirable for the individuals concerned.

As the response was authored by psychologists, it might seem appropriate to use some psychological notions to examine the document. Lucy Johnstone offers a list of the ways in which psychiatrists silence criticism of their theories, diagnosis and practice. The list will be familiar to any non-medical professionals involved in psychiatric case conferences. Johnstone includes 'irrelevant personal statement(s), disqualifying the counter-evidence' and 'attributing all improvement to medical intervention'.[70] As a more visceral example of inter-professional disharmony I once had a copy of *Toxic Psychiatry* thrown at me by an enraged child psychiatrist during a disagreement.

'Quoting important-sounding research' is another discounting manoeuvre.[71] To close readers of the BPS response this might appear ironic; the two-page introductory *General Comments* section addends seven references. To criticise such praxis is to criticise the *essence* of scientific discourse, a discourse wholly dependent on the notion that 'research' is a necessary endeavour and publication axiomatic.[72] As scientist-practitioners, the authors of the response naturally turn to 'quoting important-sounding research' as a silencing move.

Mary Boyle has noted that psychology focuses on intra-psychic attributes and 'has *invented* a great many of them ...'. In the case of, for example, hearing voices and expressing unusual beliefs, positivist psychological theorists propose a number of 'abnormal' psychological causative factors; '... defective judgement; abnormal perceptual biases; defective speech processing mechanisms; defective reality testing; parasitic memories; pathologically stored linguistic information; deficits in internal monitoring systems and an abnormal self-serving bias ...'.[73] Clinical psychologists may claim – as in the BPS response – that social and contextual factors should be considered when analysing distress but the causative factors outlined here are internal and utilise a pathologising defect discourse.

For Boyle clinical psychology has 'extreme insecurity' about its acceptance as a science. '[B]y minimizing or denying the importance of life experiences and social context ... mainstream psychology gains the double advantage of both appearing more 'scientific' and also avoiding the risk of the powerful by seeming to implicate them in the distress of others ...' and, '... there is more going on here than a craving to be recognized as a science ... Modern psychology presents its subject matter as the study of individual minds ....' Citing Sampson, Boyle continues, '... this choice of subject matter functions to maintain the ideological and social status quo ... by cutting people off ... from effective action to change their *actual* circumstances rather than their *subjective understanding* ....'[74]

Though, as quoted above, Boyle attributes an individualised concept – 'extreme insecurity' – to a discipline as a whole rather than to individual psychologists (itself a rhetorical device implying specialist knowledge), the phrase resonates. Applying a more individualistic analysis it seems that envy, particularly financial envy, is a more accurate, if less complimentary attribution; in over 20 years as director of a Department of Psychological Therapies with more than 75 Psy professionals, I witnessed hundreds of accusations that psychiatrists were paid too much and few claims of 'insecurity'. This position is explored by Smail in his discussion of how individual psychological and psychotherapeutic practitioners tend to focus on the *internal* and *invisible* worlds of their patients rather than their *material* circumstances.[75]

In June 2013 the DCP issued a position statement to further clarify its views on psychiatric diagnoses. This statement took full account of the importance of *ICD*.[76] The summary states, '… it is timely and appropriate to affirm publicly that the current classification system as outlined in DSM and ICD, in respect of the functional psychiatric diagnoses, has significant conceptual and empirical limitations.' As a consequence, the summary suggests the need for a 'paradigm shift in relation to the experiences that these diagnoses refer to' and a conceptual system not based on a 'disease' model.[77] As I have discussed in previous chapters, conceptual and empirical limitations of psychiatric nosologies have been discussed both within and outside the Psy complex since the earliest classificatory systems of the mid-19th century. The statement's suggestion that a public affirmation of these concerns is 'timely' is difficult to analyse. Perhaps, as suggested earlier, the timeliness is inherent to the present needs of the BPS and DCP to show public solidarity with critics of psychiatry in a shifting *Zeitgeist*. The increasing prominence of UK clinical psychologists who have received diagnosis and psychiatric intervention with little benefit may have influenced a sense of timeliness. The statement also distances DCP members from other members of the HCPC. It emphasises the difference between clinical psychologists as post-graduate scientists at a time when the professional discipline of psychology is being subsumed under a new registration body previously exclusively concerned with non-doctoral-level practitioners. The 'paradigm shift' envisaged is one which privileges psychological formulation while recognising the influence of non-psychological factors. In passing, it is tempting to remark that a paradigm shift will only occur if professions cease to use words like 'paradigm'.

The statement acknowledges that the DCP '... has historically held mixed views about psychiatric classification and its implications in theory and practice, reflecting its position as representing clinical practitioners in a wide range of specialisms and as a scientific body.' As in the BPS response to *DSM-5*, there is a re-affirmation of the scientific credentials of clinical psychologists to add weight to the official position. The historical holding of 'mixed views' appears to place such disagreement in the past. A scan through any psychological journal will show, however, that these views – as inferred from the text – remain mixed. The need to publish in peer-reviewed journals still dictates the language used. That language, not least for ease of access by search engines, continues to be the argot of psychiatric diagnosis.

The statement posits as a core theme that, 'The needs of services users should be central to any system of classification. Service users express a wide range of views on psychiatric diagnosis, and the DCP recognises the importance of being respectful of their perspectives.' [78] I have discussed elsewhere the construction of service 'users', a construction that positions frequently powerless people as equal to service providers. Various psychiatric activists prefer the terminology 'recipient' or 'survivor', the former term implying passivity, the latter activism.[79] Again, the statement highlights 'needs' rather than 'wants', terminology which implies professional control over definition.

The statement highlights various negative effects of being diagnosed: discrimination and social exclusion, stigmatisation and negative impact on identity, marginalising knowledge from lived experience (this term is again a shibboleth, this time with an inherent paradox – can the reader imagine *un*-lived experience?), for example, material circumstances, decision-making linked to disempowerment and an over-reliance on medication. All of these negative effects fall under the rubric of death-making. The profession of clinical psychology makes no claims to be aligned to death-making as a guiding principle. As a profession, however, the discipline might be held responsible for many of the 'wounds' outlined by Wolfensberger.[80]

The summary section concludes with five action points, three concerning more work with service user and carer allies. The fourth maintains the disciplinary nature of the profession as part of the gaze in proposing that psychosocial perspectives '... *are included in the electronic health record*'. And last, the statement prompts the DCP, '... *to continue to promote the use of psychological formulation*' (my italics).[81]

Not unexpectedly, these action points concern professional and professionalising praxis. It is a praxis which could be positioned as arising from the very prejudices that the anti-discriminatory project suggested in the statement aims to oppose.[82] This analysis positions professional psychology as part of the problem not the solution. I shall return to this theme in the final chapter.

Summarising the profession

Perhaps my brother, a groundsman, nailed it in one when I told him of my retirement: 'Well that's one less bloody 'ologist.' Experts hold an ambivalent position for the general public. Whether they be meteorologists accurately predicting changes in the weather about half the time or climatologists changing their position on global warming to a discourse of 'climate change' their expertise is continuously held up to criticism. This is frequently based on the observer's personal experience. Psychologists and clinical psychologists can be positioned as sages as often as fools or people paid well for telling us what we know already. As such they become public entertainment, sometimes literally as their words fill agony aunt columns or they appear on radio to offer advice or televised opinion on reality shows. Had Mary Maryatt been a clinical psychologist, I would have been no less intrigued by the readers' letters (most corrected for grammar and generalised) as I browsed her page in *Women's Weekly* while awaiting the dentist all those years ago.

This chapter may appear to have positioned clinical psychology in George Bernard Shaw's phrase as a 'conspiracy against the laity'. This has not been my intention. Rather, I hope to have shown that in the UK, clinical psychology has held to a position of being a science. In doing so it has failed to scientifically determine the best ways to train its members and has yet to solve the perceived problem of a lack of diversity amongst its practitioners who remain overwhelmingly white and, in the case of new entrants to the profession, young women. This is not inherently a problem as the profession could, in theory, stop attempts to match the demographics of diverse communities and instead, as implied by Mays and Albee, focus on a demographic closer to its own.[83] Public statements on behalf of the profession are commissioned by a small group of hard-working DCP officers and may not be read by many people, including the membership of the DCP. For those wishing to promote clinical psychology – in local services or the media – these are undeniably useful documents. It is unclear to me how useful they are for members of communities that publicly funded clinical psychologists serve. In some cases they may act as a deterrent to increasing the availability of clinical psychologists, as commissioners regard them as documents betraying self-interest in a profession more expensive to train and employ than similar staff with similar skills. Business jargon such as 'added value' is no longer the rhetoric employed in selling clinical psychology as a profession in part because, for commissioners of services, it is direct clinical work rather than research that is required. As noted in Chapter 3, clinical psychologists in both the USA and the UK, in any case prefer practising therapy to research. In the final chapter I shall give some examples where this is not the case and clinical psychologists combine an awareness of their political position with a more rounded professional praxis.

Endnotes

1. See Klein, M. (1975). *Envy and Gratitude and Other Works.* London: The Hogarth Press and the Institute of Psycho-analysis. NB. Since a divorce in the early eighties I have met any number of professionals; without a couple of socio-politically minded solicitors, a fine architect and two clinical psychology managers, life would have been tougher. Without the auspices of ambulance staff, a helicopter rescue pilot, a workaholic neurosurgeon, a cardio-thoracic surgeon and equally committed nurses in a high dependency unit, I would be dead. Psy colleagues were invaluable and inspirational. Along the way, I came across poor GPs, a lawyer who cost me a great deal with little return, solicitors who never seemed to be around when wanted, a hopeless architect and members of Psy who, despite my best efforts to appreciate their contextual struggles, I found hard to be around. Maybe it's just me.

2. Mollon, P. (1989). Narcissus, Oedipus and the psychologist's fraudulent identity. *Clinical Psychology Forum, 23,* 7–11.

3. Harper, D. (2004). Psychology and the 'War on Terror'. *Journal of Critical Psychology, Counselling and Psychotherapy, 4*(1), 1–10.

4. Stein, D. B. (2012). *The Psychology Industry Under the Microscope!* Plymouth, UK: University Press of America Inc.

5. Retrieved 12 March 2013 from http://www.bps.org.uk/psychology-public/introduction-psychology/introduction-psychology

6. Newnes, C. (2000). Training, the Institute and Clinical Psychology. *Clinical Psychology Forum, 145,* 4–5.

7. Retrieved 5 May 2013 from http://www.leeds.ac.uk/chpccp/Courses.html

8. *Ibid.*

9. *Ibid.*

10. *Ibid.*

11. *Ibid.*

12. ACT may be usurping CBT as a market leader for clinical psychologists in training. Unlike CBT there is no attempt to teach better control of thoughts and feelings. Rather ACT practitioners encourage patients to 'just notice', and accept sensations, especially previously unwanted ones. As with all other therapies there is debate about the efficacy and philosophy of ACT. See Zettle, R. D. (2005). The evolution of a contextual approach to therapy: From comprehensive distancing to ACT. *International Journal of Behavioral Consultation and Therapy, 1*(2), 77–89;

Gaudiano, B. A. (2009). Öst's (2008) methodological comparison of clinical trials of acceptance and commitment therapy versus cognitive behavior therapy: Matching apples with oranges? *Behaviour Research and Therapy, 47*(12), 1066–1070; Öst, L.G. (2008). Efficacy of the third wave of behavioral therapies: A systematic review and meta-analysis. *Behaviour Research and Therapy, 46,* 296–321.

13. Miller, K. & Clark, D. (2008). 'Knife before wife' – An exploratory study of gender and the UK medical profession. *Journal of Health Organization and Management, 22*(3), 238–253.

14. Turpin, G. & Coleman, G. (2010). *Clinical Psychology and Diversity: Progress and continuing challenges.* Leicester: British Psychological Society.

15. *Ibid.,* p. 1.

16. See Davenhill, R., Hunt, H., Pillary, H. M., Harris, A. & Klein, Y. (1989). Training and selection issues in clinical psychology for black and minority ethnic groups from an equal opportunities perspective. *Clinical Psychology Forum, 21,* 34–36 and Bender, M. & Richardson, A. (1990). The ethnic composition of clinical psychology in Britain. *The Psychologist, 2,* 250–252.

17. Patel, N., Bennett, E., Dennis, M., Dosanjh, N., Mahtani, A., Miller, A. & Nadirshaw, Z. (Eds.). (2000). *Clinical Psychology, 'Race' and Culture: A training manual.* Leicester: British Psychological Society.

18. Albee, G. W. (1969). A conference on the recruitment of Black and ethnic minority students and faculty. *American Psychologist, 24,* 720–723.

19. Heckler, M. M. (1986). *Report of the Secretary's Task Force on Black and Minority Health.* US Department of Health and Human Services, Washington, DC: US Government Printing Office.

20. Mays, V. M. & Albee, G. W. (1992). Psychotherapy and ethnic minorities. In D. K. Freedheim (Ed.), *History of Psychotherapy: A century of change.* Washington, DC: American Psychological Association, pp. 552–570.

21. Bender, M. & Richardson, A. (1990). The ethnic composition of clinical psychology in Britain. *The Psychologist, 2,* 250–252; British Psychological Society. (2004). *English Survey of Applied Psychologists in Health and Social Care in the Probation and Prison Service.* Leicester: British Psychological Society; Turpin, G. & Fensom, P. (2004). *Widening Access within Undergraduate Psychology Education and Its Implications for Professional Psychology: Gender, disability and ethnic diversity.* Leicester: British Psychological Society, pp. 1–80.

22. Turpin, G. & Coleman, G. (2010). *Clinical Psychology and Diversity: Progress and continuing challenges.* Leicester: British Psychological Society, p. 6.

23. *Ibid.,* p. 6.

24. *Ibid.,* p. 12.

25. Mays and Albee note that ethnic minorities are more likely to be poor, live in substandard housing, suffer educational disadvantages and other examples of discrimination. At the same time they are more likely to suffer a wide range of physical health problems from increased tooth decay to cirrhosis. Citing, amongst others, Flaskerud, they suggest that members of ethnic minorities more often seek help from traditional healers, root doctors, clergy, herbalists and family and friends. By contrast there are more psychotherapists per capita in Washington DC than anywhere else in the *world* – the majority from the white area of Northwest Washington. Mays, V. M. & Albee, G. W. (1992). Psychotherapy and ethnic minorities. In D. K. Freedheim (Ed.), *History of Psychotherapy: A century of change.* Washington, DC: American Psychological Association, pp. 552–570, pp. 553–559; Flaskerud, J. H. (1986). The effects of culture-compatible intervention on the utilization of mental health services by minority clients. *Community Mental Health Journal, 22*(2), 127–141.

26. An example of the speed of change of the wider employment context is provided by contributors to a conference in early 1990. At the time leading members of the profession heralded the implementation the NHS White Paper, 'Community Care: Agenda for Action' (due to become law in April 1991), examined the implications of the recently published White Papers 'Working for Patients' and 'Caring for People', and discussed the – barely understood – likely outcomes of the 'purchaser–provider split' wherein NHS regions lost their monopoly on service provision. They were replaced by commissioning consortia (frequently employing the *same* senior staff as the old regions, districts and areas) whose role, in a new 'business ethos' was to buy services from new provider agencies and NHS trusts (most often employing the *same* staff the new commissioners had previously managed).

27. British Psychological Society. (2011). *Guidelines for Clinical Psychology Services.* Leicester: British Psychological Society.

28. *Ibid.,* p. 4.

29. *Ibid.,* p. 5.

30. See, for example, Dillon, J. (2013). Just saying it as it is: Names matter; language matters; truth matters. *Clinical Psychology Forum, 243,* 15–19.

31. See, for example, Deenan, T. (1999). *Manufacturing Victims: What the psychology industry is doing to people.* London: Constable.

32. World Health Organization. (1978). *International Classification of Procedures in Medicine* (ICPM), Vols 1 and 2. Geneva: World Health Organization.

33. Reed, G. M. (2010). Toward ICD-11: Improving the clinical utility of WHO's International Classification of Mental Disorders. *Professional Psychology: Research and Practice, 41*(6), 457–464.

34. World Health Organization. (2013). *The ICD-10 Classification of Mental and Behavioural Disorders: Clinical descriptions and diagnostic guidelines.* Geneva: World Health Organization.

35. Reed, G. M. (2010). Toward ICD-11: Improving the clinical utility of WHO's International Classification of Mental Disorders. *Professional Psychology: Research and Practice 41, 6,* 457–464.

36. See, for example, Beutler, L. W. & Malik, M. L. (Eds.). (2002). *Rethinking the DSM: A psychological perspective.* Washington, DC: American Psychological Association and Charney, D. S., Barlow, D. H., Botteron, K., Cohen, J. D., Goldman, D., Gur, R. E. & Zalcman, S. J. (2002). Neuroscience research agenda to guide development of a pathophysiologically based classification system. In D. J. Kupfer, M. B. First & D. A. Regier (Eds.), *A Research Agenda for DSM-V.* Arlington, VA: American Psychiatric Association, pp. 31–83.

37. Retrieved 15 April 2013 from http://apps.bps.org.uk/_publicationfiles/consultation-responses/DSM-5%202011%20-%20BPS%20response.pdf

38. Retrieved 15 April 2013 from http://www.ipetitions.com/petition/dsm5/

39. Retrieved 12 March 2013 from http://www.huffingtonpost.com/allen-frances/dsm-5-reliability-tests_b_1490857.html

40. See, for example, Pilgrim, D. (2007). The survival of psychiatric diagnoses. *Social Science & Medicine, 65*(3), 536–547 and Rogers, A. & Pilgrim, D. (2010). *A Sociology of Mental Health and Illness* (4th ed.). Maidenhead: Open University Press.

41. Johnstone, L. (2000). *Users and Abusers of Psychiatry: A critical look at psychiatric practice.* London: Routledge.

42. Harper, D. J. (1994). The professional construction of 'paranoia' and the discursive use of diagnostic criteria. *British Journal of Medical Psychology, 67*(2), 131–143.

43. Bentall, R. P. (1990). *Reconstructing Schizophrenia.* London: Routledge and (2003). *Madness Explained: Psychosis and human nature.* Harmondsworth:

Penguin. Bentall is also co-editor of the PCCS series, *Straight-talking Introductions to Mental Health Problems*: 2009 and continuing.

44. Rapley, M., Moncrieff, J. & Dillon, J. (Eds). (2011). *De-medicalizing Misery: Psychiatry, psychology and the human condition.* Basingstoke: Palgrave Macmillan. Dillon, J., Moncrieff, J. & Speed, E. (Eds.). (in press). *De-medicalizing Misery II.* Basingstoke: Palgrave Macmillan.

45. Smail, D. (2005). *Power, Interest and Psychology.* Ross-on-Wye: PCCS Books.

46. Szasz, T. (1994). *Cruel Compassion: Psychiatric control of psychiatry's unwanted.* Chichester: John Wiley & Sons.

47. Breggin, P. (1991). *Toxic Psychiatry: Why therapy, empathy and love must replace the drugs, electroshock, and biochemical theories of the 'new psychiatry'.* New York: St. Martin's Press.

48. In the UK the work of the *Critical Psychiatry Network* represents an in-house attempt to subvert the psychiatric project, albeit without relinquishing the right to interfere with the lives of others via professional authority. See, for example, Bracken, P. & Thomas, P. (2010). From Szasz to Foucault: On the role of critical psychiatry. *Philosophy, Psychology and Psychiatry, 17*(3), 219–228.

49. See, for example, Masson, J. M. (1988). *Against Therapy: Emotional tyranny and the myth of psychological healing.* London: HarperCollins.

50. Wolfensberger, W. (1987). *The New Genocide of Handicapped and Afflicted People.* New York: University of Syracuse. 'Deathmaking' refers to human service practices causing spiritual or physical harm (including hastening death) to their recipients. Notably, *DSM-5* lists neuroleptic-induced brain disorders such as tardive dyskinesia as 'mental disorders' rather than iatrogenic assaults. See, Newnes, C. (2011). Toxic psychology. In M. Rapley, J. Moncrieff & J. Dillon (Eds.), *De-medicalizing Misery: Psychiatry, psychology and the human condition.* Basingstoke: Palgrave Macmillan, pp. 211–225.

51. Pilgrim, D. (2013). *DSM-5* and forms of cultural imperialism. *The Journal of Critical Psychology, Counselling and Psychotherapy, 13*(2), 117–125.

52. Retrieved 15 April 2013 from http://apps.bps.org.uk/_publicationfiles/consultation-responses/DSM-5%202011%20-%20PS%20response.pdf

53. Goldie, N. (1977). The division of labour among the mental health professions. In M. Stacey, M. Reid, C. Heath & R. Dingwall (Eds.), *Health and the Division of Labour.* London: Croom Helm, pp. 141–161.

54. Leo, J. (1985) Battling over masochism. *Time,* Dec. 2, 76.

55. Cromby, J., Diamond, B., Kelly, P., Moloney, P., Priest P. & Smail, D. (Eds.). (2006). Critical and community psychology. Special issue of *Clinical Psychology Forum, 163,* June.

56. Heriot-Maitland, C., Knight, M. & Peters, E. (2012). A qualitative comparison of psychotic-like phenomena in clinical and non-clinical populations. *British Journal of Clinical Psychology, 51*(1), 37–53.

57. Rosario, V. A. (1997) *The Erotic Imagination: French histories of perversity.* New York: Oxford University Press.

58. Retrieved 15 April 2013 from http://apps.bps.org.uk/_publicationfiles/consultation-responses/DSM-5%202011%20-%20BPS%20response.pdf; Moncrieff, J. (2007). *The Myth of the Chemical Cure: A critique of psychiatric drug treatment.* Basingstoke: Palgrave MacMillan.

59. *Ibid.*

60. Pickles, C. (2011). Lives without reason? The imperialism of scientific explanation in psychology. *The Journal of Critical Psychology, Counselling and Psychotherapy, 11*(4), 208–216.

61. A Libertarian position, the principle advocate for which in relation to psychiatry has been Thomas Szasz; see Barker, P. & Buchanan-Barker, P. (2010). No excuses: The reality cure of Thomas Szasz. *Journal of Critical Psychology, Counselling and Psychotherapy, 10*(2), 69–75.

62. Farber, S. (1993). From victim to revolutionary: An interview with Leonard Frank. In *Madness, Heresy, and the Rumor of Angels: The revolt against the mental health system.* Chicago and La Salle: Open Court, pp. 190–240.

63. Newnes, C. (2011). Toxic psychology. In M. Rapley, J. Moncrieff & J. Dillon (Eds.), *De-medicalizing Misery: Psychiatry, psychology and the human condition.* Basingstoke: Palgrave Macmillan, pp. 211–225.

64. Retrieved 15 April 2013 from http://apps.bps.org.uk/_publicationfiles/consultation-responses/DSM-5%202011%20-%20BPS%20response.pdf (p. 2)

65. *Ibid.*

66. *Ibid.*

67. See, for example online tests for (all retrieved 5 May 2013):
Asperger's Syndrome: http://webcache.googleusercontent.com/search?q=cache:http://iautistic.com/test_AS.php
Autistic Spectrum Disorder: http://www.wired.com/wired/archive/9.12/aqtest.html

Depression – sponsored by Pfizer and NHS Direct:

http://www.nhs.uk/Tools/Pages/depression.aspx

Attention Deficit Hyperactivity Disorder: http://www.dore.co.uk/learning-difficulties/adhd/?gclid=CM-N9N2Xv7lCFUEMfAodiR4Ang

Schizophrenia: http://psychcentral.com/quizzes/schizophrenia.htm

68. Publication by clinical psychologists supports publishing houses in promoting these notions, nonsensical or not; see, for example, *The Oxford Handbook of Personality Disorders* and the fifth edition of the Minnesota Multiphasic Personality Inventory (MMPI-2 Assessing *Personality* and *Psychopathology* – my italics): Widiger, T. A. (Ed.). (2012). *The Oxford Handbook of Personality Disorders.* Oxford: Oxford University Press (£105); Graham, J. R. (2012). *MMPI-2: Assessing personality and psychopathology* (5th ed.). Oxford: Oxford University Press (£70).

69. Newnes, C. & Holmes, G. (1999). Introduction. In C. Newnes, G. Holmes & C. Dunn (Eds.) *This is Madness: A critical look at psychiatry and the future of mental health services* (pp. 1–5). Ross-on-Wye: PCCS Books.

70. Johnstone, L. (1997). Psychiatry: Are we allowed to disagree? *Clinical Psychology Forum, 100,* 31–4, p. 32.

71. *Ibid.,* p. 32.

72. For a parody of the need to quote research, see Newnes, C. (1992). References. *Clinical Psychology Forum, 42,* 27–29.

73. Boyle, M. (2011). Making the world go away, and how psychology and psychiatry benefit. In M. Rapley, J. Moncrieff & J. Dillon (Eds.), *De-medicalizing Misery: Psychiatry, psychology and the human condition.* Basingstoke: Palgrave Macmillan, pp. 27–43, pp. 28–9, my italics.

74. *Ibid.,* p. 39.

75. Smail, D. (2005). *Power, Interest and Psychology: Elements of a social materialist understanding of distress.* Ross-on-Wye: PCCS Books.

76. Division of Clinical Psychology. (2013). *Position Statement on the Classification of Behaviour and Experience in Relation to Functional Psychiatric Diagnoses: Time for a paradigm shift.* Leicester: British Psychological Society.

77. *Ibid.,* p. 1.

78. *Ibid.,* p. 3.

79. Newnes, C. (2005). Constructing the service user. *Clinical Psychology, 50,* 16–19.

80. Wolfensberger, W. (1987). *The New Genocide of Handicapped and Afflicted People.* New York: University of Syracuse.

81. Division of Clinical Psychology. (2013). *Position Statement on the Classification of Behaviour and Experience in Relation to Functional Psychiatric Diagnoses: Time for a paradigm shift.* Leicester: British Psychological Society, p. 5.

82. Reicher, S. D. (2005). Rethinking prejudice. *Clinical Psychology Forum, 153,* 8–10.

83. Mays, V. M. & Albee, G. W. (1992). Psychotherapy and ethnic minorities. In D. K. Freedheim (Ed.), *History of Psychotherapy: A century of change.* Washington, DC: American Psychological Association, pp. 552–570.

CHAPTER 8

And now? What to do?

'My father often said, "Ah, my boy we're on the brink of great discoveries … I won't live to see them but you will." I used to think how fortunate I was. Now I realise life changes; it doesn't improve.'[1]

Unsure how to structure this chapter, I toyed with the idea of it comprising exclusively footnotes, then considered using only one reference (the opening quote) as the author, with a novelist's ear for brevity, seemed to say pretty much everything I intended using far fewer words. There was the 'blank page' option, readers being invited to write their conclusions to be returned to me for further comment.[2] There may yet be some kind of summary of the previous seven chapters – as if this final chapter is a logical outcome of what has gone before. This book won't have been read in a similar way by different people and I don't want to be didactic in my own conclusions in case the reader feels my reading is the *right* one – after all, I only wrote it; I didn't know where it was going.

Thematic analysis is a 'mysterious' process.[3] In constructing the preceding chapters I appear to have identified themes – scientism, professionalisation, 'wounds', and illustrated them by reference to various texts. But *how* these themes emerged as a reading of critical texts and research is impossible to divine:

'Powerful understandings ... of what was important in the "texts" seemed to present themselves independently of any "analytic process" ... we – literally – could not ignore them.' And, '... we were not even able to be confident the analysis was produced by us rather than us being produced by the analysis.'[4] I have sympathy with this view. It is one that must be familiar to anyone who has reflected on a therapy session. *Why* did it seem so important to return to discussions of a particular childhood incident? *How was it* that the conversation kept returning to money? *Who* was directing the therapy – the therapist attempting to stay within a particular psychological discourse, or the patient turning talk to events more meaningful? And why *those* events? Why *that particular* psychological discourse? And what was the 'outcome' of the therapy – *who* changed more, patient or therapist? In other words, an analysis of moment-by-moment 'decisions' in creating (or 'discovering') themes will not be transparent. Rather than the research (or therapy, or reading) 'leading to' certain conclusions, the conclusions may already be in place and the research and reading (and therapy) a justification of those conclusions, a position with which Sartre would have had sympathy. Equally, I should guess that *any* of the chapters in this volume might have been written by arbitrarily using only research published by those with the letter D as their first initial (which would have included the Davids Pilgrim, Smail and Stein but excluded Foucault, Szasz and Wolfensberger). The conclusions, already foregone, would have only needed the research gloss provided by supportive 'evidence' to give the appearance of arising from that research.

There is, notwithstanding the above, an internal logic to this final chapter. I shall return to the themes of writing and research in clinical psychology and the nature of the profession. I shall attempt to give examples of politically and socially conscious praxis whilst simultaneously critiquing that praxis. With the indulgence of my extraordinarily tolerant publisher I shall probably include a stab at humour.

Writing (righting) clinical psychology

Tristram Shandy was published in nine volumes between 1759 and 1767. Supposedly autobiographical, part of the joke is that the narrator abjures simple explanations and includes so many diversions that Tristram isn't born until the third volume.[5] He resembles clinical psychology authors who take thousands of words to say what might be said in fifty. This volume might well fall into the same category.[6] Along the way the narrator discusses at length sexual practices, insults, the influence of one's name (three centuries before the transactional analyst Eric Berne did the same thing), obstetrics, siege warfare, and philosophy.

Praised for its originality, nobody noticed until long after Sterne's death that he had incorporated passages from, amongst others, Francis Bacon, Rabelais and Robert Burton's *The Anatomy of Melancholy*. In ridiculing the latter, Sterne satirises the style whereby indisputable facts are established by quotations from respected sources; another feature of the writings of clinical psychologists and, again, a style to be found in this volume. It is also standard practice in clinical psychology authorship to plagiarise *oneself*, a feature of Burton's work parodied in *Tristram Shandy*.

There are certain patterns in the writing of clinical psychologists. Research papers are formularised along the lines explicated in Chapter 3. Books tend to loosely follow an outline of 'Problems with existing theory and practice' followed by a rationalisation for a new praxis, frequently presented as more effective, more ethical or both.[7] Psy journals have a consistent style frequently presenting scientistic research and will have occasional special issues devoted to particular themes. Amidst the more orthodox issues of *Clinical Psychology Forum*, for example, guest editors and commissioned authors have demonstrated a commitment to race, gender, psychotherapy, assessment, training and community psychology in special issues published every three months or so.[8]

Patterns within the development of individual practitioners mirror those of the profession. Consistent change rather than consistency is a hallmark of both. For recently trained clinical psychologists in the UK, for example, *further* training is high on the agenda.[9] Whatever school of therapy is privileged by the training course, the majority of professionals soon train in additional modalities. They might see this as a 'progression' or refinement of their 'skills'. For a minority, particularly those trained psychoanalytically, their original praxis may obtain for much of their subsequent careers. For the majority, however, the trend is toward further training in therapy techniques and work in a burgeoning number of specialities. Clinical psychologists in the UK can be found working in palliative care, memory clinics, projects for Turkish-speaking mothers, Asian elders, primary schools – the size of the list begins to approach the number of clinical psychologists actually practising. Some of this endeavour may, for localised administrative reasons, be subsumed under broader categories such as 'community', 'adult' or 'child' services. Despite concerns that today's NHS places more constraints on praxis, clinical psychologists remain one of the least harnessed professions. Being subsumed under the auspices of the HCPC rather than the BPS has increased form-filling but barely touched on practitioners' autonomy; as described earlier day-to-day practice remains invisible. Reluctance to engage in research and publication maintains that invisibility.

For the profession early commitment to promoting, again broadly, psychoanalytic or behavioural approaches changed as the profession diversified. The 1960s and 1970s saw a privileging of humanistic therapies. CBT was enthusiastically embraced in the decades following as was narrative and systemic praxis. The current shibboleth, psychological formulation, continues to be promoted by the DCP in descriptions of training and the profession. Though clumsy, the notion of a clinical psychologist as a 'psychological formulator' is replacing dated notions of 'scientist practitioner'.

This smorgasbord of therapeutic styles and professional sanctions can be seen as evidence that some clinical psychologists still seek the grail of 'successful' therapy and the profession continues to struggle to find a marketable 'brand'. The variety can, in systemic terms, be regarded as an inevitable product of the open nature of organic systems. Here, human systems continuously respond to new information in efforts to adapt to and survive in a constantly changing environment. This is no less true of, say, the profession of architecture as practising architects incorporate new ideas and technologies into the overall architecture project.

For a profession presented as scientific, the changes *need* to be presented as progressive rather than the result of individual fads or responses to a shifting *Zeitgeist*. This is just as problematic for conceptual notions such as 'psychological formulation' as it was for humanistic practitioners claiming their therapeutic work to be an 'art' based on the subtleties of relationships, frequently presented as examples of the fetishised I–Thou type.[10] It is difficult to imagine *how* one would research 'psychological formulation' not least because any particular therapy used as an outcome of the formulation is, by necessity, unique to the individuals concerned. The approach bears some resemblance to psychoanalytic encounters where each *session* is regarded as a unique scientific experiment. As discussed previously, one potential difficulty with the possibility of psychological formulation is that the process can be viewed as – in itself – countertransference; those clinical psychologists who attempt to use it after further training in psychoanalysis might find that their efforts are undermined by the very theoretical model they prefer to use (see Chapter 7).

In summary, professionals and professions change. One narrative might describe this in terms of conflict and conflict resolution (between competing theories or therapies), another as positioning within a changing and highly competitive marketplace. The promotion of the concept of 'narrative' is, in itself, an example of this positioning.

W(h)ither clinical psychology

To some, clinical psychology must appear more as a guild than a profession. It has a language derived from medicine and the parent discipline of psychology. There are rituals via assessment techniques designed to re-language and categorise experience. Its therapies can be seen as further ritual and obscurantism and its professional hierarchy attempts to maintain its place in society via codes and public proclamation. It has its own texts, some considered radical, the majority orthodox. To some the profession is barely visible amongst related enterprises such as counselling. For others it holds the promise of individual help from practitioners who counter the medical hegemony. For many the profession represents the more benign face of that same hegemony. For some graduates it holds the prospect of employment in a post-doctoral 'helping profession'.

For those graduates, the guild-like nature of clinical psychology can be determined via a reading of the clearing house website section covering experience seen as necessary to gain a place on one of the UK's 30 training programmes. 'Relevant' experience, in addition to at least an upper-second-class honours degree in psychology, 'includes part-time or full-time, voluntary or paid work, involving caring or service roles with clients, whether in the public, private or charitable sectors ... work in other areas is also relevant. As examples, many successful applicants have worked in Social Services, in services for people with disabilities, or in the charitable sector ... course centres may value clinical experience which has been supervised by a qualified clinical psychologist over other types of experience ... you should seek regular supervision or contact from a qualified clinical psychologist ... you may benefit by making contact with local clinical psychologists.'[11]

These experiences draw the potential clinical psychology trainee into the professionalised discourse of the Psy endeavour. A summary of the proposed experiences might be, 'Try to spend as much time in a caring role (preferably alongside practising clinical psychologists) as possible'.

The experiences might be regarded an apprenticeship. To me they seem inconsistent with the publicised aims of the profession. These aims include inclusiveness, an appreciation of cultural and other distal influences and concerns about the mismatched demographics of the profession and the populations it professes to serve. Caring for a relative is not excluded as relevant experience. The experiences do not, however, include, for example, being a diagnosed patient, a parent, a divorcee, a historian, lawyer, a member of an oppressed minority or an activist. None of these are excluded (indeed all can be found amongst clinical psychologists cited in this volume) but knowledge of the praxis of a qualified clinical psychologist is privileged. Becoming a clinical psychologist may enable people to maintain their preferred role as spokespeople for the oppressed, the training simply a necessary hurdle. *Surviving* the process of professional indoctrination becomes the main aim in these cases.

This ambiguity of being part of an oppressive system whilst hoping to change it was claimed as motivation for clinical psychology trainees who came to me for their six-month elective (third year) placement. Entitled 'The Critical Psychology Placement', it enabled trainees to work alongside service survivors and discuss the ironies of being paid by a 'helping' system that often seemed to do more harm than good.[12] The placement might be construed as part of a professionalising discourse wherein protest is harnessed and the *academic* pursuit of liberatory ends privileged. The position is encapsulated in the Leonard Cohen lyric: 'They sentenced me to twenty years of boredom for trying to change the system from within.'[13]

Clinical psychology as a 'servant of power'

I think it fair to say that clinical psychology is in a muddle politically. Many practitioners might espouse broadly egalitarian views whilst simultaneously decrying any attempts to bring their salaries into line with less-well-paid employees. They might deplore the living conditions of some of their patients without having *experienced* similar conditions. As members of a predominantly white, middle-class profession they can be viewed as oppressors who view themselves as oppressed when faced with the stultifying bureaucracy of the NHS or demands to see more patients.

The ways in which those in power decree how people – as *subjects* – should be has been described by sociologists such as Foucault and Rose and neo-liberal political scientists such as Minogue. The latter was particularly concerned that democracy, rather than meaning government by the people, had come to mean government of the people and (*pace* Foucault) the governance of the self.[14] Citizens are informed they are bad parents, smoke or drink too much and eat the wrong kind of food. This 'way of reconfiguring selves and the social order in accord with the demands of market economies' has been described as 'governmentality'.[15]

Clinical psychologists, particularly those involved in 'wellbeing' projects, might be viewed as an expert element in this chain. Governmentality also requires that work is seen as good and when work is unavailable, voluntarism or so-called entrepreneurship are substituted. This form of neo-liberalism is some distance from the *experience* of those seeking work, many of whom, like UK conscripts from the first part of the 20th century, see themselves as cannon fodder.

Previous chapters have discussed the lack of validity in psychometric testing and lack of construct validity in aspects of 'personality' that testers claim to measure. The UK Government's Behavioural Insights Team, however, requires benefits claimants to submit to online psychometric testing. The test is a version of the Values in Action (VIA) 'Inventory of Signature Strengths', an assessment of personality or character.[16] Those failing to complete the test (to a short deadline) are warned that they might lose benefits. Psychometric testing used in this way has been described as, '… flawed, unethical, and unlikely to help claimants to find work'.[17]

Clinical psychologists in the UK – many of whom no longer use psychometrics – have been promoted as supervisors in the UK Government's Improving Access to Psychological Therapies scheme (IAPT) (see Chapter 4). The scheme has been criticised as a cynical exercise aimed at giving the appearance of making efforts to return people to paid employment (in the absence of actual jobs) and, as noted previously, in terms of its reversal of an assumed 'cause and effect'; people are no longer unhappy because they have no paid work, they can't work because they are unhappy ('depressed').[18] For the profession, IAPT was seen as another opportunity, perhaps to increase the number of clinical psychologists but, more probably, to establish a role for practitioners to become involved in training and supervising IAPT workers. The outcome of IAPT interventions has been less successful than the UK Government predicted.

The project, which started in May 2006, was launched with £173 million 'baseline funds'. The *Programme Review* from 2011 would be of interest to epidemiologists. As in many official documents of this type (most of which are sent to the general media with easy-to-reproduce sound bites), estimates appear as statements of fact. The authors reproduce psychologised terminology which is neither explained nor, given the invalidity of the concept of mental disorder, explicable. The authors claim, for example, '… one in six adults is *known* to suffer from mental ill-health' (my italics) giving a 'morbidity estimate' of six million adults with common mental health problems of whom 15 per cent would be expected to seek psychological therapy.[19] With a target of 900,000 people entering treatment with a newly trained workforce of CBT-oriented IAPT workers the review suggests that 600,000 would complete treatment by 2015. The outcome would be 50 per cent recovering and 25,000 'off sick pay'. An unspecified proportion of IAPT recipients would enter or return to employment. By 2011 the target of 648,974 people entering therapy was some 216,766 short. Of those who had completed therapy 28,133 were off sick pay.[20]

Employment prospects for newly trained IAPT workers were not encouraging: 'It is also of concern that in some cases there appears to be divergence in service and education commissioning strategies with the potential for newly trained therapists not being able to secure employment in future IAPT services.'[21] In *addition* to the baseline funds for the initial programme of £173m, over £400m was allocated ('prioritised') for the programme. This represents a cost in the region of £20,000 per person removed from sick pay. Changes in the benefits system would make a cost–benefit analysis of IAPT extremely complicated. Employing a similar process of estimation, however, and assuming that 'relapse' for recipients of IAPT help is similar to that for patients receiving similar approaches, perhaps 70 per cent of the 28,133 people no longer receiving sick pay *would* again be entitled to it. Had the benefits system (essentially a change in the criteria for receipt of 'job seeker's allowance') not changed this would leave only 7,000 people 'off sick pay' – at a cost approaching £80,000 per person.

Such projects are not limited to employment. Concerns that were for centuries a family matter such as, for example, caring (or not) for elderly relatives have been monopolised by the state; '… concerns arising in the "household sector" become part of public and political concern … arise in … "social policy", "child welfare", "health and mental health", "education" all of these subordinated to economic policy'.[22] The professions of clinical and educational psychology are beneficiaries of this overall economic policy. A, perhaps, harsh critic might argue that, even when acting as 'community' clinical psychologists, the expert status further removes power and agency from citizens and their households. A balancing argument would posit that *some* households are so toxic to family life that the only humane response is to reduce their influence. As noted previously, Szasz suggests this leads to an essentially Judeo-Christian position whereby compassion is the justification for psychologists' interventions.

Love thy neighbour?

The separation of the roles of citizen, patient and professional is a feature of the post-industrial world. It is evident in the 'us and them' positioning of everyday media coverage where a report that, say, men are more likely to lie than women makes no reference to the fact that the writer is male. Some clinical psychologists embrace identities that subvert this separation. They may, for example, be explicitly feminist in their approach. Others may hope to avoid the necessary connections in person-to person encounters, preferring the relative safety of the professional–patient divide.

Consider the following vignette. You are a clinical psychologist about to encounter a new patient. You may have read a referral letter or a personal account of the client's life from another source. There may be psychiatric case notes available or a general medical history. You have prepared the room. Just before the client arrives you take a phone call from a distressed colleague who can't make a meeting later. Slightly flustered you welcome the client, noticing immediately the scuffed, muddy shoes and the torn coat. The latter vaguely reminds you that you need to go to a charity shop later and, then, from seemingly nowhere you remember that you didn't lock your front door. Thoughts, fantasies, memories, anxieties old and new continue for the next hour. No doubt the client is experiencing something similar as they monitor what they say, how you react, what you are wearing, your age, sex, ethnicity and the mud on your carpet. They will be making guesses at your sexuality and whether you seem like you can help. They are also horribly conscious that they have left the front door unlocked. Meanwhile you are both realising that this isn't your first encounter. You are both regulars at a local pizza takeaway and the last time you saw each other you were forcefully admonishing your three-year-old for clambering onto another customer's child's buggy.

We are multiply identitied. We might say that we have multiple selves. Miller Mair has discussed the idea of a community of selves and John Rowan the presence of sub-personalities.[23] Our experience of ourselves in any given situation is not static; it is fluid and changing. The vignette above includes many identities: professional, client, helper, helped, friend, the person who is eager to please, the homeowner, the potential lover, neighbour and so on. We can appear reasonably solid in our professional identity but, for some, the experience within that identity is one of constantly switching through other selves.[24] For patients the preferred identity *may* be one based on diagnosis. There are, for example, over 50 self-help groups in England for those marked 'bipolar'.[25]

Clinical psychologists might be described as 'entrepreneurs of identity'.[26] They are selling identity, or at least the hope of a new identity, to patients. The profession, as represented by its officers and public statements, simultaneously sells an identity of clinical psychologists to funding bodies, the public, the media and clinical psychologists themselves. That identity includes the magician-like power to change others. The presence of clinical psychologists in the media demonstrates a willingness to add to the numerous websites and self-help books promising personal control over change – scientism is now substituted for magic. This praxis has an older history than some might imagine.

Millions of cheaply printed 'chapbooks' were produced by presses in the larger cities of England and Ireland from the 17th to the 19th centuries. Sold wherever an outlet was available (market stalls, shops, fairs, etc.) they were eventually superseded by newspapers, magazines and more substantial printed books in the 19th century. Subject matter included traditional tales, songs, rhymes and lists of the meanings of dreams or more specialist areas such as astrology or love divination. Arising from a different context (one explicitly magical) the latter might be seen as a forebear of the agony aunts found in current magazines and newspapers or the expert advice available via television or the Internet. Chapbooks were the basic reading matter '... of the working and lower middle classes ...' and, like the ubiquitous horoscope, relied on superstition.[27] The reader might wonder if the expert opinion of clinical psychologists also now available via the media bears some similarity to the chapbook phenomena, magic having been replaced by the mysteries of science and a style of publication that also frequently involves the inclusion of impressive charts, 'flow diagrams' and predictive formulae providing the reader 'follows the instructions'.

Accounting for clinical psychology

An account *criticising* the clinical psychology project might read: Research (funded by those with vested interests) and regulation (by the very bodies that have an interest in their own survival) continue to foster the illusion of progress in helping those in distress or deemed mad. Such research is an implausible project as there remains little reliability and no validity for the so-called conditions it attempts to explore. As it is based on a fallacious model of Psy as a natural science in comparison to research in areas of true physical scientific endeavour, research in psychology is contaminated by both the subject matter (human beings) and the values of the researchers (human beings). Regulation might be regarded as another ploy by Psy to gain credibility. This strategy has been compromised by the subjugation of the BPS by the HCPC.

A second *professionalised* account might read: Clinical psychology continues to match the wry comment of its then chair (and soon to be president of the BPS) made at an executive committee meeting in the 1990s: (to paraphrase), 'Clinical psychology has won. We're everywhere.' The spread into specialities as diverse as childhood cancer and pre-senile dementia services is evidence of the success of the professional project. This project has been described as 'giving psychology away'.[28] Notwithstanding the last decade's *Zeitgeist* privileging the Psy project in all aspects of the media and public life, clinical psychology has achieved remarkable prominence in the NHS. This is, in part, due to the efforts of individuals working in a medicalised system who speak out at case conferences or in the media. Several clinical psychologists have attained national prominence as media pundits, columnists in national newspapers or, more locally, as 'agony aunts' on radio stations and television. In turn this demonstrates the success of the BPS press office.[29]

An analysis highlighting ambiguity suggests pockets of liberatory and class-conscious praxis where clinical psychologists work alongside service survivors as allies, use a degree of political awareness to aid change within services towards a more equal allocation of resources and actively participate in community projects as partners of oppressed minorities. In one-to-one work with patients these clinical psychologists do not privilege a psychological discourse but retain a narrative based on exposing the subjectification of citizens. The ambiguity emerges in a reading of the published work of these clinical psychologists, some of whom acknowledge that *psychological* theories don't feature in their work. Rather, the discourse is wholly political, raising the question of how – other than their projected status as *expert* – they are better placed to raise consciousness than, say, trade unionists and politicians (there are a very few clinical psychologists who do exactly this in the former role).

One possible reading reveals the profession and individual

practitioners in a mixed position. Carried out just after the millennium a DCP-sponsored research exercise predicted – accurately – that clinical psychology courses in the UK would place more emphasis on trainees' 'personal awareness' and on 'core competencies' including consultancy skills, qualitative research methods, multidisciplinary work and the cultural context of health. Health and forensic psychology were seen to be growth areas and the evidence-based scientist-practitioner model endorsed. 'On the negative side' the results suggested that gender and ethnic imbalances in recruitment would remain and 'manuals, protocols and guidelines' would 'have an impact'.[30] 'Endorsement' of the scientist-practitioner model, however has not translated into more research publications by clinical psychologists.[31] As noted in previous chapters it remains impossible to *know* if clinical psychologists follow manualised treatment protocols or treatment guidelines – *appearing* to play by the rules is a tactic well known to other professions, particularly nursing, within the Psy complex. Also unclear to me is whether a predominantly young, white and female profession is welcomed in a 'consultancy role' in a context where individualistic clinical praxis is demanded by employers.

A critical reading is more demanding; there are numerous perspectives – cultural, linguistic, political – from which to view the profession. Each of these positions is open to a further critical account from similar cultural, linguistic, political and psychological perspectives. Critical analysology might well suggest that a genuinely critical reading is impossible due to the way in which moment-by-moment reflection by the analyst of the analytic process shifts.[32] Why, for example, highlight vested interest in clinical psychology endeavour? Is such an approach not also open to an analysis of the analyst? Is the primarily academic examination of clinical psychology praxis not an *exclusively* academic praxis contextualised by university demands to publish? This kind of analysis of analysis resembles an ever-decreasing but never-ending spiral indistinguishable from nihilism.

What then might the fate of this volume be? The proximal and distal forces acting on practising clinical psychologists make it unlikely many will read it cover to cover. I had originally thought it might only be read by 'the converted'. But converted to what? I hope the reader has found the text challenging and reasonably well argued. But the overall project seems to be a neutral endeavour. The introduction seems clear that the book isn't aimed at changing much. This is more an acknowledgement that the process of change is beyond the power of the individual, a kind of resignation that things are just the way they are. Professional praxis is subservient to the *Zeitgeist* and rarely welcomes (at the level of the individual or profession) the type of evidence presented here. One fate is for the volume to be quoted in further academic publications; another might be that some individual practitioners find creative ways to act on some of the ideas presented in previous chapters. If the reader is urged to effect some change, allies will be needed, preferably allies with social power. That change will be, by necessity, small and local and will require a surprising amount of effort.

What then?

Two potential projects occur to me – one for the profession in the UK, the other for both the profession and individual practitioners. The reader might find the target – ECT – an odd one given the numerous areas in which clinical psychologists might work and the wide-ranging ambit of the profession. For me, however, it is an example of a 'hittable' target. The public are barely aware of its ongoing use and much of the profession has little contact with either ECT survivors or services using it. There are, however, several websites devoted to its eradication and some activists with a wealth of data available. It is a procedure used principally against old, less powerful women and one which continues to inflict wounds, from memory loss to death. Chapter 6 looked in detail at its history and current usage worldwide, a usage that appears to be entirely at the discretion of particular psychiatrists who favour it. As such, it fails the test of being a scientific praxis.

To join with an oppressed minority such as ECT survivors might, by some, be seen as an 'anti-professional' step; ECT survivors can, however, be found amongst practising clinical psychologists and other members of Psy. I don't present this option as an 'anti-psychiatric' action *per se* but, by not joining in public protest, clinical psychologists can be seen as bystanders, *de facto* members of a silent majority of Psy professionals. This position might be viewed as a human rights perspective. Clinical psychologist allies of organisations such as the World Network for Users and Survivors of Psychiatry promote the position of psychiatric survivors as citizens. Similarly, clinical psychology has been represented amongst feminist critics and those concerned with the rights of people coerced into arranged marriage or victims of torture. Some recipients of ECT regard it as a form of torture which overrides a human right to safe and effective treatments.

If the profession remains sincere in its stated aim of changing the profile of its trainees then a second aim might be suggested. I should guess that the constraints of fulfilling my second suggestion are such that it is close to unachievable. There is no *evidence* that those with an undergraduate degree in *psychology* make the best clinical psychologists. There can't be – a degree in psychology has been a definitive qualification for training since the profession's inception. The DCP should change the guild-like nature of the profession; if, for reasons demanded by the academy, a degree is necessary then, perhaps, other degrees might, in rotation be considered along with fluency in at least one (also in rotation) other language. If that language were, say, Urdu this change might well simultaneously change one aspect of the cultural ground of the profession as well as its resemblance to a guild.[33]

This suggestion betrays the first tenet of making change – think small – but it does have the advantage of being (mostly) within the power of the profession. Clinical psychologists are under the auspices of the HCPC, though the BPS retains a lead professional role. The change would, by necessity have to be agreed within the BPS itself, raising the considerable challenge that potential clinical psychology trainees, as non-psychologists, may not be considered eligible for membership.

In part to illustrate the contextualised nature of change I produced a 'How to change your life' volume. One proposal was its publication as a calendar with one change per day. As I only came up with 64 suggestions it stayed on my hard-drive. A feature of the list is that it acknowledges that any given change might not result in particularly positive movement from the user's viewpoint due to the numerous factors militating against life feeling more tolerable. It does have the advantage of being brief – one line per page with no extraneous material, not unlike the Ten Commandments with a codicil to the effect that sticking with all ten will be quite a trial. The suggested changes are not *obviously* driven by a health agenda but were written after I survived the car crash and subsequent injuries that came close to killing me (see introduction). They are based instead on a list of things I do which has the advantage that they avoid the charge of hypocrisy (Montaigne claimed hypocrisy was the *first* lesson[34]) and means I can act on one of the early ones: 'Don't suggest to others they do things you haven't done yourself – they may need some back-up.' The difficulty of achieving these changes outside of the context of a privileged and reasonably comfortable materially secure place in society is revealed immediately by the injunction to 'Eat by candlelight every night'. Fine for those with a room of their own but a challenge for those living in sheltered accommodation. As a clinical psychologist I see the list as analogous to some of the suggestions made by practitioners to patients; if eating by candlelight (or throwing away your television or visiting the Great Blasket) is difficult, how much more challenging is it for patients to 'keep a thought diary' or even respond to the rhetorical question, 'Can you come next Wednesday at 9.30?' (Rhetorical because both practitioner and patient know only 9.30 on Wednesday is available.)

In short, change happens continuously but in a context over which people have no control. To suggest for clinical psychology the two changes outlined above is to simultaneously acknowledge they can only be achieved in a changing political and inter-personal *Zeitgeist*. And that assumes a *Zeitgeist* change favourable towards the protection of older women and a genuine inclusivity for clinical psychology as a profession.

Towards politicised praxis

Louis XIV ordered the grand incarceration in 1656. It was a police roundup of the odd and mad. The reasons for incarceration in the Salpêtrière and Bicêtre (part of the Paris General Hospital) were social (disruption to society) and ethical (potential self-harm); the aim of the edict was to prevent 'mendicancy and idleness as the source of all disorders'.[35] The responsibility for deciding on those to be hospitalised lay with the Chief of Police. Pinel was appointed as physician of Bicêtre in 1793 and Salpêtrière in 1795. In 1838 he classed some as aliénés (insane) to be treated in hospital – hence, 'aliénistes', the precursors of psychiatrists. Less than 60 years later there were many huge hospitals for the mad in the US and Europe, a practice soon mirrored around the world (see Chapter 6). The incarceration of so many people *necessitated* the development of means to control unruly inmates. Except for the more resistant patients, straitjackets were rapidly superseded by a techno-pharmacopoeia including: bromides, cocaine, caffeine, paraldehyde, electroshock, insulin, psycho-surgery, major tranquillisers such as lithium and chlorpromazine (marketed as drugs to combat supposed conditions such as manic depression and schizophrenia), ECT (marketed as a specific treatment for schizophrenia and depression on an age range from 4 to 104), Librium, amphetamines, Valium, Ativan, the so-called atypical anti-psychotics, Prozac, Ritalin and Adderall (effectively amphetamines now popular as 'study' drugs and soon to re-appear as slimming pills[36]). Like names of new cars, drug names are carefully selected – 'Valium' suggests becoming valiant, 'Librium' was to liberate the recipient and so on.

There is a discernible 'evolution' in physical treatments for the mad. Underlying the change, a pattern can be detected whereby new approaches are heralded as 'breakthroughs'. As in the marketing of any product, the faults of the previous product are emphasised and the (frequently known) adverse effects of the newest procedure downplayed. The fundamental problem that all so-called conditions are linguistic constructions is ignored in marketing campaigns – rather like ignoring the carbon footprint in the manufacturing process of 'green' automobiles (or the fact it is greener to walk, cycle or take the bus).

Therapies are similarly branded, three-letter acronyms being popular. The more technicalised therapies have proven a marketing success amongst clinical psychologists as psychoanalysis and behaviour therapy incorporated other elements to become cognitive analytic therapy and cognitive behaviour therapy. For those more interested in clinical work with families, different forms of family therapy have been subsumed under 'narrative' approaches. As noted in Chapter 6 there are some 500 therapies, offering clinical psychologists the opportunity to train in modalities to which they find themselves better suited. The growth of psychological formulation would suggest that, if a particular clinical psychologist hopes to offer a choice of treatments based on a particular understanding of a person's difficulties then that psychologist should train in a number of individualistic therapies *and* family therapy. This seems to me a tall order as a thorough training in *any* therapy will take many years.

For a troublesome minority the de-institutionalisation of the 1960s and 1970s has become a re-institutionalisation of people supposedly sharing similar characteristics (and diagnoses) – 'eating disorder' units or 'low-secure' establishments. In something of a return to the hospice movement of the half millennium before the 1600s there are also now a few (formal and funded) retreats for those deemed mad in the UK and Europe. Essentially asylum from the excesses of modern life the schemes tend to be short-lived, dependent on one or two energetic individuals and well-placed allies and, to a lesser extent, deeply suspicious of the Psy complex. The Wokingham MIND Crisis House, for example, survived for over 20 years. Run by a radical separatist the house took in up to three 'guests' who found life overwhelming. Some were referred by psychiatrists or social workers and 'escaped' to the house rather than spend time in psychiatric hospital. This was despite the fact that the house kept only the barest details of the guests and *banned* visits from Psy professionals. The sitting room resembled nothing less than a lower-middle class living room *circa* 1960, countless small porcelain knick-knacks on display, bottles of alcohol freely available (sherry appeared at 11 each morning), several cats and, apart from a fairly antagonistic poster about social workers, no obvious signs of any connection with statutory services. There may have been a notice with information concerning what to do in the event of a fire, but I didn't notice it on visits with clinical psychology trainees exploring alternatives to psychiatry. The house had been an 'independent' branch of the local MIND; on the organiser's retirement, the house was subsumed under the local social services.[37] Adopting a model similar to that of the original Soteria houses, there is a proposed further Soteria-style retreat in the UK. Like the Wokingham project, there is no particular view of medication and potential residents will be expected to self-monitor its use. Funding is haphazard and dependent on a few committed individuals.[38]

The Berlin Runaway House is of a different order. Explicitly opened for those rejecting psychiatric hospitalisation it has continued to take in psychiatric 'runaways' for the last 20 years. There is a contrast here with various small 'crisis' projects, monitored by social services and only open to those marked with a psychiatric diagnosis.[39]

Beyond these projects there are numerous – unheralded – schemes for offering refuge to distressed people, the majority entirely informal; people are, indeed, being 'good neighbours'. It is in these local schemes that professional psychologists (clinical and community) may be found, frequently working voluntarily. It might be added that these volunteer professionals are *not* using psychological theory to justify their input. Nor do they use, for example, the theories of French and Raven on social power to develop strategies on local influence.[40] This seems to me entirely *possible* but, as with their paid employment, these clinical psychologists may have found that their status *requires* no theoretical justification of their actions.

Such justification can be found in the work of Penny Priest, Guy Holmes and Carl Harris (see Chapter 1). All three are clinical psychologists. The first combined methods from grounded theory and ethnography to explore members' experience of a mental health service walking group, with regard to benefits of the physical activity (walking), being outdoors and the social benefits of being a group member. These themes were brought together in a *Healing Balm* model, which sought to explicate the healing properties of the experience. These included: *Striving, Getting Away, Being Closer to What is More Natural, Finding Meaning, Feeling Safe, Being Part,* and *Being Me*.[41]

It might be possible to take context and complexity into account. That lives are contextual is undeniable – someone waking up to the sounds of birds and a view from the bedroom window of a productive vegetable patch is likely to start the day differently from someone woken up by yells from a local gang known to terrorise the local council housing estate. Someone getting up at five to cycle to an underpaid job through that same housing estate may be less keen on the day ahead than the well-paid commuter imagining that the most challenging part of the day will be completing the cryptic crossword by 8.30. So far, so stereotypic. But what of the relationships between these people and their families, partners, cultures and histories? What of the dialects they speak, sometimes a local argot, sometimes a language the clinical psychologist has only heard before from a television programme? What of the person's age, experience, attitude to professionals? It seems to me hubristic for those who promote psychological formulation as the future of the profession to expect context-bound clinical psychologists to grasp this degree of complexity. Limiting interventions to sharing an account of how tough life can be may have none of the gloss of science but has the advantage of being *possible*.

The work of Guy Holmes may fall into this category. For some years he has organised walking groups in Shrewsbury. These are loosely based on the *Healing Balm* approach, are open to all and widely promoted in local health and other service venues thus attracting people, some with psychiatric labels, others without. These people walk – and talk. No agenda but a degree of companionship. Shy and newer members are 'shepherded' for the first few walks. In 2013 the project included a series of discussions at a town centre coffee house and open access learning venue. The series – Toxic Mental Environments – involved local clinical psychologists facilitating discussion about what brings us down. The events were open to the criticism that 'experts' were being asked to tell people what they already knew, but the *ordinariness* of these meetings and their potential for generating local action stands in stark contrast to the formalised and individualised techno-therapies promoted by the profession.[42]

Finally, it might seem unduly optimistic, given earlier comments about the low numbers of qualified clinical psychologists carrying out research, but one research avenue seems to suggest itself. It is research which fulfils the expectations of some service survivors and seems to place researchers in the area of human rights rather than Psy, *per se*. Various psychiatric survivor groups have, for many years, been concerned with the involuntary and coercive nature of psychiatric practice. It was the main concern of the libertarian psychiatrist, Szasz. Despite no legal qualifications those with powers under the UK's Mental Health Act can incarcerate citizens against their will for different periods according to their perceived dangerousness to themselves or others. Survivors are interested in: the longer-term effects of forced interventions and coercive treatments, the impact coercion has on compliance, whether there is an increase in non-compliance after patients have been coerced, and whether there is an increase in treatment avoidance among people who have been coerced. These are all empirical questions that clinical psychology research could help to answer.

Unifying psychology theory and practice

There is nothing, in theory, to prevent clinical psychologists utilising psychological theories to inform their work in a less traditional way than suggested by the profession's reactionary history. Theories of scapegoating, for example, can be used in examining the positioning of people as 'mad' in much the same way that analytic ideas concerning 'projection' are used to understand why some members of families are seen as deviant. A project developing a definition of 'mental health' analysed group discussions including diagnosed patients and Psy professionals.

The analysis revealed that *only* characteristics (the ability to work, love, make people laugh) viewed as culturally positive had been mentioned. The project undermined local attempts to define mental health in terms of an absence of illness and showed that diagnosed individuals were, in the terms of the project's definition, 'mentally healthy'.[43] Psychological interventions would thus focus not on 'helping' those who are diagnosed, but on identifying the vested interests of those doing the diagnosing. This is a project undertaken by many of the clinical psychologists referenced in this volume but not one embraced by the profession; the majority of clinical psychologists, though not diagnosing, continue to see those who are diagnosed as 'in need' of help rather than emancipation.

The CAMH early intervention service in Luton uses systemic theory and practice to inform its model of service, and supports systems around young persons. The service works with children's centres, primary care professionals, schools systems and children's social services. Workers in child-related agencies are encouraged to change their perception of mental health to one that is relational in concept. A similar project in Shropshire co-facilitated by a GP and a clinical psychologist acting as a wellbeing consultant was also briefly commissioned by the local health authority (2003–2009).[44]

Some primarily academic clinical psychologists have privileged public health approaches in their work. The Neighbourhood Networks project was started in Salford, then moved to Aberdeen and was adopted in Australia when its founder moved there two years later. There are similar schemes worldwide.[45] The project's founder also founded the journal *Care in Place*.[46]

The Centre for Disability Research at the University of Lancaster, also directed by a clinical psychologist, applies public health praxis to intellectual disability. Researchers explore social, cultural and economic bases of health and social inequalities faced by disabled children, their families and adults with intellectual or developmental disabilities. The Centre builds resilience amongst this group, designing and implementing early intervention programmes through the facilitation of social support systems. There is a focus on education of the public and empowerment to maximise the coping skills of the *community*.[47] This work has echoes of Wolfensberger's ideas concerning revaluing the *perceived* position of devalued groups seeking community integration.[48]

Established by a community clinical psychologist and others in 2010, the Great Yarmouth Fathers Project utilised a number of psycho-theoretical models to inform design and praxis.[49] Social action theory, for example, guides praxis while power-mapping guides thinking about where resources need to be targeted.[50]

Influenced by post-structuralist theory, 'critical psychology' in Europe, North America and Australasia is less practical than in Latin America. The psychology of liberation, despite the sustained interest amongst academic psychologists, remains only on the margins, even in Latin America where it originated.[51] Contributing psychology activists can be found in '… South Africa, the Philippines, Australia, Ireland, the UK, Canada and the USA'. The psychology of liberation is, however, '… not a branch of psychology but an orientation to its theory and practice'.[52] Here, it is the way psychological theory and practice are used that matters. An analysis of the way psychology is used provokes questions concerning emancipatory versus oppressive praxis. For liberation psychology three areas of application might be: community social psychology, work with victims of state oppression (disappearances, genocide), and social analysis, including policy analysis and ideology critique.[53]

The start

Stories don't end. This book has been a story – a kind of biography. As a form of confession I'll conclude this phase with a confession. In David Lodge's *Changing Places* the narrator tells the tale of a post-conference social meeting of various professors of English who play a game of who can name the book everyone assumes they will have read but, actually, he or she never got round to it. To mutual horror, one of the players names *Hamlet*.[54] I live and work in various communities – like the reader I occupy a community of selves. As an erstwhile critical community psychologist complete with clinical credentials I have read a great deal. Conspicuous by its absence is Prilleltensky's work on community psychology.[55] For those aspiring to make a mark I should recommend his curriculum vitae.[56]

Training as a clinical psychologist didn't get me away from working nights (see Introduction). Discounting the number of times I saw patients in the evening because of their work commitments I found myself interviewing ward staff in the early hours for a thesis on uniform.[57] Years later I ran seminars on social role valorisation for night-shift workers who seemed relieved at the break in routine. I had the advantage that I could leave at two in the morning while they worked on until six. To date, clinical psychology is a career retaining those kinds of advantages for those who navigate their way through the guild-like nature of training. For those who can draw on allies and the kind of liberatory praxis outlined in this chapter, it will remain a challenge to facilitate small change. Context will determine both what changes are possible and the moral dimension in which changes are seen as for the good.

And, finally … my eldest daughter recently accused me of critiquing everything; a characteristic she finds simultaneously stimulating, nihilistic and depressing. Once diagnosable as Oppositional Disorder, it is a characteristic that brings few rewards in the context of NHS management, a degree of success in therapeutic encounters and, had I taken a more academic career route, might have seen me floating around the more abstruse world of French post-structuralism. Or: 'I' (a barely understood self) 'critique' (an unanalysable praxis) 'everything' (hubris). Hence the dedication at the start of this book.

Endnotes

1.   Manning, O. (1985). *The Doves of Venus.* London: Virago, p. 138. (Original work published 1955)

2.   Comments will be welcomed via craignewnes76@gmail.com

3.   Fryer, D. & Easpaig, B. N. G. (2013). Critical analysology: The critical theorising of analysis. *Journal of Critical Psychology, Counselling and Psychotherapy, 13*(2), 67–72, p. 70.

4.   *Ibid.,* p. 71.

5.   Sterne, L. (1759–1767/1970). *The Life and Opinions of Tristram Shandy, Gentleman.* Nine volumes/One volume. London: The Folio Society. See also: http://www.gutenberg.org/ebooks/1079. Schopenhauer, Marx and Goethe were fans of Sterne and the novel has been regarded a forerunner of modernist and postmodernist literature. Page 357, for example, is left blank in recognition of the 'concupiscible' widow Wadman and the reader invited to '… call for pen and ink [and] … paint her to your own mind'.

6.   Dorothy Rowe has suggested to me more than once that most of what she has written can be summarised in a few cartoons.

7.   This format is illustrated in Stein, D. B. (2012). *The Psychology Industry Under a Microscope!* Plymouth, UK: University Press of America Inc and in Newnes, C. & Radcliffe, N. (Eds.). (2005). *Making and Breaking Children's Lives.* Ross-on-Wye: PCCS Books.

8.   The first issue of *Clinical Psychology Forum* I edited was 'Developing Community Services'. It was entirely commissioned as the departing editors had left me with no copy. There is a confrontational editorial describing the confusion around the notion of 'community' (frequently a vague term meaning 'outside the hospital') and ending with, 'Our challenge is to use the concepts of group psychology in our understanding of the numerous communities which exist within as well as outside the places where we hide people others would rather not see', Editorial (1988). *Clinical Psychology Forum, 16,* 2.

9.   Whilst a low response rate leads the researchers to interpret their results with caution, Urquhart-Law, McCarron and Wright's survey of pre-qualification trainees showed that the majority wanted high salaries and the opportunity for further study in their first job. Few saw research opportunities or the availability of psychometric resources as important. Urquhart-Law, G., McCarron, L. A. & Wright, C. (1999). What do trainees want in their first job after qualification? *Clinical Psychology Forum, 123,* 56.

10. Feltham, C. (2013). *Counselling and Counselling Psychology: A critical examination.* Ross-on-Wye: PCCS Books, p. 185.

11. Retrieved 5 February 2013 from http://www.leeds.ac.uk/chpccp/BasicEqualopps. html

12. Newnes, C. (1997). Teaching critical psychiatry and clinical psychology. *Clinical Psychology Forum, 109,* 37–40.

13. Cohen, L. (1988). First We Take Manhattan. From *I'm Your Man*. Columbia Records.

14. Minogue, K. (2010). *The Servile Mind: How democracy erodes the moral life*. New York: Encounter.

15. Cromby, J. & Willis, E. H. (in press). Nudging into subjectification: Governmentality and psychometrics. *Critical Social Policy.*

16. Retrieved 3 July 2013 from http://www.behaviourlibrary.com/strengths.php

17. Cromby, J. & Willis, E. H. (in press). Nudging into subjectification: Governmentality and psychometrics. *Critical Social Policy.* Preprint publication 15 October 2013 doi: 10.1177/0261018313500868

18. NHS. (2011). *Improving Access to Psychological Therapies: Programme Review December 2011*. London: NHS. See also Walker, C. (2009). The Improving Access to Psychological Therapies programme, globalisation and the credit crunch: Is this how we put politics into depression? *Journal of Critical Psychology, Counselling and Psychotherapy, 9*(2), 66–74.

19. NHS. (2011). *Improving Access to Psychological Therapies: Programme Review December 2011*. London: NHS, p. 5.

20. *Ibid.*, p. 7.

21. *Ibid.*, p. 9.

22. Davey, B. (2013). Household economy. *Journal of Critical Psychology, Counselling and Psychotherapy, 13*(3), 4–9, p. 4.

23. Perrin, A. & Newnes, C. (2002). Professional identity and the complexity of therapeutic relationships. *Clinical Psychology, 15,* 18–22.

24. Newnes, C. (2008). Diary 2. *Journal of Critical Psychology, Counselling and Psychotherapy, 8*(2), 89–95.

25. Retrieved 10 July 2013 from http://www.bipolaruk.org.uk/self-help-group-map.html

26. Reicher, S. D. & Hopkins, N. (2004). On the science of the art of leadership. In D. van Knippenberg & M. A. Hogg (Eds.), *Leadership, Power and Identity.* London: Sage, pp. 197–209.

27. Roud, S. (2003). *The Penguin Guide to the Superstitions of Britain and Ireland.* Harmondsworth: Penguin, p. 75.

28. Lyon, J. & Smith, P. (1987). Trying to give psychology away. *Clinical Psychology Forum, 12,* 21–24; Harper, D. (1989). Are we selling psychological skills or just selling psychology away? *Clinical Psychology Forum, 20,* 23–25.

29. In regard to media prominence the profession owes a debt to Jonathan Calder, DCP

press officer for many years. Jon was also the copy-editor for *Clinical Psychology Forum* for the last 15 years of my tenure as co-ordinating editor. A staunch, working-class liberal and Victorian Studies postgraduate, his comments in the margins of the journal should have been published as a separate volume. One remark went something along the lines, 'Funny how, for such a supposedly citizen-friendly profession, so many of you have addresses like "The Old Vicarage" or "Field House".' I was one of two clinical psychologists with this last address.

30. Kennedy, P. & Llewellyn, S. (2001). Does the future belong to the scientist practitioner? *The Psychologist, 14*(2), 74–78, p. 76.

31. Jones claims that the scientific identity of clinical psychology is fraudulent as training doesn't aim to help practitioners meet the majority of patients' needs. Jones, A. (1998). 'What's the bloody point?' More thoughts on fraudulent identity. *Clinical Psychology Forum, 112*, 3–9.

32. Fryer, D. & Easpaig, B. N. E. (2013). Critical analysology: The critical theorizing of analysis. *Journal of Critical, Psychology, Counselling and Psychotherapy, 13*(2), 67–72.

33. Under these circumstances I would never have gained a training place; it is hard to picture poorly remembered Yiddish being a qualifier.

34. Shklar, J. N. (1984). *Ordinary Vices.* Cambridge, MA: Harvard University Press.

35. Foucault, M. (1972). *Histoire de la Folie à l'Âge Classique.* Paris: Gallimard, p. 47.

36. Studies reported in *The Wall Street Journal online* seem to show that the so-called 'cognitive enhancing' effects of drugs like Ritalin and Adderall is a myth, notwithstanding the finding that 20 per cent of the 2.5 million US children prescribed the drugs *share* them with friends. The finding has echoes of the 1960s when teenagers smoked dried banana skins hoping to get similar effects to marihuana. Retrieved 9 July 2013 from http://online.wsj.com/article/SB10001 4241278873233687045785936603843622292.html

37. Jenkinson, P. (1999). The duty of community care: The Wokingham MIND Crisis House. In C. Newnes, G. Holmes & C. Dunn (Eds.), *This is Madness: A critical look at psychiatry and the future of mental health services.* Ross-on-Wye: PCCS Books, pp. 227–239.

38. Soteria UK in Bradford is raising funds for a safe house for one person experiencing overwhelm and likely to be seen as psychotic. Contact: http://www.soterianetwork. org.uk/local/bradford/index.html

Soteria UK in Brighton hosts regular meetings for those deemed psychotic.

Contact: http://soteriabrighton.co.uk/

39. Wehde, U. (1992). The Runaway-House: Human support instead of inhuman psychiatric treatment. *Changes, 10,* 154–160.

40. French, J. R. P. & Raven, B. (1959). The bases of social power. In D. Cartwright & A. Zander (Eds.), *Group dynamics.* New York: Harper & Row, pp. 150–167.

41. Priest, P. (2007). The healing balm effect: Using a walking group to feel better. *Journal of Health Psychology, 12,* 36–52.

42. Holmes, G. (2010). *Psychology in the Real World: Community based groupwork.* Ross-on-Wye: PCCS Books.

43. Newnes, C. (1994). Defining mental health. *Nursing Times, 90*(19), 46. Newnes, C. (1993). What is mental health? *Clinical Psychology Forum 51,* 32–33. See also Parker, I., Georgaca, E., Harper, D., McLaughlin, T. & Stowell-Smith, M. (1995). *Deconstructing Psychopathology.* London: Sage.

44. Bandak, R. (2005). Empowering vulnerable children and families. In C. Newnes & N. Radcliffe (Eds.), *Making and Breaking Children's Lives.* Ross-on-Wye: PCCS Books, pp. 123–137.

45. See, for example, http://www.neighbourhoodnetworks.org/ Retrieved 10th July 2013.

46. A similar venture, *Health and Place*, publishes research on the impact of environment on conduct (http://www.journals.elsevier.com/health-and-place/).

47. Emerson, E., Vick, B., Graham, H., Hatton, C., Llewellyn, G., Madden, R. et al. (2012). Disablement and health. In N. Watson, A. Roulstone & C. Thomas (Eds.), *The Routledge Handbook of Disability Studies.* New York: Routledge, pp. 253–270.

48. One of Wolfensberger's projects involved countering local protest against a proposed residential facility for people with profound disabilities by simply giving each resident a valued title like 'Doctor'. The protest rapidly changed to comments about how remarkable it was that the new residents had completed doctorates despite their disabilities.

49. Taggart, D. (in press). The fathers group. *Journal of Critical Psychology, Counselling and Psychotherapy.*

50. Holland, S. (1992). From social abuse to social action: A neighbourhood psychotherapy and social action project for women. *Changes: An International Journal of Psychology and Psychotherapy, 10*(2), 146–53; Hagan, T. & Smail, D. (1997). Power-mapping I. Background and basic methodology. *Journal of Community and Applied Social Psychology, 7,* 257–267. Power-mapping can be

subjected to the criticism that those involved, subject to similar distal powers (culture, the macro-economy, etc.) are still responding to the proximal power of each other. The distal power behind the 'expert' in the room makes it likely (though not inevitable) that the expert analysis will be privileged.

51. Martín-Baró, I. (1996). Toward a liberation psychology. In A. Aron & S. Corne (Eds.), *Writings for a Liberation Psychology.* Cambridge, MA: Harvard University Press, pp. 198–220. (Original publication: Hacia una psicología de la liberación. *Boletin de Psicología* (UCA), *22*, 219–31.)

52. Burton, M. (2013). A second psychology of liberation? Valuing and moving beyond the Latin American. *Journal of Critical Psychology, Counselling and Psychotherapy, 13*(2), 96–107, p. 102.

53. Burton, M. & Kagan, C. (2005). Liberation social psychology: Learning from Latin America. *Journal of Community and Applied Social Psychology, 15*(1), 63–78. In the UK, the Centre for Research and Socio-cultural Change at the University of Manchester and the Open University carries out research that is interdisciplinary rather than psychological (there are no clinical psychologists) and aimed at tracing the complexities of social and cultural change in finance, the media, cities, technologies and social exclusions. The Centre also investigates the social implications of research methods.

54. Lodge, D. (1975). *Changing Places.* Harmondsworth: Penguin.

55. Nelson, G. & Prilleltensky, I. (Eds.). (2010). *Community Psychology: In pursuit of liberation and well-being* (2nd ed.). Basingstoke: Palgrave Macmillan (Original work published 2005).

56. Retrieved 10 July 2013 from http://www.education.miami.edu/facultystaff/CVs/163.pdf

57. Newnes, C. D. (1981). Black stockings and frilly caps. *Nursing Mirror,* Oct. 28, 28–30.

INDEX

Critical Examinations –
new series edited by Craig Newnes

Critical evaluation is an essential element of academic study. Any theory is only as strong as its capacity to withstand sustained critical examination of the assumptions it makes about the world. The individual volumes in this series, written by prominent experts and insider critics in their field, critically examine the theories and practices of the main branches of psychology in an accessible style.

Counselling and Counselling Psychology: A critical examination
Colin Feltham
ISBN 978 1 906254 58 2
April 2013

Clinical Psychology: A critical examination
Craig Newnes
ISBN 978 1 906254 59 9

Psychology: A critical examination
David Fryer
ISBN 978 1 906254 60 5
(Spring 2014)

Psychotherapy: A critical examinaton
Keith Tudor
ISBN 978 1 906254 61 2
(Spring 2015)